Schiller's Poems And Ballads

Friedrich Schiller

In the interest of creating a more extensive selection of rare historical book reprints, we have chosen to reproduce this title even though it may possibly have occasional imperfections such as missing and blurred pages, missing text, poor pictures, markings, dark backgrounds and other reproduction issues beyond our control. Because this work is culturally important, we have made it available as a part of our commitment to protecting, preserving and promoting the world's literature. Thank you for your understanding.

SCHILLER'S POEMS AND BALLADS

TRANSLATED BY

EDWARD, LORD LYTTON

WITH AN INTRODUCTION BY

HENRY MORLEY

LL.D., PROFESSOR OF ENGLISH LITERATURE AT UNIVERSITY COLLEGE, LONDON

LONDON
GEORGE ROUTLEDGE AND SONS
BROADWAY, LUDGATE HILL
GLASGOW AND NEW YORK
1887

INTRODUCTION.

JOHANN CHRISTOPH FRIEDRICH SCHILLER was born of an ancestry of village bakers, who transmitted their business from father to son, at Bittenfeld, near Waiblingen, in Würtemberg. But Schiller's father, Johann Kaspar, having been left fatherless at ten years old, abandoned the family trade, trained himself for medical practice, went to the wars as surgeon to a regiment of hussars, and served also as non-commissioned officer until the peace. He then practised medicine, married an innkeeper's daughter, wrote verse, went again to the wars, and in the autumn of 1759, the year in which (on the 10th of November) the son Friedrich was born, Johann Kaspar became lieutenant in a regiment of infantry.

During the first four years of Schiller's life, his father was at the wars, and his mother had sole charge of him. The father was promoted to the rank of captain, and retired upon the post of superintendent of shrubberies to the Duke of Würtemberg. He gave his mind to the new work, planted 60,000 trees, and wrote a book upon their culture. At six years old young Schiller's home was in the village of Lorch, under the influence of a Pastor Moser, whose name he afterwards gave to a good priest in his play of "The Robbers.' His own first choice of a career in life was to be such a Pastor. He went to school, therefore, at Ludwigsburg, became skilful in Latin versification, studied Greek and Hebrew and wrote also some German verse.

In 1770 the Duke of Würtemberg built a Military Orphan House, chiefly for the education of poor soldiers' children, and in 1772 Friedrich Schiller, then thirteen years old, being a clever boy, was drafted into the new school with some others, and with the chief teacher from Ludwigsburg. Education was offered to young Schiller at the Duke's expense in this school, which was called, after 1772, a Military Academy. Father and mother hesitated to allow the transfer; as it meant abandonment of education for the ministry. But the Duke urged; refusal might affect the fortunes of the family; and the boy went to his free education under a contract signed by his parents that he "should devote himself unreservedly to the service of the Ducal House of Würtemberg," an unwelcome exchange for the service of the House of God.

Law now became Schiller's study, but as he grew to manhood, his poet's mind was seized by the new enthusiasm of the day for freedom to move away from dead traditions and to lift the world. In 1775, the Academy was transferred to Stuttgard, and Schiller transferred his own studies there from law to medicine. Goethe, ten years older than Schiller, had published "Goetz von Berlichingen" in 1773. Schiller joined himself in friendship to the young poets of the Military Academy, and, as he said, would gladly have given his last shirt to be free to soar. In 1777, at the age of eighteen, Schiller began to write "The Robbers," which was first printed in 1781, and he had from time to time written poems in the Swabian Magazine, before he passed from his studies at the Academy to the office of surgeon in a regiment of grenadiers. But he disliked official life, and paid too little attention to its formal duties. When no publisher would venture on "The Robbers," Schiller printed his play at his own expense. It was first acted at Mannheim on the 13th of January, 1782, and in that year appeared the second revised edition. Schiller's "Robbers" passed immediately from theatre to theatre, and its fame spread throughout Europe. Like Goethe's first successes, it expressed much of the passionate feeling and impatience of established wrongs that preceded the fall of the Bastille.

In the same year, 1782, Schiller printed some of his earlier poems in an "Anthology for 1782," which he edited in critical antagonism to a Swabian Anthology that had been published in 1781, with too little regard to the new stir of life, and too much regard to the formalities of the French classicism against which the most vigorous writers of that day were asserting their own claim to be true to themselves and to the best hopes of man.

Schiller was now forbidden by his patron, the Duke, to leave Würtemberg; forbidden also to write more poetry. He slipped away again to see his play acted at Mannheim. He was put under arrest. He began another play. At last he escaped by secret flight to Mannheim, where he wrote to the Duke, who replied with a gracious order to him to return at once, but did not remove the interdict from his poetry. At the same time Schiller read his "Fiesko" to the actors; but he was so bad a reader of his own work that they thought the play abominable until they had read it for themselves. Schiller remained a deserter, and to avoid chance of arrest, he and the friend who had shared his flight, moved on to Frankfort. Money was not to be had. "Fiesko" was declined by the actors; and Schiller was in serious straits when a home was offered to him at Bauerbach, in a house belonging to the Frau Henrietta von Wolzogen, a widow of eight-and-thirty, with five children.

In December, 1782, the Duke of Würtemberg filled up the place that Schiller had vacated, and took no further thought for his return.

At the beginning of 1783 Schiller published "Fiesko." At ease in Bauerbach, he began his play of "Don Karlos." In July, 1783, he went to Mannheim. "Fiesko," revised for the third time, was acted; its success was great. "Cabal and Love" followed.

In 1784 the poet became journalist, and proposed to publish every two months "The Rhenish Thalia." The first number appeared in March, 1785. "Don Karlos" was first tried on the stage at Hamburg on the 30th of August, 1787. Then Schiller was for a time at Weimar. He worked hard for his bread, and became in 1789 a Professor Extraordinary at the University of Jena, reading himself in with an Introductory Lecture upon Universal History. In the summer of 1789 he was betrothed to Charlotte von Lengefeld, and he was married to her in February, 1790. He had debts to pay, and toiled incessantly. He worked hard at his "History of the Thirty Years' War;" thought over "Wallenstein;" and had a severe illness that increased his difficulties. After recovery for a short time, this illness returned upon him. The personal charm of Schiller's character, and the reasonable spirit of brotherhood that always overcomes the mere instinct of rivalry between men of true genius who learn to know each other, overcame Goethe's antipathy to Schiller. The two chief poets of Germany came out of a lecture-room at Jena side by side, talked of the lecture, walked to Schiller's house, went in, talked on, and were friends thenceforward.

Goethe readily agreed to contribute to a new poetical journal, "Die Horen," that Schiller was then planning, and which came out at the end of 1794. Within four months in 1795, while suffering severe illness, Schiller poured out his poems on "The Poetry of Life;" "The Power of Song;" "Pegasus in the Yoke;" "The Dance;" "The Ideal and Life;" "Genius;" "The Ideal;" "The Veiled Image at Sais;" "Dignity of Women;" "German Fidelity;" "The Walk;" "Columbus;" "Evening;" "The Partition of the Earth;" and others. Most critics attacked "Die Horen." Schiller and Goethe gave the critics a return fire with epigrams of the "Xenien."

Then Schiller bought a garden-hut at Jena which he built into a cottage. There was beautiful scenery about it, and there, in 1797, he wrote ballads—"The Diver;" "The Glove;" "Knight of Toggenburg;" "The Ring of Polycrates;" "The Cranes of Ibycus;" and "Fridolin." Next year followed "Rudolf of Hapsburg," and others. "The Song of the Bell," conceived in 1788, was taken up again in 1797, and finished in September, 1799. It appeared in the "Musen Almanach" of 1800, the last that Schiller edited. He had given up "Die Horen" in 1798. Then followed the trilogy of "Wallenstein;" the "Piccolomini," produced in February, 1799; "Wallenstein's Death," in May, but "Wallenstein's Camp" was not produced until December, 1803. The play of "Mary Stuart" followed; then an engagement at the Court Theatre of Weimar. Then came "The Maid of Orleans," "The Bride of Messina," "William Tell." And Schiller obtained a Patent of Nobility before his death in May, 1805. He entered the world Schiller, and went out of it with a "von" before his name.

H. M.

June, 1887.

CONTENTS.

POEMS AND BALLADS OF SCHILLER.

	PAGE
THE DIVER. A BALLAD	15
THE GLOVE. A TALE	21
THE KNIGHT OF TOGGENBURG	23
THE MEETING	26
THE ASSIGNATION	27
THE SECRET	29
TO EMMA	30
THE POET TO HIS FRIENDS. (WRITTEN AT WEIMAR.)	31
EVENING. (FROM A PICTURE.)	32
THE LONGING	33
THE PILGRIM	34
THE DANCE	35
THE SHARING OF THE EARTH	37
THE INDIAN DEATH-DIRGE	38
THE LAY OF THE MOUNTAIN	39
THE ALP HUNTER	41
RUDOLF OF HAPSBURG. A BALLAD	42
THE FIGHT WITH THE DRAGON	46
DITHYRAMB	54
THE KNIGHTS OF ST. JOHN	55
THE MAIDEN FROM AFAR (OR FROM ABROAD)	55
THE TWO GUIDES OF LIFE—THE SUBLIME AND THE BEAUTIFUL	56
THE FOUR AGES OF THE WORLD	57
THE MAIDEN'S LAMENT	69
THE IMMUTABLE	60
THE VEILED IMAGE AT SAIS	61
THE CHILD IN THE CRADLE	63
THE RING OF POLYCRATES. A BALLAD	64

CONTENTS.

	PAGE
HOPE	67
THE SEXES	67
HONOURS	69
POMPEII AND HERCULANEUM	69
LIGHT AND WARMTH	71
BREADTH AND DEPTH	72
THE PHILOSOPHICAL EGOIST	72
FRIDOLIN; OR, THE MESSAGE TO THE FORGE	73
THE YOUTH BY THE BROOK	80
TO THE IDEAL	81
PHILOSOPHERS	84
PUNCH SONG	85
PUNCH SONG. TO BE SUNG IN THE NORTH	86
PEGASUS IN HARNESS	88
HERO AND LEANDER. A BALLAD	90
THE PLAYING INFANT	98
CASSANDRA	98
THE VICTORY FEAST	102
THE CRANES OF IBYCUS	107
THE HOSTAGE. A BALLAD	113
THE COMPLAINT OF CERES	117
THE ELEUSINIAN FESTIVAL	122
PARABLES AND RIDDLES	129
THE MIGHT OF SONG	135
HONOUR TO WOMAN. (LITERALLY "DIGNITY OF WOMEN.")	137
THE WORDS OF BELIEF	138
THE WORDS OF ERROR	139
THE MERCHANT	140
THE GERMAN ART	141
THE WALK	141
THE LAY OF THE BELL	150
THE POETRY OF LIFE	163
THE ANTIQUE AT PARIS. (FREE TRANSLATION.)	164
THE MAID OF ORLEANS	165
THEKLA. (A SPIRIT VOICE.)	165
WILLIAM TELL	166
ARCHIMEDES	167
CARTHAGE	167
COLUMBUS	168
NÆNIA	168
JOVE TO HERCULES	169
THE IDEAL AND THE ACTUAL LIFE	169

CONTENTS. xiii

	PAGE
THE FAVOUR OF THE MOMENT	175
THE FORTUNE-FAVOURED	176
THE SOWER	179
SENTENCES OF CONFUCIUS	179
THE ANTIQUE TO THE NORTHERN WANDERER	180
GENIUS. (FREE TRANSLATION.)	181
ULYSSES	183

VOTIVE TABLETS:
- MOTTO TO THE VOTIVE TABLETS 183
- THE GOOD AND THE BEAUTIFUL (ZWEIERLEI WIRKUNGSARTEN) 183
- VALUE AND WORTH 184
- THE DIVISION OF RANKS 184
- TO THE MYSTIC 184
- THE KEY 184
- WISDOM AND PRUDENCE 184
- THE UNANIMITY 185
- THE SCIENCE OF POLITICS 185
- TO ASTRONOMERS 185
- THE BEST GOVERNED STATE 186
- MY BELIEF 186
- FRIEND AND FOE 186
- LIGHT AND COLOUR 186
- FORUM OF WOMEN 186
- GENIUS 186
- THE IMITATOR 187
- CORRECTNESS. (FREE TRANSLATION.) . . . 187
- THE MASTER 187
- EXPECTATION AND FULFILMENT 187
- THE EPIC HEXAMETER. (TRANSLATED BY COLERIDGE.) . 187
- THE ELEGIAC METRE. (TRANSLATED BY COLERIDGE.) . 188

OTHER EPIGRAMS, &c.:
- THE PROSELYTE MAKER 188
- THE CONNECTING MEDIUM 188
- THE MORAL POET 188
- THE SUBLIME THEME 189
- SCIENCE 189
- KANT AND HIS COMMENTATORS 189

TO THE HEREDITARY PRINCE OF SAXE-WEIMAR, ON HIS JOURNEY TO PARIS. WRITTEN FEBRUARY, 1802 . . 189
TO A YOUNG FRIEND DEVOTING HIMSELF TO PHILOSOPHY . 191
THE PUPPET-SHOW OF LIFE. (DAS SPIEL DES LEBENS.) A PARAPHRASE 191

CONTENTS.

	PAGE
THE MINSTRELS OF OLD	192
THE COMMENCEMENT OF THE NEW CENTURY	193
HYMN TO JOY	196
THE INVINCIBLE ARMADA	199
THE CONFLICT	200
RESIGNATION	201
THE GODS OF GREECE	203
THE ARTISTS	207
THE CELEBRATED WOMAN. AN EPISTLE BY A MARRIED MAN—TO A FELLOW-SUFFERER	226
TO A FEMALE FRIEND. (WRITTEN IN HER ALBUM.)	232

FIRST PERIOD; OR, EARLY POEMS.

HECTOR AND ANDROMACHE	234
AMALIA	235
A FUNERAL FANTASIE	236
FANTASIE TO LAURA	238
TO LAURA PLAYING	240
TO LAURA. (RAPTURE.)	242
TO LAURA. (THE MYSTERY OF REMINISCENCE.)	242
MELANCHOLY; TO LAURA	244
THE INFANTICIDE	248
THE GREATNESS OF CREATION	253
ELEGY ON THE DEATH OF A YOUTH	254
THE BATTLE	257
ROUSSEAU. (FREE TRANSLATION.)	259
FRIENDSHIP	259
A GROUP IN TARTARUS	261
ELYSIUM	262
THE REFUGEE	263
THE FLOWERS	264
TO MINNA	265
TO THE SPRING	266
THE TRIUMPH OF LOVE. (A HYMN.)	267
TO A MORALIST	271
FORTUNE AND WISDOM	272
COUNT EBERHARD, THE QUARRELLER (DER GREINER) OF WURTEMBERG	272
FAREWELL TO THE READER. (TRANSFERRED FROM THE THIRD PERIOD.)	275

THE POEMS AND BALLADS

OF

SCHILLER.

THE DIVER.

A BALLAD.

[The original of the story on which Schiller has founded this ballad, matchless perhaps for the power and grandeur of its descriptions, is to be found in Kircher. According to the true principles of imitative art, Schiller has preserved all that is striking in the legend, and ennobled all that is commonplace. The name of the Diver was Nicholas, surnamed the Fish. The King appears, according to Hoffmeister's probable conjectures, to have been either Frederic I. or Frederic II., of Sicily. Date from 1295 to 1377.]

"OH, where is the knight or the squire so bold,
   As to dive to the howling charybdis below?—
I cast in the whirlpool a goblet of gold,
   And o'er it already the dark waters flow;
Whoever to me may the goblet bring,
Shall have for his guerdon that gift of his king."

He spoke, and the cup from the terrible steep,
   That, rugged and hoary, hung over the verge
Of the endless and measureless world of the deep,
   Swirl'd into the maëlstrom that madden'd the surge,
"And where is the diver so stout to go—
I ask ye again—to the deep below?"

And the knights and the squires that gather'd around,
   Stood silent—and fix'd on the ocean their eyes;
They look'd on the dismal and savage Profound,
   And the peril chill'd back every thought of the prize.
And thrice spoke the monarch—"The cup to win,
Is there never a wight who will venture in?"

And all as before heard in silence the king—
 Till a youth with an aspect unfearing but gentle,
'Mid the tremulous squires—stept out from the ring,
 Unbuckling his girdle, and doffing his mantle.;
And the murmuring crowd as they parted asunder,
On the stately boy cast their looks of wonder.

As he strode to the marge of the summit, and gave
 One glance on the gulf of that merciless main;
Lo! the wave that for ever devours the wave,
 Casts roaringly up the charybdis again;
And, as with the swell of the far thunder-boom,
Rushes foamingly forth from the heart of the gloom.

And it bubbles and seethes, and it hisses and roars,*
 As when fire is with water commix'd and contending,
And the spray of its wrath to the welkin up-soars,
 And flood upon flood hurries on, never-ending.
And it never *will* rest, nor from travail be free,
Like a sea that is labouring the birth of a sea.

Yet, at length, comes a lull o'er the mighty commotion,
 As the whirlpool sucks into black smoothness the swell
Of the white-foaming breakers—and cleaves thro' the ocean
 A path that seems winding in darkness to hell.
Round and round whirl'd the waves—deeper and deeper
   still driven,
Like a gorge thro' the mountainous main thunder-riven!

The youth gave his trust to his Maker! Before
 That path through the riven abyss closed again—
Hark! a shriek from the crowd rang aloft from the shore,
 And, behold! he is whirl'd in the grasp of the main!
And o'er him the breakers mysteriously roll'd,
And the giant-mouth closed on the swimmer so bold.

---

* "Und es wallet, und siedet, und brauset, und zischt," &c. Goethe was particularly struck with the truthfulness of these lines, of which his personal observation at the Falls of the Rhine enabled him to judge. Schiller modestly owns his obligations to Homer's descriptions of Charybdis, Odyss. l. 12. The property of the higher order of imagination to reflect truth, though not familiar to experience, is singularly illustrated in this description. Schiller had never seen even a Waterfall.

THE DIVER.

O'er the surface grim silence lay dark; but the crowd
    Heard the wail from the deep murmur hollow and fell;
They harken and shudder, lamenting aloud—
    "Gallant youth—noble heart—fare-thee-well, fare-thee-well!"
More hollow and more wails the deep on the ear—
More dread and more dread grows suspense in its fear.

If thou shouldst in those waters thy diadem fling,
    And cry, "Who may find it shall win it and wear;"
God wot, though the prize were the crown of a king—
    A crown at such hazard were valued too dear.
For never shall lips of the living reveal
What the deeps that howl yonder in terror conceal.

Oh, many a bark, to that breast grappled fast,
    Has gone down to the fearful and fathomless grave;
Again, crash'd together the keel and the mast,
    To be seen, toss'd aloft in the glee of the wave.—
Like the growth of a storm ever louder and clearer,
Grows the roar of the gulf rising nearer and nearer.

And it bubbles and seethes, and it hisses and roars,
    As when fire is with water commix'd and contending;
And the spray of its wrath to the welkin up-soars,
    And flood upon flood hurries on, never ending;
And as with the swell of the far thunder-boom,
Rushes roaringly forth from the heart of the gloom.

And, lo! from the heart of that far-floating gloom,*
    What gleams on the darkness so swanlike and white?
Lo! an arm and a neck, glancing up from the tomb!—
    They battle—the Man's with the Element's might.
It is he—it is he! in his left hand behold,
As a sign—as a joy!—shines the goblet of gold!

And he breathèd deep, and he breathèd long,
    And he greeted the heavenly delight of the day.
They gaze on each other—they shout, as they throng—
    "He lives—lo the ocean has render'd its prey!

    * The same rhyme as the preceding line in the original.

And safe from the whirlpool and free from the grave,
Comes back to the daylight the soul of the brave!"

And he comes, with the crowd in their clamour and glee,
  And the goblet his daring has won from the water,
He lifts to the king as he sinks on his knee;—
  And the king from her maidens has beckon'd his daughter—
She pours to the boy the bright wine which they bring,
And thus spake the Diver—"Long life to the king!

"Happy they whom the rose-hues of daylight rejoice,
  The air and the sky that to mortals are given!
May the horror below never more find a voice—
  Nor Man stretch too far the wide mercy of Heaven!
Never more—never more may he lift from the sight
The veil which is woven with Terror and Night!

"Quick-brightening like lightning—it tore me along,
  Down, down, till the gush of a torrent, at play
In the rocks of its wilderness, caught me—and strong
  As the wings of an eagle, it whirl'd me away.
Vain, vain was my struggle—the circle had won me,
Round and round in its dance, the wild element spun me.

"And I call'd on my God, and my God heard my prayer
  In the strength of my need, in the gasp of my breath—
And show'd me a crag that rose up from the lair,
  And I clung to it, nimbly—and baffled the death!
And, safe in the perils around me, behold
On the spikes of the coral the goblet of gold.

"Below, at the foot of the precipice drear,
  Spread the gloomy, and purple, and pathless Obscure!
A silence of Horror that slept on the ear,
  That the eye more appall'd might the Horror endure!
Salamander—snake—dragon—vast reptiles that dwell
In the deep—coil'd about the grim jaws of their hell.

"Dark-crawl'd—glided dark the unspeakable swarms,
  Clump'd together in masses, misshapen and vast—
Here clung and here bristled the fashionless forms—
  Here the dark-moving bulk of the Hammer-fish pass'd—

And with teeth grinning white, and a menacing motion,
Went the terrible Shark—the Hyæna of Ocean.

"There I hung, and the awe gather'd icily o'er me,
  So far from the earth, where man's help there was none!
The One Human Thing, with the Goblins before me—
  Alone—in a loneness so ghastly—ALONE!
Fathom-deep from man's eye in the speechless profound,
With the death of the Main and the Monsters around.

"Methought, as I gazed through the darkness, that now
  IT * saw—the dread hundred-limbed creature—its prey!
And darted—O God! from the far flaming-bough
  Of the coral, I swept on the horrible way;
And it seized me, the wave with its wrath and its roar,
It seized me to save—King, the danger is o'er!"

On the youth gazed the monarch, and marvell'd; quoth he,
  "Bold Diver, the goblet I promised is thine,
And this ring will I give, a fresh guerdon to thee,
  Never jewels more precious shone up from the mine;
If thou'lt bring me fresh tidings, and venture again;
To say what lies hid in the *innermost* main?"

Then outspake the daughter in tender emotion:
  "Ah! father, my father, what more can there rest?
Enough of this sport with the pitiless ocean—
  He has served thee as none would, thyself has confest.
If nothing can slake thy wild thirst of desire,
Let thy knights put to shame the exploit of the squire!"

The king seized the goblet—he swung it on high,
  And whirling, it fell in the roar of the tide:
"But bring back that goblet again to my eye,
  And I'll hold thee the dearest that rides by my side;
And thine arms shall embrace, as thy bride, I decree,
The maiden whose pity now pleadeth for thee."

---

* "——da kroch's heran," &c.
The *It* in the original has been greatly admired. The poet thus vaguely represents the fabulous misshapen monster, the Polypus of the ancients.

In his heart, as he listen'd, there leapt the wild joy—
   And the hope and the love through his eyes spoke in fire,
On that bloom, on that blush, gazed delighted the boy;
   The maiden—she faints at the feet of her sire!
Here the guerdon divine, there the danger beneath;
He resolves! To the strife with the life and the death!

They hear the loud surges sweep back in their swell,
   Their coming the thunder-sound heralds along!
Fond eyes * yet are tracking the spot where he fell:
   They come, the wild waters, in tumult and throng,
Roaring up to the cliff—roaring back, as before,
But no wave ever brings the lost youth to the shore.

   This ballad is the first composed by Schiller, if we except his early and ruder lay of "Count Eberhard, the Quarreller," which really, however, has more of the true old ballad spirit about it than those grand and artistic tales elaborated by his riper genius and belonging to a school of poetry, to which the ancient Ballad singer certainly never pretended to aspire. . . The old Ballad is but a simple narrative, without any symbolical or interior meaning. . . But in most of the performances to which Schiller has given the name of Ballad, a certain purpose, not to say philosophy, in conception, elevates the Narrative into Dramatic dignity. . . . Rightly, for instance, has "The Diver" been called a Lyrical Tragedy in two Acts—the first act ending with the disappearance of the hero amidst the whirlpool; and the conception of the contest of Man's will with physical Nature, ... together with the darkly hinted moral, not to stretch too far the mercy of Heaven, . . . belong in themselves to the design and the ethics of Tragedy.
   There is another peculiarity in the art which Schiller employs upon his narrative poems.—Though he usually enters at once on the interest of his story, and adopts, for the most part, the simple and level style of recital, he selects a subject admitting naturally of some striking picture, upon which he lavishes those resources of description that are only at the command of a great poet; . . . thus elevating the ancient ballad not only into something of the Drama, by conception, but into something of the Epic by execution.—The reader will recognise this peculiarity in the description of the Charybdis and the Abyss in the Ballad he has just concluded—in that of the Storm in "Hero and Leander"—of the Forge and the Catholic Ritual in "Fridolin"—of the Furies in the "Cranes of Ibycus," &c. . . . We have the more drawn the reader's notice to these distinctions between the simple ballad of the ancient minstrels, and the artistical narratives of Schiller—because it seems to us, that our English critics are too much inclined to consider that modern Ballad-writing succeeds or fails in proportion as it seizes merely the spirit of the ancient. . . . But this would but lower genius to an exercise of the same imitative ingenuity which a school-boy or a college prizeman displays upon Latin Lyrics . . . in which the merit consists in the avoidance of originality. The Great Poet cannot be content with only imitating what he studies: And he succeeds really in proportion not

---

* Viz.: the King's Daughter. Hoffmeister, Sup. iv. 301.

to his fidelity but his innovations ... that is, in proportion as he improves upon what serves him as a model.

In the ballad of "The Diver," Schiller not only sought the simple but the sublime.—According to his own just theory—"The Main Ingredient of Terror is the Unknown." He here seeks to accomplish as a poet what he before perceived as a critic. ... And certainly the picture of his lonely Diver amidst the horrors of the Abyss, dwells upon the memory amongst the sublimest conceptions of modern Poetry.

THE GLOVE.

A TALE.

[The original of this well-known story is in St. Foix—(*Essai sur Paris*) date the reign of Francis I.]

Before his lion-court,
To see the griesly sport,
  Sate the king;
Beside him group'd his princely peers,
And dames aloft, in circling tiers,
  Wreath'd round their blooming ring.
King Francis, where he sate,
Raised a finger—yawn'd the gate,
And, slow from his repose,
A LION goes!
Dumbly he gazed around
The foe-encircled ground;
And, with a lazy gape,
He stretch'd his lordly shape,
And shook his careless mane,
And—laid him down again!

A finger raised the king—
And nimbly have the guard
A second gate unbarr'd;
  Forth, with a rushing spring,
    A TIGER sprung!
Wildly the wild one yell'd
When the lion he beheld;
And, bristling at the look,
With his tail his sides he strook,
  And roll'd his rabid tongue;

In many a wary ring
He swept round the forest king,
  With a fell and rattling sound;—
  And laid him on the ground,
    Grommelling!
The king raised his finger; then
Leap'd two LEOPARDS from the den
  With a bound;
And boldly bounded they
Where the crouching tiger lay
  Terrible!
And he griped the beasts in his deadly hold;
In the grim embrace they grappled and roll'd;
  Rose the lion with a roar!
  And stood the strife before;
  And the wild-cats on the spot,
  From the blood-thirst, wroth and hot,
    Halted still!

Now from the balcony above,
A snowy hand let fall a glove:—
Midway between the beasts of prey,
Lion and tiger; there it lay,
  The winsome lady's glove!

Fair Cunigonde said, with a lip of scorn,
To the knight DELORGES—"If the love you have sworn
Were as gallant and leal as you boast it to be,
I might ask you to bring back that glove to me!"

The knight left the place where the lady sate;
The knight he has pass'd thro' the fearful gate;
The lion and tiger he stoop'd above,
And his fingers have closed on the lady's glove!

All shuddering and stunn'd, they beheld him there—
The noble knights and the ladies fair;
But loud was the joy and the praise the while
He bore back the glove with his tranquil smile!

With a tender look in her softening eyes,
That promised reward to his warmest sighs,

Fair Cunigonde rose her knight to grace,
He toss'd the glove in the lady's face!
"Nay, spare me the guerdon, at least," quoth he;
And he left for ever that fair ladye!

THE KNIGHT OF TOGGENBURG.

[In this beautiful ballad, Schiller is but little indebted to the true legend of Toggenburg, which is nevertheless well adapted to Narrative Poetry. Ida, wife of Henry Count of Toggenburg, was suspected by her husband of a guilty attachment to one of his vassals, and ordered to be thrown from a high wall. Her life, however, was miraculously saved; she lived for some time as a female hermit in the neighbouring forest, till she was at length discovered, and her innocence recognised. She refused to live again with the Lord whose jealousy had wronged her, retired to a convent, and was acknowledged as a saint after her death. This Legend, if abandoned by Schiller, has found a German Poet not unworthy of its simple beauty and pathos. Schiller has rather founded his poem, which sufficiently tells its own tale, upon a Tyrolese Legend, similar to the one that yet consecrates Rolandseck and Nonnenwörth on the Rhine. Hoffmeister implies that, unlike "The Diver," and some other of Schiller's Ballads, "The Knight of Toggenburg" dispenses with all intellectual and typical meaning, draws its poetry from feeling, and has no other purpose than that of moving the heart. Still upon Feeling itself are founded those ideal truths which make up the true philosophy of a Poet. In these few stanzas are represented the poetical chivalry of an age—the contest between the earthly passion and the religious devotion, which constantly agitated human life in the era of the Crusades. How much of deep thought has been employed to arouse the feelings—what intimate conviction of the moral of the middle ages, in the picture of the Knight looking up to the convent—of the Nun bowing calmly to the vale!]

"KNIGHT, a sister's quiet love
   Gives my heart to thee!
Ask me not for other love,
   For it paineth me!
Calmly could'st thou greet me now,
   Calmly from me go;
Calmly ever,—why dost thou
   Weep in silence, so?"

Sadly—(not a word he said!)—
   To the heart she wrung,
Sadly clasp'd he once the maid,
   On his steed he sprung!
"Up, my men of Swisserland!"
   Up awake the brave!
Forth they go—the Red-Cross band,
   To the Saviour's grave!

High your deeds, and great your fame,
   Heroes of the tomb!
Glancing through the carnage came
   Many a dauntless plume.
Terror of the Moorish foe,
   Toggenburg, thou art!
But thy heart is heavy! Oh,
   Heavy is thy heart!

Heavy was the load his breast
   For a twelvemonth bore:
Never can his trouble rest!
   And he left the shore.
Lo! a ship on Joppa's strand,
   Breeze and billow fair,
On to that beloved land,
   Where she breathes the air!

Knocking at her castle-gate
   Was the pilgrim heard;
Woe the answer from the grate!
   Woe the thunder-word!
"She thou seekest lives—a Nun!
   To the world she died!
When, with yester-morning's sun,
   Heaven received a Bride!"

From that day, his father's hall
   Ne'er his home may be;
Helm, and hauberk, steed and all,
   Evermore left he!
Where his castle-crownèd height
   Frowns the valley down,
Dwells unknown the hermit-knight,
   In a sackcloth gown.

Rude the hut he built him there,
   Where his eyes may view
Wall and cloister glisten fair
   Dusky lindens through.*

---

* In this description (though to the best of our recollection, it has escaped the vigilance of his many commentators) Schiller evidently has his

There, when dawn was in the skies,
　　Till the eve-star shone,
Sate he with mute wistful eyes,
　　Sate he there—alone!

Looking to the cloister, still,
　　Looking forth afar,
Looking to her lattice—till
　　Clink'd the lattice-bar.
Till—a passing glimpse allow'd—
　　Paused her image pale,
Calm and angel-mild, and bow'd
　　Meekly tow'rds the vale.

Then the watch of day was o'er,
　　Then, consoled awhile,
Down he lay, to greet once more,
　　Morning's early smile.
Days and years are gone, and still
　　Looks he forth afar,
Uncomplaining, hoping—till
　　Clinks the lattice-bar:

Till,—a passing glimpse allow'd,—
　　Paused her image pale,
Calm, and angel-mild, and bow'd
　　Meekly tow'rds the vale.
So, upon that lonely spot,
　　Sate he, dead at last,
With the look where life was not
　　Tow'rds the casement cast!

eye and his mind upon the scene of his early childhood at Lorch, a scene to which in later life he was fondly attached.

The village of Lorch lies at the foot of a hill crowned with a convent, before the walls of which springs an old linden or lime tree. The ruined castle of Hohenstaufen is in the immediate neighbourhood.

THE MEETING.

[This poem and the two that immediately follow, appear to have been inspired by Charlotte von Lengefeld, whom Schiller afterwards married.]

I.

I SEE her still, with many a fair one nigh,
   Of every fair the stateliest shape appear:
Like a lone sun she shone upon my eye—
   I stood afar, and durst not venture near.
Seized, as her presence brighten'd round me, by
   The trembling passion of voluptuous fear,
Yet, swift, as borne upon some hurrying wing,
The impulse snatch'd me, and I struck the string!

II.

What then I felt—what sung—my memory hence
   From that wild moment would in vain invoke—
It was the life of some discover'd sense
   That in the heart's divine emotion spoke;
Long years imprison'd, and escaping thence
   From every chain, the SOUL enchanted broke,
And found a music in its own deep core,
Its holiest, deepest deep, unguess'd before.

III.

Like melody long hush'd, and lost in space,
   Back to its home the breathing spirit came:
I look'd, and saw upon that angel face
   The fair love circled with the modest shame;
I heard (and heaven descended on the place)
   Low-whisper'd words a charmèd truth proclaim—
Save in thy choral hymns, O spirit-shore,
Ne'er may I hear such thrilling sweetness more!

IV.

"I know the worth within the heart which sighs,
   Yet shuns, the modest sorrow to declare;
And what rude Fortune niggardly denies,
   Love to the noble can with love repair.
The lowly have the birthright of the skies;
   Love only culls the flower that love should wear;

And ne'er in vain for love's rich gifts shall yearn
The heart that feels their wealth—and can return!"*

THE ASSIGNATION.

[NOTE.—In Schiller the eight long lines that conclude each stanza of this charming love-poem, instead of rhyming alternately, as in the translation, chime somewhat to the tune of Byron's *Don Juan*—six lines rhyming with each other, and the two last forming a separate couplet. In other respects the translation, it is hoped, is sufficiently close and literal.]

I.

HEAR I the creaking gate unclose?
  The gleaming latch uplifted?
No—'twas the wind that, whirring, rose,
  Amidst the poplars drifted!

Adorn thyself, thou green leaf-bowering roof,
  Destined the Bright One's presence to receive,
For her, a shadowy palace-hall aloof
  With holy Night, thy boughs familiar weave.
And ye sweet flatteries of the delicate air,
  Awake and sport her rosy cheek around,
When their light weight the tender feet shall bear,
  When Beauty comes to Passion's trysting-ground.

II.

Hush! what amidst the copses crept—
  So swiftly by me now?
No—'twas the startled bird that swept
  The light leaves of the bough!

Day, quench thy torch! come, ghost-like, from on high,
  With thy loved Silence, come, thou haunting Eve,
Broaden below thy web of purple dye,
  Which lullèd boughs mysterious round us weave.
For love's delight, enduring listeners none,
  The froward witness of the light will flee;
Hesper alone, the rosy Silent One,
  Down-glancing may our sweet Familiar be!

---

* This is the only one of Schiller's poems that reminds us of the Italian poets.—It has in it something of the sweet mannerism of Petrarch.

III.

What murmur in the distance spoke,
   And like a whisper died?
No!—'twas the swan that gently broke
   In rings the silver tide!

Soft to my ear there comes a music-flow;
   In gleesome murmur glides the waterfall;
To Zephyr's kiss the flowers are bending low;
   Through life goes joy, exchanging joy with all.
Tempt to the touch the grapes—the blushing fruit,*
   Voluptuous swelling from the leaves that hide;
And, drinking fever from my cheek, the mute
   Air sleeps all liquid in the Odour-Tide!

IV.

Hark! through the alley hear I now
   A footfall? Comes the maiden?
No,—'twas the fruit slid from the bough,
   With its own richness laden!

Day's lustrous eyes grow heavy in sweet death,
   And pale and paler wane his jocund hues,
The flowers too gentle for his glowing breath,
   Ope their frank beauty to the twilight dews.
The bright face of the moon is still and lone,
   Melts in vast masses the world silently;
Slides from each charm the slowly-loosening zone;
   And round all beauty, veilless, roves the eye.

V.

What yonder seems to glimmer?
   Her white robe's glancing hues?—
No,—'twas the column's shimmer
   Athwart the darksome yews!

O, longing heart, no more delight-upbuoy'd
   Let the sweet airy image thee befool!
The arms that would embrace her clasp the void:
   This feverish breast no phantom-bliss can cool.

* The Peach.

O, waft her here, the *true*, the *living* one!
Let but my hand *her* hand, the tender, feel—
The very shadow of her robe alone!—
So into life the idle dream shall steal!

* * * * *

As glide from heaven, when least we ween,
The rosy hours of bliss,
All gently came the maid, unseen:—
He waked beneath her kiss!

THE SECRET.

AND not a word by her was spoken;
For many a listener's ear was by,
But sweetly was the silence broken,
For eye could well interpret eye.
Soft to thy hush'd pavilion stealing,
Thou fair, far-spreading Beech, I glide,
Thy favouring veil our forms concealing,
And all the garish world denied.

From far, with dull, unquiet clamour,
Labours the vex'd and busy day,
And, through the hum, the sullen hammer
Comes heaving down its heavy way.
Thus man pursues his weary calling,
And wrings the hard life from the sky.
While happiness unseen is falling
Down from God's bosom silently.

O, all unheard be still the lonely
Delights in our true love embrac'd.
The hearts that never loved can only
Disturb the well they shun to taste.
The world but searches to destroy her,
The Bliss conceal'd from vulgar eyes—
In secret seize, in stealth enjoy her,
Ere watchful Envy can surprise.

Soft, upon tiptoe, comes she greeting,
  Thro' silent night she loves to stray,
A nymph, that fades to air, if meeting
  One gaze her mysteries to betray.
Roll round us, roll, thou softest river,*
  Thy broad'ning stream, a barrier given,
And guard with threat'ning waves for ever
  This one last Heritage of Heaven!

TO EMMA.

I.

Amidst the cloud-grey deeps afar
  The Bliss departed lies;
How linger on one lonely star
  The loving wistful eyes!
Alas—a star in truth—the light
Shines but a signal of the night!

II.

If lock'd within the icy chill
  Of the long sleep, thou wert—
My faithful grief could find thee still
  A life within my heart;—
But, oh, the worse despair to see
Thee live to earth, and die to me!

III.

Can those sweet longing hopes, which make
  Love's essence, thus decay?
Can that be love which doth forsake?—
  That love—which fades away?
That earthly gifts are brief, I knew—
Is that all heaven-born mortal too?

---

* Probably the river Saale, on the banks of which Schiller was accustomed to meet his Charlotte.

THE POET TO HIS FRIENDS.
(WRITTEN AT WEIMAR.)

I.

FRIENDS, fairer times have been
(Who can deny?) than we ourselves have seen;
And an old race of more majestic worth.
Were History silent on the Past, in sooth,
A thousand stones would witness of the truth
   Which men disbury from the womb of earth.
But yet that race, if more endowed than ours
   Is past!—no joy to death can glory give;
But we—we *are*—to us the breathing hours,
   They have the best—who live!

II.

Suns are of happier ray
Than where, not ill, we while our life away,
If the far-wandering traveller speaks aright;
   But much which Nature hath to us denied
   Hath not kind Art, the genial friend, supplied,
And our hearts warm'd beneath her mother-light!
Tho' native not beneath our winters keen,
   Or bays or myrtle—for our mountain shrines
And hardy brows, their lusty garlands green
   Weave the thick-clustering vines.

III.

Well may proud hearts take pleasure
Where change four worlds their intermingled treasure,
And Trade's great pomp the wanderer may behold,
   Where, on rich Thames, a thousand sails unfurl'd
   Or seek or leave the market of the world—
And throned in splendour sits the Earth-god,—GOLD.
But never, in the mire of troubled streams,
   Swell'd by wild torrents from the mountain's breast,
But on the still wave's mirror, the soft beams
   Of happy sunshine rest.*

---

* These lines afford one of the many instances of the peculiar tenacity with which Schiller retained certain favourite ideas. At the age of

Prouder and more elate
Than we o' the North, beside the Angel's Gate *
The beggar basking views eternal Rome!
    Round to his gaze bright-swarming beauties given,
      And, holy in the heaven, a second heaven,
The world's large wonder, hangs St. Peter's Dome.
But Rome in all her glory is a grave,
The Past, that ghost of power, alone is hers,
Strew'd by the green Hours, where the young leaves wave
    Breathes all the life that stirs!

Elsewhere are nobler things
Than to our souls our scant existence brings:
The *New* beneath the sun hath never been.
    Yet still the greatness of each elder age
    We see—the conscious phantoms of the stage—
As the world finds its symbol on the scene.†
Life but repeats itself, all stale and worn;
    Sweet Phantasy alone is young for ever;
What ne'er and nowhere on the earth was born ‡
    Alone grows aged never.

EVENING.

(FROM A PICTURE.)

SINK, shining god—tired Nature halts; and parch'd
Earth needs the dews; adown the welkin arch'd
      Falter thy languid steeds;—
      Sink in thy ocean halls!
Who beckons from the crystal waves unto thee?
Knows not thy heart the smiles of love that woo thee?
      Quicken the homeward steeds!
      The silver Thetis calls!

---

seventeen he had said, "Not on the stormy sea, but on the calm and glassy stream, does the sun reflect itself."—See Hoffmeister, Part iv., p. 39.

  * St. Peter's Church.
  † The signification of these lines in the original has been disputed—we accept Hoffmeister's interpretation.—Part vi., p. 40.
    ‡ "The light that never was on sea or land,
        The Consecration and the Poet's Dream."—WORDSWORTH.

Swift to her arms he springs, and, with the bridle
Young Eros toys—the gladdening steeds (as idle
    The guideless chariot rests)
    The cool wave bend above;
And Night, with gentle step and melancholy,
Breathes low through heaven; with her comes Love the
    holy—
    Phœbus the lover rests,—
    Be all life, rest and love!

THE LONGING.

From out this dim and gloomy hollow,
  Where hang the cold clouds heavily,
Could I but gain the clue to follow,
  How blessed would the journey be!
Aloft I see a fair dominion,
  Through time and change all vernal still;
But where the power, and what the pinion,
  To gain the ever-blooming hill?

Afar I hear the music ringing—
  The lulling sounds of heaven's repose,
And the light gales are downward bringing
  The sweets of flowers the mountain knows.
I see the fruits, all golden-glowing,
  Beckon the glossy leaves between,
And o'er the blooms that there are blowing
  Nor blight nor winter's wrath hath been.

To suns that shine for ever, yonder,
  O'er fields that fade not, sweet to flee:
The very winds that there may wander,
  How healing must their breathing be!
But lo, between us rolls a river—
  O'er which the wrathful tempest raves;
I feel the soul within me shiver
  To gaze upon the gloomy waves.

A rocking boat mine eyes discover,
　But, woe is me, the pilot fails!—
In, boldly in—undaunted over!
　And trust the life that swells the sails!
Thou must *believe*, and thou must *venture*,
　In fearless faith thy safety dwells;
* By miracles alone men enter
　The glorious Land of Miracles!

THE PILGRIM.

Youth's gay spring-time scarcely knowing
　Went I forth the world to roam—
And the dance of youth, the glowing,
　Left I in my Father's home.
Of my birthright, glad-believing,
　Of my world-gear took I none,
Careless as an infant, cleaving
　To my pilgrim staff alone.
For I placed my mighty hope in
　Dim and holy words of Faith,
"Wander forth—the way is open
　Ever on the upward path—
Till thou gain the Golden Portal,
　Till its gates unclose to thee.
There the Earthly and the Mortal,
　Deathless and Divine shall be!"
Night on Morning stole, on stealeth,
　Never, never stand I still,
And the Future yet concealeth,
　What I seek, and what I will!
Mount on mount arose before me,
　Torrents hemm'd me every side,
But I built a bridge that bore me
　O'er the roaring tempest-tide.
Towards the East I reach'd a river,
　On its shores I did not rest;
Faith from Danger can deliver,
　And I trusted to its breast.

* "Wo kein Wunder geschicht, ist kein Beglückter zu sehn."
　　　　　　　　　　Schiller. *Das Glück*.

THE DANCE.

Drifted in the whirling motion,
  Seas themselves around me roll—
Wide and wider spreads the ocean,
  Far and farther flies the goal.
While I live is never given
  Bridge or wave the goal to near—
Earth will never meet the Heaven,
  Never can the THERE be HERE!

The two poems of "The Longing" and "The Pilgrim" belong to a class which may be said to allegorise *Feeling*, and the meaning, agreeably to the genius of allegory or parable, has been left somewhat obscure. The commentators agree in referring both poems to the illustration of the *Ideal*. "The Longing" represents the desire to escape from the real world into the higher realms of being. "The Pilgrim" represents the active labour of the idealist to reach "the Golden Gate." The belief in what is beyond Reality is necessary to all who would escape from the Real; and in "The Longing" it is intimated that that belief may attain the end. But "The Pilgrim," after all his travail, finds that the earth will never reach the heaven, and the *There* never can be *Here*. The two poems are certainly capable of an interpretation at once loftier and more familiar than that which the commentators give to it. They are apparently intended to express the natural human feeling—common not to poets alone, but to us all—the human feeling which approaches to an instinct, and in which so many philosophers have recognised the inward assurance of a hereafter, viz., the desire to escape from the coldness and confinement, "the valley and the cloud" of actual life, into the happier world which smiles, in truth, evermore upon those who *believe* that it exists: the desire of the poet is identical with the desire of the religious man. He who longs for another world—only to be attained by abstraction from the low desires of this—longs for what the Christian strives for. And if he finds, with Schiller's Pilgrim, that in spite of all his longing and all his labour, the goal cannot be reached below, still, as Schiller expresses it elsewhere, "He has had *Hope*—his belief has been his reward." That Heaven which "The Longing" yearns for, which "The Pilgrim" seeks, may be called "The Ideal," or whatever else refiners please; but, in plain fact and in plain words, that Ideal is the Hereafter—is Heaven!

THE DANCE.

SEE how like lightest waves at play, the airy dancers
    fleet;
And scarcely feels the floor the wings of those harmonious
    feet.
Oh, are they flying shadows from their native forms set
    free?
Or phantoms in the fairy ring that summer moonbeams
    see?

As, by the gentle zephyr blown, some light mist flees in air,
As skiffs that skim adown the tide, when silver waves are fair,
So sports the docile footstep to the heave of that sweet measure,
As music wafts the form aloft at its melodious pleasure,
Now breaking through the woven chain of the entangled dance,
From where the ranks the thickest press, a bolder pair advance,
The path they leave behind them lost—wide opes the path beyond,
The way unfolds or closes up as by a magic wand.
See now, they vanish from the gaze in wild confusion blended;
Ah, in sweet chaos whirl'd again, that gentle world is ended!
No!—disentangled glides the knot, the gay disorder ranges—
The only system ruling here, a grace that ever changes.
For aye destroy'd—for aye renew'd, whirls on that fair creation;
And yet one peaceful law can still pervade in each mutation.
And what can to the reeling maze breathe harmony and vigour,
And give an order and repose to every gliding figure?
That each a ruler to himself doth but himself obey,
Yet through the hurrying course still keeps his own appointed way.
What, would'st thou know? It is in truth the mighty power of Tune,
A power that every step obeys, as tides obey the moon;
That threadeth with a golden clue the intricate employment,
Curbs bounding strength to tranquil grace, and tames the wild enjoyment.
And comes THE WORLD'S wide harmony in vain upon thine ears?
The stream of music borne aloft from yonder choral spheres?

And feel'st thou not the measure which Eternal Nature
   keeps?
The whirling Dance for ever held in yonder azure deeps?
The suns that wheel in varying maze?—*That* music thou
   discernest?
No! Thou canst honour that in sport which thou for-
   gett'st in earnest.

NOTE.—This poem is very characteristic of the noble ease with which
Schiller often loves to surprise the reader, by the sudden introduction of
matter for the loftiest reflection, in the midst of the most familiar subjects.
What can be more accurate and happy than the poet's description of the
national dance, as if such description were his only object—the outpouring,
as it were, of a young gallant, intoxicated by the music, and dizzy with the
waltz? Suddenly and imperceptibly the reader finds himself elevated from
a trivial scene. He is borne upward to the harmony of the spheres. He
bows before the great law of the universe—the young gallant is transformed
into the mighty teacher; and this without one hard conceit—without one
touch of pedantry. It is but a flash of light; and where glowed the playful
picture, shines the solemn moral.

THE SHARING OF THE EARTH.

"TAKE the world," cried the God from his heaven
   To men—"I proclaim you its heirs;
To divide it amongst you 'tis given,
   You have only to settle the shares."

Each takes for himself as it pleases,
   Old and young have alike their desire;
The Harvest the Husbandman seizes,
   Through the wood and the chase sweeps the Squire.

The Merchant his warehouse is locking—
   The Abbot is choosing his wine—
Cries the Monarch, the thoroughfares blocking,
   "Every toll for the passage is mine!"

All too late, when the sharing was over,
   Comes the Poet—He came from afar—
Nothing left can the laggard discover,
   Not an inch but its owners there are.

"Woe is me, is there nothing remaining,
   For the son who best loves thee alone!"
Thus to Jove went his voice in complaining,
   As he fell at the Thunderer's throne.

"In the land of the dreams if abiding,"
  Quoth the God—"Canst thou murmur at ME?
Where wert *thou*, when the Earth was dividing?"
  "I WAS," said the Poet, "BY THEE!"

"Mine eye by thy glory was captur'd—
  Mine ear by thy music of bliss,
Pardon him whom *thy* world so enraptur'd—
  As to lose him his portion in this!"

"Alas," said the God—"Earth is given!
  Field, forest, and market, and all!—
What say you to quarters in Heaven?
  We'll admit you whenever you call!"

THE INDIAN DEATH-DIRGE.

[The idea of this Poem is taken from Carver's Travels through North America. Goethe reckoned it amongst Schiller's best poems of the kind, and wished he had made a dozen such. But, precisely because Goethe admired it for its *objectivity*, William von Humboldt, found it wanting in ideality. See Hoffmeister, pp. 3, 311.]

SEE on his mat—as if of yore,
  All life-like, sits he here!
With that same aspect which he wore
  When light to him was dear.
But where the right hand's strength?—and where
  The breath that loved to breathe,
To the Great Spirit aloft in air,
  The peace-pipe's lusty wreath?
And where the hawk-like eye, alas!
  That wont the deer pursue,
Along the waves of rippling grass,
  Or fields that shone with dew?
Are these the limber, bounding feet,
  That swept the winter snows?
What stateliest stag so fast and fleet?
  Their speed outstript the roe's!
These arms that then the sturdy bow
  Could supple from its pride,
How stark and helpless hang they now
  Adown the stiffen'd side!

Yet weal to him—at peace he strays
  Where never fall the snows;
Where o'er the meadows springs the maize
  That mortal never sows:
Where birds are blithe on every brake—
  Where forests teem with deer—
Where glide the fish through every lake—
  One chase from year to year!
With spirits now he feasts above;
  All left us—to revere
The deeds we honour with our love,
  The dust we bury here.
Here bring the last gifts!—loud and shrill
  Wail, death-dirge for the brave!
What pleased him most in life may still
  Give pleasure in the grave.
We lay the axe beneath his head
  He swung, when strength was strong—
The bear on which his banquets fed—
  The way from earth is long!
And here, new-sharpen'd, place the knife
  That sever'd from the clay,
From which the axe had spoil'd the life,
  The conquer'd scalp away!
The paints that deck the Dead, bestow—
  Yes, place them in his hand—
That red the Kingly Shade may glow
  Amidst the Spirit-Land!

THE LAY OF THE MOUNTAIN.

[The scenery of Gotthardt is here personified.]
The three following ballads, in which Switzerland is the scene, betray their origin in Schiller's studies for the drama of William Tell.

To the solemn abyss leads the terrible path,
  The life and the death winding dizzy between;
In thy desolate way, grim with menace and wrath,
  To daunt thee the spectres of giants are seen;
That thou wake not the Wild One,* all silently tread—
Let thy lip breathe no breath in the pathway of Dread!

  * The avalanche—the *équivoque* of the original, turning on the Swiss

High over the marge of the horrible deep
  Hangs and hovers a Bridge with its phantom-like span,*
Not by man was it built, o'er the vastness to sweep;
  Such thought never came to the daring of Man!
The stream roars beneath—late and early it raves—
But the bridge which it threatens, is safe from the waves.

Black-yawning a Portal, thy soul to affright,
  Like the gate to the kingdom, the Fiend for the king—
Yet beyond it there smiles but a land of delight,
  Where the Autumn in marriage is met with the Spring.
From a lot which the care and the trouble assail,
Could I fly to the bliss of that balm-breathing vale!

Through that field, from a fount ever hidden their birth,
  Four Rivers in tumult rush roaringly forth;
They fly to the fourfold divisions of earth—
  The sunrise, the sunset, the south, and the north.
And, true to the mystical mother that bore,
Forth they rush to their goal, and are lost evermore.

High over the races of men in the blue
  Of the ether, the Mount in twin summits is riven;
There, veil'd in the gold-woven webs of the dew,
  Moves the Dance of the Clouds—the pale Daughters of Heaven!
There, in solitude circles their mystical maze,
Where no witness can hearken, no earthborn surveys.

August on a throne which no ages can move,
  Sits a Queen, in her beauty serene and sublime,†
The diadem blazing with diamonds above
  The glory of brows, never darken'd by time,

---

word *Lawine*, it is impossible to render intelligible to the English reader. The giants in the preceding line are the rocks that overhang the pass which winds now to the right, now to the left, of a roaring stream.

* The Devil's Bridge. The Land of Delight (called in Tell "a serene valley of joy") to which the dreary portal (in Tell the black rock gate) leads, is the Urse Vale. The four rivers, in the next stanza, are the Reus, the Rhine, the Tessin, and the Rhône.

† The everlasting glacier. See William Tell, act v: scene 2.

His arrows of light on that form shoots the sun—
And he gilds them with all, but he warms them with
   none!

THE ALP HUNTER.

[Founded on a legend of the Valley of Ormond, in the Pays de Vaud.]

"Wilt thou not, thy lamblings heeding,
  (Soft and innocent are they!)
Watch them on the herbage feeding,
  Or beside the brooklet play?"
"Mother, mother, let me go,
  O'er the mount to chase the roe."

"Wilt thou not, around thee bringing,
  Lure the herds with lively horn?—
Gaily go the clear bells ringing,
  Through the echoing forest borne!"
"Mother, mother, let me go,
  O'er the wilds to chase the roe."

"Wilt thou not (their blushes woo thee!)
  In their sweet beds tend thy flowers;
Smiles so fair a garden to thee,
  Where the savage mountain lours?"
"Leave the flowers in peace to blow;
Mother, mother, let me go!"

On and ever onwards bounding,
  Scours the hunter to the chase,
On and ever onwards hounding
  To the mountain's wildest space.—
Swift, as footed by the wind,
Flies before the trembling hind.

Light and limber, upwards driven,
  On the hoar crag quivering,
Or through gorges thunder-riven
  Leaps she with her airy spring!
But behind her still the Foe—
Near, and near the deadly bow!

Fast and faster on—unslack'ning;
　Now she hangs above the brink,
Where the last rocks, grim and black'ning,
　Down the gulf abruptly sink.
Never pathway there may wind,
Chasms below—and death behind!

To the hard man—dumb-lamenting,
　Turns she with her look of woe;
Turns in vain—the Unrelenting
　Meets the look—and bends the bow.—
Sudden—from the darksome deep,
Rose the Spirit of the Steep!—

And his godlike hand extending,
　From the hunter snatch'd the prey,
"Wherefore, woe and slaughter sending,
　To my solitary sway?—
Why should my herds before thee fall?—
THERE'S ROOM UPON THE EARTH FOR ALL!"

RUDOLF OF HAPSBURG.

A BALLAD.

[Hinrichs properly classes this striking ballad (together with the yet grander one of the "Fight with the Dragon") amongst those designed to depict and exalt the virtue of Humility. The source of the story is in Ægidius Tschudi, a Swiss chronicler; and Schiller appears to have adhered, with much fidelity, to the original narrative.]

At Aachen, in imperial state,
　In that time-hallow'd hall renown'd,
At solemn feast King Rudolf sate,
　The day that saw the hero crown'd!
Bohemia and thy Palgrave, Rhine,
Give this the feast, and that the wine;*

---

* The office, at the coronation feast, of the Count Palatine of the Rhine (Grand Sewer of the Empire and one of the Seven Electors) was to bear the Imperial Globe and set the dishes on the board; that of the King of Bohemia was cup-bearer. The latter was not, however, present, as Schiller himself observed in a note (omitted in the editions of his collected works), at the coronation of Rudolf.

The Arch Electoral Seven,
Like choral stars around the sun,
Gird him whose hand a world has won,
  The anointed choice of Heaven.

In galleries raised above the pomp,
  Press'd crowd on crowd their panting way,
And with the joy-resounding tromp,
  Rang out the million's loud hurra!
For closed at last the age of slaughter,
When human blood was pour'd as water—
  Law dawns upon the world! *
Sharp force no more shall right the wrong,
And grind the weak to crown the strong—
  War's carnage-flag is furl'd!

In Rudolf's hand the goblet shines—
  And gaily round the board look'd he;
"And proud the feast, and bright the wines
  My kingly heart feels glad to me!
Yet where the Gladness-Bringer—blest
In the sweet art which moves the breast
  With lyre and verse divine?
Dear from my youth the craft of song,
And what as knight I loved so long,
  As Kaisar, still be mine."

Lo, from the circle bending there,
  With sweeping robe the Bard appears,
As silver white his gleaming hair,
  Bleach'd by the many winds of years;
"And music sleeps in golden strings—
Love's rich reward the minstrel sings,
  Well known to him the All
High thoughts and ardent souls desire!
What would the Kaisar from the lyre
  Amidst the banquet-hall?"

---

* Literally, "*A judge (ein Richter)* was again upon the earth." The word substituted in the translation is introduced in order to recall to the reader the sublime name given, not without justice, to Rudolf of Hapsburg, viz., "The Living Law."

The Great One smiled—"Not mine the sway—
　　The minstrel owns a loftier power—
A mightier king inspires the lay—
　　Its hest—THE IMPULSE OF THE HOUR!"
As through wide air the tempests sweep,
As gush the springs from mystic deep,
　　Or lone untrodden glen;
So from dark hidden fount within,
Comes SONG, its own wild world to win
　　Amidst the souls of men!"

Swift with the fire the minstrel glow'd,
　　And loud the music swept the ear:—
"Forth to the chase a Hero rode,
　　To hunt the bounding chamois-deer;
With shaft and horn the squire behind;—
Through greensward meads the riders wind—
　　A small sweet bell they hear.
Lo, with the HOST, a holy man,—
Before him strides the sacristan,
　　And the bell sounds near and near.

"The noble hunter down-inclined
　　His reverent head and soften'd eye,
And honour'd with a Christian's mind
　　The Christ who loves humility!
Loud through the pasture, brawls and raves
A brook—the rains had fed the waves,
　　And torrents from the hill.
His sandal shoon the priest unbound,
And laid the Host upon the ground,
　　And near'd the swollen rill!

"'What wouldst thou, priest?' the Count began,
　　As, marvelling much, he halted there.
'Sir Count, I seek a dying man,
　　Sore-hungering for the heavenly fare.
The bridge that once its safety gave,
Rent by the anger of the wave,
　　Drifts down the tide below.
Yet barefoot now, I will not fear
(The soul that seeks its God, to cheer)
　　Through the wild wave to go!'

"He gave that priest the knightly steed,
  He reach'd that priest the lordly reins,
That he might serve the sick man's need,
  Nor slight the task that heaven ordains.
He took the horse the squire bestrode;
On to the chase the hunter rode,
  On to the sick the priest!
And when the morrow's sun was red,
The servant of the Saviour led
  Back to its lord the beast.

"'Now Heaven forfend!' the Hero cried,
  'That e'er to chase or battle more
These limbs the sacred steed bestride
  That once my Maker's image bore;
If not a boon allow'd to thee,
Thy Lord and mine its Master be,
  My tribute to the King,
From whom I hold, as fiefs, since birth,
Honour, renown, the goods of earth,
  Life and each living thing!'

"'So may the God, who faileth never
  To hear the weak and guide the dim,
To thee give honour here and ever,
  As thou hast duly honour'd Him!
Far-famed ev'n now through Swisserland,
Thy generous heart and dauntless hand;
  And fair from thine embrace,
Six daughters bloom,* six crowns to bring,
Blest as the daughters of a KING,
  The mothers of a RACE!"

The mighty Kaisar heard amazed!
  His heart was in the days of old;
Into the minstrel's heart he gazed,
  That tale the Kaisar's own had told.

---

* At the coronation of Rudolf was celebrated the marriage-feast of three of his daughters—to Ludwig of Bavaria, Otto of Brandenburg, and Albrecht of Saxony. His other three daughters married afterwards Otto, nephew of Ludwig of Bavaria, Charles Martell, son of Charles of Anjou, and Wenceslaus, son of Ottocar of Bohemia. The royal house of England numbers Rudolf of Hapsburg amongst its ancestors.

Yes, in the bard the priest he knew,
And in the purple veil'd from view
　　The gush of holy tears !
A thrill through that vast audience ran,
And every heart the godlike man
　　Revering God—reveres!

THE FIGHT WITH THE DRAGON.

Who comes?—why rushes fast and loud,
Through lane and street the hurtling crowd,
Is Rhodes on fire?—Hurrah!—along
Faster and fast storms the throng!
High towers a shape in knightly garb—
Behold the Rider and the Barb!
Behind is dragg'd a wondrous load;
Beneath what monster groans the road?
The horrid jaws—the Crocodile,
　　The shape the mightier Dragon, shows—
From Man to Monster all the while—
　　The alternate wonder glancing goes.

Shout thousands, with a single voice,
" Behold the Dragon, and rejoice,
Safe roves the herd, and safe the swain !
Lo!—there the Slayer—here the Slain !
Full many a breast, a gallant life,
Has waged against the ghastly strife,
And ne'er return'd to mortal sight—
Hurrah, then, for the Hero Knight !"
So to the Cloister, where the vow'd
　　And peerless brethren of St. John
In conclave sit—that sea-like crowd,
　　Wave upon wave, goes thundering on.

High o'er the rest, the chief is seen—
There wends the Knight with modest mien;
Pours through the galleries raised for all
Above that Hero-council Hall,
The crowd—And thus the Victor One :—
" Prince—the knight's duty I have done.

The Dragon that devour'd the land
Lies slain beneath thy servant's hand;
Free, o'er the pasture, rove the flocks—
  And free the idler's steps may stray—
And freely o'er the lonely rocks,
  The holier pilgrim wends his way!"

A lofty look the Master gave:
"Certes," he said, "thy deed is brave;
Dread was the danger, dread the fight—
Bold deeds bring fame to vulgar knight;
But say, what sways with holier laws
The knight who sees in Christ his cause,
And wears his cross?"—Then every cheek
Grew pale to hear the Master speak;
But nobler was the blush that spread
  His face—the Victor's of the day—
As bending lowly—"Prince," he said;
  "His noblest duty—TO OBEY!"

"And yet that duty, son," replied
The chief "methinks thou hast denied
And dared thy sacred sword to wield
For fame in a forbidden field."
"Master, thy judgment, howso'er
It lean, till all is told, forbear—
Thy law, in spirit and in will,
I had no thought but to fulfil,
Not rash, as some, did I depart
  A Christian's blood in vain to shed;
But hoped by skill, and strove by art,
  To make my life avenge the dead.

"Five of our Order, in renown
The war-gems of our saintly crown,
The martyr's glory bought with life;
'Twas then thy law forbade the strife.
Yet in my heart there gnaw'd, like fire,
Proud sorrow, fed with stern desire:
In the still visions of the night,
Panting I fought the fancied fight;

And when the morrow glimmering came,
  With tales of ravage freshly done,
The dream remember'd, turn'd to shame,
  That night should dare what day should shun.

"And thus my fiery musings ran—
'What youth has learn'd should nerve the man;
How lived the great in days of old,
Whose fame to time by bards is told—
Who, heathens though they were, became
As gods—upborne to heaven by fame?
How proved they best the hero's worth?
They chased the monster from the earth—
They sought the lion in his den—
  They pierced the Cretan's deadly maze—
Their noble blood gave humble men
  Their happy birthright—peaceful days.

"'What! sacred, but against the horde
Of Mahound, is the Christian's sword?
All strife, save one, should he forbear?
No! earth itself the Christian's care.—
From every ill and every harm,
Man's shield should be the Christian's arm.
Yet art o'er strength will oft prevail,
And mind must aid where heart may fail!'
Thus musing, oft I roam'd alone,
  Where wont the Hell-born Beast to lie;
Till sudden light upon me shone,
  And on my hope broke victory!

"Then, Prince, I sought thee with the prayer
To breathe once more my native air;
The license given—the ocean past—
I reach'd the shores of home at last.
Scarce hail'd the old beloved land,
Than huge, beneath the artist's hand,
To every hideous feature true,
The Dragon's monster-model grew,
The dwarf'd, deformèd limbs upbore
  The lengthen'd body's ponderous load;
The scales the impervious surface wore,
  Like links of burnish'd harness, glow'd.

"Life-like, the huge neck seem'd to swell,
And widely, as some porch to hell,
You might the horrent jaws survey,
Griesly, and greeding for their prey.
Grim fangs and added terror gave,
Like crags that whiten through a cave.
The very tongue a sword in seeming—
The deep-sunk eyes in sparkles gleaming.
Where the vast body ends, succeed
　The serpent spires around it roll'd—
Woe—woe to rider, woe to steed,
　Whom coils as fearful e'er enfold!

"All to the awful life was done—
The very hue, so ghastly, won—
The grey, dull tint:—the labour ceased,
It stood—half reptile and half beast!
And now began the mimic chase;
Two dogs I sought, of noblest race,
Fierce, nimble, fleet, and wont to scorn
The wild bull's wrath and levell'd horn;
These, docile to my cheering cry,
　I train'd to bound, and rend, and spring,
Now round the Monster-shape to fly,
　Now to the Monster-shape to cling!

"And where their gripe the best assails,
The belly left unsheath'd in scales,
I taught the dexterous hounds to hang
And find the spot to fix the fang;
Whilst I, with lance and mailèd garb,
Launch'd on the beast mine Arab barb.
From purest race that Arab came,
And steeds, like men, are fired by fame.
Beneath the spur he chafes to rage;
　Onwards we ride in full career—
I seem, in truth, the war to wage—
　The monster reels beneath my spear!

"Albeit, when first the *destrier* * eyed
The laidly thing, it swerved aside,

* War-horse.

Snorted and rear'd—and even they,
The fierce hounds, shrank with startled bay;
I ceased not, till by custom bold,
After three tedious moons were told,
Both barb and hounds were train'd—nay, more,
Fierce for the fight—then left the shore!
Three days have fleeted since I prest
  (Return'd at length) this welcome soil,
Nor once would lay my limbs to rest,
  Till wrought the glorious crowning toil.

"For much it moved my soul to know
The unslack'ning curse of that grim foe.
Fresh rent, men's bones lay bleach'd and bare
Around the hell-worm's swampy lair;
And pity nerved me into steel:—
Advice?—I had a heart to feel,
And strength to dare! So, to the deed.—
I call'd my squires—bestrode my steed,
And with my stalwart hounds, and by
  Lone secret paths, we gaily go
Unseen—at least by human eye—
  Against a worse than human foe!

"Thou know'st the sharp rock—steep and hoar?—
The abyss?—the chapel glimmering o'er?
Built by the Fearless Master's hand,
The fane looks down on all the land.
Humble and mean that house of prayer—
Yet God hath shrined a wonder there:—
Mother and Child, to whom of old
The Three Kings knelt with gifts, behold!
By three times thirty steps, the shrine
  The pilgrim gains—and faint, and dim,
And dizzy with the height, divine
  Strength on the sudden springs to him!

"Yawns wide within that holy steep
A mghty cavern dark and deep—
By blessed sunbeam never lit—
Rank fœtid swamps engirdle it;

And there by night, and there by day,
Ever at watch, the fiend-worm lay,
Holding the Hell of its abode
Fast by the hallow'd House of God.
And when the pilgrim gladly ween'd
 His feet had found the healing way,
Forth from its ambush rush'd the fiend,
 And down to darkness dragged the prey.

"With solemn soul, that solemn height
I clomb, ere yet I sought the fight—
Kneeling before the cross within,
My heart, confessing, clear'd its sin.
Then, as befits the Christian knight,
I donn'd the spotless surplice white,
And, by the altar, grasp'd the spear:—
So down I strode with conscience clear—
Bade my leal squires afar the deed,
 By death or conquest crown'd, await—
Leapt lightly on my lithesome steed,
 And gave to God his soldier's fate!

"Before me wide the marshes lay—
Started the hounds with sudden bay—
Aghast the swerving charger slanting
Snorted—then stood abrupt and panting—
For curling there, in coilèd fold,
The Unutterable Beast behold!
Lazily basking in the sun.
Forth sprang the dogs. The fight's begun!
But lo! the hounds, in cowering, fly
 Before the mighty poison-breath—
A fierce yell, like the jackal's cry,
 Howl'd, mingling with that wind of death.

"No halt—I gave one cheering sound,
Lustily springs each dauntless hound—
Swift as the dauntless hounds advance,
Whirringly skirrs my stalwart lance—
Whirringly skirrs; and from the scale
Bounds, as a reed aslant the mail.
Onward—but no!—the craven steed

Shrinks from his lord in that dread need—
  Smitten and scar'd before that eye
Of basilisk horror, and that blast
  Of death, it only seeks to fly—
And half the mighty hope is past!

"A moment, and to earth I leapt;
Swift from its sheath the falchion swept;
Swift on that rock-like mail it plied—
The rock-like mail the sword defied:
The monster lash'd its mighty coil—
Down hurl'd—behold me on the soil!
Behold the hell-jaws gaping wide—
When lo! they bound—the flesh is found;
  Upon the scaleless parts they spring!
Springs either hound;—the flesh is found—
  It roars; the blood-dogs cleave and cling!

"No time to foil its fast'ning foes—
Light, as it writhed, I sprang, and rose;
The all-unguarded place explored,
Up to the hilt I plunged the sword—
Buried one instant in the blood—
The next, upsprang the bubbling flood!
The next, one Vastness spread the plain—
Crush'd down—the victor with the slain;
And all was dark—and on the ground
  My life, suspended, lost the sun,
Till waking—lo my squires around—
  And the dead foe!—my tale is done."

Then burst, as from a common breast,
The eager laud so long supprest—
A thousand voices, choral-blending,
Up to the vaulted dome ascending—
From groinèd roof and banner'd wall'
Invisible echoes answering all—
The very Brethren, grave and high,
Forget their state, and join the cry.
"With laurel wreaths his brows be crown'd,
  Let throng to throng his triumph tell;
Hail him all Rhodes!"—the Master frown'd,
  And raised his hand—and silence fell.

"Well," said that solemn voice, "thy hand
From the wild-beast hath freed the land.
An idol to the People be!
A foe our Order frowns on thee!
For in thy heart, superb and vain,
A hell-worm laidlier than the slain,
To discord which engenders death,
Poisons each thought with baleful breath!
That hell-worm is the stubborn Will—
  Oh! What were man and nations worth
If each his own desire fulfil,
  And law be banish'd from the earth?

"*Valour* the Heathen gives to story—
Obedience is the Christian's glory;
And on that soil our Saviour-God
As the meek low-born mortal trod.
We the Apostle-knights were sworn
To laws thy daring laughs to scorn—
Not *fame*, but *duty* to fulfil—
Our noblest offering—man's wild will.
Vain-glory doth thy soul betray—
  Begone—thy conquest is thy loss:
No breast too haughty to obey,
  Is worthy of the Christian's cross!"

From their cold awe the crowds awaken,
As with some storm the halls are shaken;
The noble Brethren plead for grace—
Mute stands the doom'd, with downward face;
And mutely loosen'd from its band
The badge, and kiss'd the Master's hand,
And meekly turn'd him to depart:
A moist eye follow'd, "To my heart
Come back, my son!"—the Master cries:
  "Thy grace a harder fight obtains;
When Valour risks the Christian's prize,
  Lo, how Humility regains!"

In the poem just presented to the reader, Schiller designed, as he wrote to Goethe, to depict the old Christian chivalry—half knightly, half monastic. The attempt is strikingly successful. Indeed, "The Fight of the Dragon" appears to us the most spirited and nervous of all Schiller's narrative poems, with the single exception of "The Diver;" and if its interest is less intense than that of the matchless "Diver," and its descriptions less poetically striking and effective, its interior meaning or philosophical conception is at once more profound and more elevated. In "The Fight of the Dragon," is expressed the moral of that humility which consists in self-conquest—even merit may lead to vain-glory—and, after vanquishing the fiercest enemies without, Man has still to contend with his worst foe,—the pride or disobedience of his own heart. "Every one," as a recent and acute, but somewhat over-refining critic has remarked, "has more or less—his own 'fight with the Dragon'—his own double victory (without and within) to achieve." The origin of this poem is to be found in the Annals of the Order of Malta—and the details may be seen in Vertot's History. The date assigned to the conquest of the Dragon is 1342. Helion de Villeneuve was the name of the Grand Master—that of the Knight, Dieu-Donné de Gozon. Thevenot declares that the head of the monster (to whatever species it really belonged), or its effigies, was still placed over one of the gates of the city in his time.—Dieu-Donné succeeded De Villeneuve as Grand Master, and on his gravestone were inscribed the words "Draconis Exstinctor."

DITHYRAMB.*

BELIEVE me, together
The bright gods come ever,
 Still as of old;
Scarce see I Bacchus, the giver of joy,
Than comes up fair Eros, the laugh-loving boy ;
 And Phœbus, the stately, behold !

  They come near and nearer,
   The Heavenly Ones all—
  The Gods with their presence
   Fill earth as their hall!

Say, how shall *I* welcome,
 Human and earthborn,
  Sons of the Sky ?
Pour out to me—pour the full life that ye live !
What to you, O ye gods ! can the mortal-one give ?

  The Joys can dwell only
   In Jupiter's palace—
  Brimm'd bright with your nectar,
   Oh, reach me the chalice !

* This has been paraphrased by Coleridge.

"Hebe, the chalice
  Fill full to the brim!
Steep his eyes—steep his eyes in the bath of the dew,
Let him dream, while the Styx is concealed from his view,
  That the life of the Gods is for him!"

  It murmurs, it sparkles,
    The Fount of Delight;
  The bosom grows tranquil—
    The eye becomes bright.

THE KNIGHTS OF ST. JOHN.

Oh, nobly shone the fearful Cross upon your mail afar,
When Rhodes and Acre hail'd your might, O lions of the war!
When leading many a pilgrim horde, through wastes of Syrian gloom;
Or standing with the Cherub's sword before the Holy Tomb.
Yet on your forms the Apron seem'd a nobler armour far,
When by the sick man's bed ye stood, O lions of the war!
When ye, the high-born, bow'd your pride to tend the lowly weakness,
The duty, though it brought no fame,* fulfilled by Christian meekness—
Religion of the Cross, thou blend'st, as in a single flower,
The twofold branches of the palm—HUMILITY AND POWER.

THE MAIDEN FROM AFAR.

(OR, FROM ABROAD.)

Within a vale, each infant year,
  When earliest larks first carol free,
To humble shepherds doth appear
  A wondrous maiden, fair to see.

* The epithet in the first edition is *ruhmlos*.

Not born within that lowly place—
   From whence she wander'd, none could tell:
Her parting footsteps left no trace,
   When once the maiden sigh'd farewell.

And blessèd was her presence there—
   Each heart, expanding, grew more gay;
Yet something loftier still than fair
   Kept man's familiar looks away.
From fairy gardens, known to none,
   She brought mysterious fruits and flowers—
The things of some serener sun—
   Some Nature more benign than ours.

With each, her gifts the maiden shared—
   To some the fruits, the flowers to some;
Alike the young, the aged fared;
   Each bore a blessing back to home.
Though every guest was welcome there,
   Yet some the maiden held more dear,
And cull'd her rarest sweets whene'er
   She saw two hearts that loved draw near.

NOTE.—It seems generally agreed that POETRY is allegorised in these stanzas; though, with this interpretation, it is difficult to reconcile the sense of some of the lines—for instance, the last in the first stanza. How can Poetry be said to leave no trace when she takes farewell?

THE TWO GUIDES OF LIFE—

THE SUBLIME AND THE BEAUTIFUL.

Two genii are there, from thy birth through weary life, to guide thee;
Ah, happy when, united both, they stand to aid, beside thee!
With gleesome play, to cheer the path, the One comes blithe with beauty—
And lighter, leaning on her arm, the destiny and duty.

With jest and sweet discourse, she goes unto the rock
      sublime,
Where halts above the Eternal Sea,* the shuddering
      Child of Time.
The Other here, resolved and mute, and solemn claspeth
      thee,
And bears thee in her giant arms across the fearful sea.
Never admit the one alone!—Give not the gentle guide
Thy honour—nor unto the stern thy happiness confide!

THE FOUR AGES OF THE WORLD.

[This Poem is one of those in which Schiller has traced the progress of Civilization, and to which the Germans have given the name of Culture-Historic.]

BRIGHT-PURPLING the glass glows the blush of the wine—
    Bright sparkle the eyes of each guest;
The POET has enter'd the circle to join—
    To the good brings the Poet the best.
Ev'n Olympus were mean, with its nectar and all,
If the lute's happy magic were mute in the hall.

Bestow'd by the gods on the poet has been
    A soul that can mirror the world!
Whate'er has been done on this earth he has seen,
    And the future to him is unfurl'd.
He sits with the gods in their council sublime,
And views the dark seeds in the bosom of Time.

The folds of this life, in the pomp of its hues,
    He broadens all justly forth,
And to him is the magic he takes from the Muse,
    To deck, like a temple, the earth.
A hut, though the humblest that man ever trod,
He can charm to a heaven, and illume with a god!

---

* By this, Schiller informs us elsewhere that he does not mean Death alone; but that the thought applies equally to every period in life, when we can divest our souls of the body, and perceive or act as pure spirits: we are truly then under the influence of the Sublime.

As the god and the genius, whose birth was of Jove,*
  In one type all creation reveal'd,
When the ocean, the earth, and the star-realm above,
  Lay compress'd in the orb of a shield;
So the poet, a shape and a type of the All,
From a sound, that is mute in a moment, can call.†

Blithe pilgrim! his footsteps have pass'd in their way,
  Every time, every far generation;
He comes from the age when the Earth was at play
  In the childhood and bloom of Creation.
Four Ages of men have decay'd to his eye,
And fresh to the Fifth he glides youthfully by.

King Saturn first ruled us, the simple and true—
  Each day as each yesterday fair:
No grief and no guile the calm shepherd-race knew—
  Their life was the absence of care;
They loved, and to love was the whole of their task—
Kind earth upon all lavish'd all they could ask.

Then the LABOUR arose, and the demi-god man
  Went the monster and dragon to seek;
And the age of the hero, the ruler, began,
  And the strong were the stay of the weak.
By Scamander the strife and the glory had birth;
But the Beautiful still was the god of the earth.

From the strife came the conquest; and Strength, like a wind,
Swept its way through the meek and the mild:
Still vocal the Muse, and in marble enshrined,
  The gods upon Helicon smiled.
Alas, for the age which fair Phantasie bore!—
It is fled from the earth, to return nevermore.

---

* Vulcan—the allusion, which is exquisitely beautiful, is to the Shield of Achilles.—HOMER, Il. i. 18.

  "There Earth, there Heaven, there Ocean, he design'd."—POPE.

† This line is obscure, not only in the translation, but so in the original. Schiller means to say that the Poet is the true generaliser of the infinite—a position which he himself practically illustrates, by condensing, in the few verses that follow, the whole history of the world. Thus, too, Homer is the condenser of the whole heroic age of Greece. In the Prologue to "Wallenstein," the same expressions, with little alteration, are employed to convey the perishable nature of the Actor's art.

The gods from their thrones in Olympus were hurl'd,
  Fane and column lay rent and forlorn;
And—holy, to heal all the wounds of the world—
  The Son of the Virgin was born.
The lusts of the senses subdued or suppress'd,
Man mused on life's ends, and took THOUGHT to his breast.*

Ever gone were those charms, the voluptuous and vain,
  Which had deck'd the young world with delight;
For the monk and the nun were the penance and pain,
  And the tilt for the iron-clad knight.
Yet, however that life might be darksome and wild,
Love linger'd with looks still as lovely and mild:

By the shrine of an altar yet chaste and divine,
  Stood the Muses in stillness and shade;
And honour'd, and household, and holy that shrine—
  In the blush—in the heart of the maid:
And the sweet light of song burn'd the fresher and truer,
In the lay and the love of the wild Troubadour.

As ever, so aye, in their beautiful band,
  May the Maid and the Poet unite:
Their task be to work, and to weave, hand in hand,
  The zone of the Fair and the Right!
Love and Song, Song and Love, intertwined evermore,
Weary Earth to the suns of its youth can restore.

* "Der Mensch griff *denkend* in seine Brust,"
i. e. Man strove by reflection to apprehend the phenomena of his own being —the principles of his own nature. The development of the philosophical, as distinguished from the natural consciousness, forms a very important æra in the history of civilization. It is in fact the great turning-point of humanity, both individually and historically. Griff, Begriff—has a peculiar logical significance in German.

THE MAIDEN'S LAMENT.

[The two first Stanzas of this Poem are sung by Thekla, in the third Act of the "Piccolomini."]

THE wind rocks the forest,
  The clouds gather o'er;
The girl sitteth lonely
  Beside the green shore;
The breakers are dashing with might, with might:
And she mingles her sighs with the gloomy night,
  And her eyes are hot with tears.

"The earth is a desert,
  And broken my heart,
Nor aught to my wishes
  The world can impart.
To her Father in Heaven may the Daughter now go;
I have known all the joys that the world can bestow—
  I have lived—I have loved"—

"In vain, oh! how vainly,
  Flows tear upon tear!
Human woe never waketh
  Dull Death's heavy ear!—
Yet say what can soothe for the sweet vanish'd love,
And I, the Celestial, will shed from above
  The balm for thy breast."

"Let ever, though vainly,
  Flow tear upon tear;
Human woe never waketh
  Dull Death's heavy ear;
Yet still when the heart mourns the sweet vanish'd love,
No balm for its wound can descend from above
  Like Love's own faithful tears!"

THE IMMUTABLE.

TIME flies on restless pinions—constant never.
Be constant—and thou chainest time for ever.

THE VEILED IMAGE AT SAIS.

A YOUTH, whom wisdom's warm desire had lured
To learn the secret lore of Egypt's priests,
To Sais came. And soon, from step to step
Of upward mystery, swept his rapid soul!
Still ever sped the glorious Hope along,
Nor could the parch'd Impatience halt, appeased
By the calm answer of the Hierophant—
"What have I, if I have not all," he sigh'd;
"And givest thou but the little and the more?
Does thy truth dwindle to the gauge of gold,
A sum that man may smaller or less small
Possess and count—subtract or add to—still?
Is not TRUTH *one* and indivisible?
Take from the Harmony a single tone—
A single tint take from the Iris bow,
And lo! what once was all, is nothing—while
Fails to the lovely whole one tint or tone!"

They stood within the temple's silent dome,
And, as the young man paused abrupt, his gaze
Upon a veil'd and giant IMAGE fell:
Amazed he turn'd unto his guide—" And what
Towers, yonder, vast beneath the veil?"
         "THE TRUTH,"
Answered the Priest.
      "And have I for the truth
Panted and struggled with a lonely soul,
And yon the thin and ceremonial robe
That wraps her from mine eyes?"
         Replied the priest,
"There shrouds herself the still Divinity.
Hear, and revere her hest: 'Till I this veil
Lift—may no mortal-born presume to raise;
And who with guilty and unhallow'd hand
Too soon profanes the Holy and Forbidden—
He,' says the goddess"—
       "Well?"
        "'SHALL SEE THE TRUTH!'"

"A wond'rous oracle; and hast *thou* never
Lifted the veil?"
                    "No! nor desired to raise!"
"What! nor desired? O strange incurious heart,
Here the thin barrier—there reveal'd the truth!"
Mildly return'd the priestly master, "Son,
More mighty than thou dream'st of, Holy Law
Spreads interwoven in yon slender web,
Air-light to touch—lead-heavy to the soul!"

The young man, thoughtful, turn'd him to his home,
And the sharp fever of the Wish to Know
Robb'd night of sleep. Around his couch he roll'd,
Till midnight hatch'd resolve—
                    "Unto the shrine!"

Stealthily on, the involuntary tread
Bears him—he gains the boundary, scales the wall,
And midway in the inmost, holiest dome,
Strides with adventurous step the daring man.

Now halts he where the lifeless Silence sleeps
In the embrace of mournful Solitude;—
Silence unstirr'd,—save where the guilty tread
Call'd the dull echo from mysterious vaults!

High from the opening of the dome above,
Came with wan smile the silver-shining moon.
And, awful as some pale presiding god,
Dim-gleaming through the hush of that large gloom,
In its wan veil the Giant Image stood.

With an unsteady step he onwards past,
Already touch'd the violating hand
The Holy—and recoil'd! a shudder thrill'd
His limbs, fire-hot and icy-cold in turns,
As if invisible arms would pluck the soul
Back from the deed.
                    "O miserable man!
What would'st thou?" (Thus within the inmost heart
Murmur'd the warning whisper.) "Wilt thou dare
The All-hallow'd to profane? 'No mortal-born

(So spake the oracular word) may lift the veil
Till I myself shall raise!' Yet said it not,
The same oracular word—' who lifts the veil
Shall see the truth?' Behind, be what there may,
I dare the hazard—I will lift the veil—"
Loud rang his shouting voice—." and I will see!"
                                                        "SEE!"

A lengthen'd echo, mocking, shrill'd again!
He spoke and rais'd the veil! And ask'st thou what
Unto the sacrilegious gaze lay bare?
I know not—pale and senseless, stretch'd before
The statue of the great Egyptian queen,
The priests beheld him at the dawn of day;
But what he saw, or what did there befall,
His lips reveal'd not. Ever from his heart
Was fled the sweet serenity of life,
And the deep anguish dug the early grave:
"Woe—woe to him"—such were his warning words,
Answering some curious and impetuous brain,
"Woe—for her face shall charm him never more!
Woe—woe to him who treads through Guilt to TRUTH!"

THE CHILD IN THE CRADLE.

WITHIN that narrow bed, glad babe, to thee
    A boundless world is spread!
Unto thy soul, the boundless world shall be
    When man, a narrow bed!"*

---

* This epigram has a considerable resemblance to the epitaph on Alexander the Great:

   Sufficit huic Tumulus, cui non suffecerat orbis:
   Res brevis huic ampla est, cui fuit ampla brevis.

A little tomb sufficeth him whom not sufficed all:
The small is now as great to him as once the great was small.
              Vide BLACKWOOD'S MAGAZINE, *April*, 1838, p. 556.

THE RING OF POLYCRATES.

A BALLAD.

Upon his battlements he stands—
And proudly looks along the lands—
    His Samos and the Sea!
"And all," he said, "that we survey,
Egyptian king, my power obey—
    Own, Fortune favours me!"

"With thee the Gods their favour share,
And they who once thine equals were,
    In thee a monarch know!
Yet one there lives to avenge the rest,
Nor can my lips pronounce thee blest,
    While on thee frowns the Foe!"

He spoke, and from Miletus sent,
There came a breathless man, and bent
    Before the tyrant there.
"Let incense smoke upon the shrine,
And with the lively laurel twine,
    Victor, thy godlike hair!

"The foe sunk, smitten by the spear;
With the glad tidings sends me here,
    Thy faithful Polydore."
And from the griesly bowl he drew
(Grim sight they well might start to view!)
    A head that dripp'd with gore.

The Egyptian king recoil'd in fear,
"Hold not thy fortune yet too dear—
    Bethink thee yet," he cried,
"Thy Fleets are on the faithless seas;
Thy Fortune trembles in the breeze,
    And floats upon the tide."

THE RING OF POLYCRATES.

Ere yet the warning word was spoken—
Below, the choral joy was broken—
　　Shouts ring from street to street!
Home-veering to the crowded shore—
Their freight of richest booty bore
　　The Forests of the Fleet.

Astounded stood that kingly guest,
"Thy luck this day must be confest,
　　Yet trust not the Unsteady!
The banners of the Cretan foe
Wave war, and bode thine overthrow—
　　They near thy sands already!"

Scarce spoke the Egyptian King—before
Hark, "Victory—Victory!" from the shore,
　　And from the seas ascended;
"Escaped the doom that round us lower'd,
Swift storm the Cretan has devoured,
　　And war itself is ended!"

Shudder'd the guest—"In sooth," he falter'd,
"To-day thy fortune smiles unalter'd,
　　Yet more thy fate I dread—
The Gods oft grudge what they have given,
And ne'er unmix'd with grief has Heaven
　　Its joys on Mortals shed!

"No less than thine my rule has thriven,
And o'er each deed the gracious heaven
　　Has, favouring, smiled as yet.
But one beloved heir had I—
God took him!—I beheld him die,
　　His life paid fortune's debt.

"So, would'st *thou* 'scape the coming ill—
Implore the dread Invisible—
　　Thy sweets themselves to sour!
Well ends his life, believe me, never,
On whom, with hands thus full for ever,
　　The Gods their bounty shower.

"And if thy prayer the Gods can gain not
This counsel of thy friend disdain not—
 Thine own afflictor be!
And what of all thy worldly gear
Thy deepest heart esteems most dear,
 Cast into yonder sea!"

The Samian thrill'd to hear the king—
"No gems so rich as deck this ring,
 The wealth of Samos gave:
By this—O may the Fatal Three
My glut of fortune pardon me!"
 He cast it on the wave—

And when the morrow's dawn began,
All joyous came a fisherman
 Before the prince.—Quoth he,
"Behold this fish—so fair a spoil
Ne'er yet repaid the snarer's toil,
 I bring my best to thee!"

The cook to dress the fish began—
The cook ran fast as cook could run—
 "Look, look!—O master mine—
The ring—the ring the sea did win,
I found the fish's maw within—
 Was ever luck like thine!"

In horror turns the kingly guest—
"Then longer here I may not rest,
 I'll have no friend in thee!
The Gods have marked thee for their prey,
To share thy doom I dare not stay!"
 He spoke—and put to sea.

NOTE.—This story is taken from the well-known correspondence between Amasis and Polycrates, in the third book of Herodotus. Polycrates—one of the ablest of that most able race, the Greek tyrants,—was afterwards decoyed into the power of Orœtes, Governor of Sardis, and died on the cross. Herodotus informs us, that the ring Polycrates so prized, was an emerald set in gold, the workmanship of Theodorus the Samian. Pliny, on the contrary, affirms it to have been a sardonyx, and in his time it was supposed still to exist among the treasures in the Temple of Concord. It is worth while to turn to Herodotus (c. 40—43, book 3), to notice the admirable art with which Schiller has adapted the narrative, and heightened its effect.

HOPE.

We speak with the lip, and we dream in the soul,
    Of some better and fairer day;
And our days, the meanwhile, to that golden goal
    Are gliding and sliding away.
Now the world becomes old, now again it is young,
But "*The Better*" 's for ever the word on the tongue

At the threshold of life Hope leads us in—
    Hope plays round the mirthful boy;
Though the best of its charms may with youth begin,
    Yet for age it reserves its toy.
When we sink at the grave, why the grave has scope,
And over the coffin Man planteth—Hope!

And it is not a dream of a fancy proud,
    With a fool for its dull begetter;
There's a voice at the heart that proclaims aloud—
    We are born for a something Better!"
And that Voice of the Heart, oh, ye may believe,
Will never the Hope of the Soul deceive!

THE SEXES.

See in the babe two loveliest flowers united—yet in truth,
While in the bud they seem the same—the virgin and the youth!
But loosen'd is the gentle bond, no longer side by side—
From holy Shame the fiery Strength will soon itself divide.
Permit the youth to sport, and still the wild desire to chase,
For, but when sated, weary strength returns to seek the grace.
Yet in the bud, the double flowers the future strife begin,
How precious all—yet nought can still the longing heart within.

In ripening charms the virgin bloom to woman shape hath
　　grown,
But round the ripening charms the pride hath clasp'd its
　　guardian zone;
Shy, as before the hunter's horn the doe all trembling
　　moves,
She flies from man as from a foe, and hates before she
　　loves!
From lowering brows this struggling world the fearless
　　youth observes,
And, harden'd for the strife betimes, he strains the willing
　　nerves;
Far to the armèd throng and to the race prepared to
　　start,
Inviting glory calls him forth, and grasps the troubled
　　heart:—
Protect thy work, O Nature now! one from the other
　　flies,
Till thou unitest each at last that for the other sighs.
There art thou, mighty one! where'er the discord darkest
　　frown,
Thou call'st the meek harmonious Peace, the godlike
　　soother down.
The noisy chase is lull'd asleep, day's clamour dies afar,
And through the sweet and veilèd air in beauty comes the
　　star.
Soft-sighing through the crispèd reeds, the brooklet glides
　　along,
And every wood the nightingale melodious fills with
　　song.
O virgin! now what instinct heaves thy bosom with the
　　sigh?
O youth! and wherefore steals the tear into thy dreaming
　　eye?
Alas! they seek in vain within the charm around be-
　　stow'd,
The tender fruit is ripen'd now, and bows to earth its
　　load.
And restless goes the youth to feed his heart upon its
　　fire,
Ah, where the gentle breath to cool the flame of young
　　desire!

And now they meet—the holy love that leads them lights
    their eyes,
And still behind the wingèd god the wingèd victory flies.
O heavenly Love!—'tis thy sweet task the human flowers
    to bind,
For aye apart, and yet by thee for ever intertwined!

HONOURS.

[DIGNITIES would be the better title, if the word were not so essentially
unpoetical.]

WHEN the column of light on the waters is glass'd,
    As blent in one glow seem the shine and the stream;
But wave after wave through the glory has pass'd,
    Just catches, and flies as it catches, the beam:
So Honours but mirror on mortals their light;
Not the MAN but the PLACE that he passes is bright.

POMPEII AND HERCULANEUM.

WHAT wonder this?—we ask the lymphid well,
O Earth! of thee—and from thy solemn womb
What yield'st thou?—Is there life in the abyss—
Doth a new race beneath the lava dwell?
Returns the Past, awakening from the tomb?
Rome—Greece!—O, come!—Behold—behold! For this
Our living world—the old Pompeii sees;
And built anew the town of Dorian Hercules!
House upon house—its silent halls once more
Opes the broad Portico!—O, haste and fill
Again those halls with life!—O, pour along
Through the seven-vista'd theatre the throng!
Where are ye, mimes?—Come forth, the steel prepare
For crown'd Atrides, or Orestes haunt,
Ye choral Furies with your dismal chaunt!
The Arch of Triumph!—whither leads it?—still
Behold the Forum!—On the curule chair
Where the majestic image? Lictors, where
Your solemn fasces?—Place upon his throne

The Prætor—here the Witness lead, and there
Bid the Accuser stand!
                —O God! how lone
The clear streets glitter in the quiet day—
The footpath by the doors winding its lifeless way!
The roofs arise in shelter, and around
The desolate Atrium—every gentle room
Wears still the dear familiar smile of Home!
Open the doors—the shops—on dreary night
Let lusty day laugh down in jocund light!
See the trim benches ranged in order!—See
The marble-tesselated floor—and there
The very walls are glittering livingly
With their clear colours. But the artist where?
Sure but this instant he hath laid aside
Pencil and colours!—Glittering on the eye
Swell the rich fruits, and bloom the flowers!—See all
Art's gentle wreaths still fresh upon the wall!
Here the arch Cupid slyly seems to glide
By with bloom-laden basket. There the shapes
Of Genii press with purpling feet the grapes.
Here springs the wild Bacchante to the dance,
And there she sleeps [while that voluptuous trance
Eyes the sly faun with never-sated glance]
Now on one knee upon the centaur-steeds
Hovering — the Thyrsus plies. — Hurrah! — away she
    speeds!
Come—come, why loiter ye?—Here, here, how fair
The goodly vessels still! Girls, hither turn,
Fill from the fountain the Etruscan urn!
On the wing'd sphinxes see the tripod.—
                              Ho!
Quick—quick, ye slaves, come—fire!—the hearth prepare!
Ha! wilt thou sell?—this coin shall pay thee—this,
Fresh from the mint of mighty Titus!—Lo!
Here lie the scales, and not a weight we miss!
So—bring the light! The delicate lamp!—what toil
Shaped thy minutest grace!—quick, pour the oil!
Yonder the fairy chest!—come, maid, behold
The bridegroom's gifts—the armlets—they are gold,
And paste out-feigning jewels!—lead the bride
Into the odorous bath—lo, unguents still—

And still the crystal vase the arts for beauty fill!
But where the men of old—perchance a prize
More precious yet in yon papyrus lies,
And see ev'n still the tokens of their toil—
The waxen tablets—the recording style.
  The earth, with faithful watch, has hoarded all!
Still stand the mute Penates in the hall;
Back to his haunts returns each ancient God.
Why absent only from their ancient stand
The Priests?—waves Hermes his Caducean rod,
And the wing'd victory struggles from the hand.
Kindle the flame—behold the Altar there!
Long hath the God been worshipless—To prayer!

LIGHT AND WARMTH.

In cheerful faith that fears no ill
  The good man doth the world begin;
And dreams that all without shall still
  Reflect the trusting soul within.
Warm with the noble vows of youth,
Hallowing his true arm to the truth;

Yet is the littleness of all
  So soon to sad experience shown,
That crowds but teach him to recall
  And centre thought on self alone;
Till love, no more, emotion knows,
And the heart freezes to repose.

Alas! though truth may *light* bestow,
  Not always *warmth* the beams impart,
Blest he who gains the BOON TO KNOW,
  Nor buys the knowledge with the heart.
For warmth and light a blessing both to be,
Feel as the Enthusiast—as the World-wise see.

BREADTH AND DEPTH.

Full many a shining wit one sees,
　　With tongue on all things well-conversing;
The what can charm, the what can please,
　　In every nice detail rehearsing.
Their raptures so transport the college,
It seems one honeymoon of knowledge.

Yet out they go in silence where
　　They whilome held their learned prate;
Ah! he who would achieve the fair,
　　Or sow the embryo of the great,
Must hoard—to wait the ripening hour—
In the least point the loftiest power.

With wanton boughs and pranksome hues,
　　Aloft in air aspires the stem;
The glittering leaves inhale the dews
　　But fruits are not conceal'd in *them*.
From the small kernel's undiscerned repose
The oak that lords it o'er the Forest grows.

THE PHILOSOPHICAL EGOIST.

Hast thou the infant seen that yet, unknowing of the love
Which warms and cradles, calmly sleeps the mother's heart above—
Wandering from arm to arm, until the call of passion wakes,
And glimmering on the conscious eye—the world in glory breaks?—
And hast thou seen the mother there her anxious vigil keep,
Buying with love that never sleeps the darling's happy sleep?
With her own life she fans and feeds that weak life's trembling rays,
And with the sweetness of the care, the care itself repays.

And dost thou Nature then blaspheme—that, both the child
    and mother
Each unto each unites, the while the one doth need the
    other?—
All self-sufficing wilt thou from that lovely circle stand—
That creature still to creature links in faith's familiar
    band?
Ah! dar'st thou, poor one, from the rest thy lonely self
    estrange?
Eternal Power itself is but all powers in interchange!

FRIDOLIN;

OR, THE MESSAGE TO THE FORGE.

[Schiller speaking of this Ballad, which he had then nearly concluded, says that "accident had suggested to him a very pretty theme for a Ballad;" and that "after having travelled through air and water," alluding to "The Cranes of Ibycus" and "The Diver," "he should now claim to himself the Element of Fire."—Hoffmeister supposes from the name of Savern, the French orthography for Zabern, a town in Alsatia, that Schiller took the material for his tale from a French source; though there are German Legends analogous to it. The general style of the Ballad is simple almost to homeliness, though not to the puerility affected by some of our own Ballad writers.—But the pictures of the Forge and the Catholic Ritual are worked out with singular force and truthfulness.]

A HARMLESS lad was Fridolin,
    A pious youth was he;
He served and sought her grace to win,
    Count Savern's fair ladye;
And gentle was the Dame as fair,
And light the toils of service there;
And yet the woman's wildest whim
In her—had been but joy to him.

Soon as the early morning shone,
    Until the vesper bell,
For her sweet hest he lived alone
    Nor e'er could serve too well.
She bade him oft not labour so:
But then his eyes would overflow. . .
It seemed a sin if strength could swerve,
From that one thought—her will to serve!

And so of all her House, the Dame
  Most favour'd him always;
And from her lip for ever came
  His unexhausted praise.
On him, more like some gentle child,
Than serving-youth, the lady smiled,
And took a harmless pleasure in
The comely looks of Fridolin.

For this, the Huntsman Robert's heart
  The favour'd Henchman cursed;
And long, till ripen'd into art,
  The hateful envy nursed.
His Lord was rash of thought and deed:
And thus the knave the deadly seed,
(As from the chase they homeward rode,)
That poisons thought to fury, sow'd—

"Your lot, great Count, in truth is fair,
  (Thus spoke the craft suppress'd;)
The gnawing tooth of doubt can ne'er
  Consume your golden rest.
He who a noble spouse can claim,
Sees love begirt with holy shame;
Her truth no villain arts ensnare—
The smooth seducer comes not there.

"How now!—bold man, what sayest thou?"
  The frowning Count replied—
"Think'st thou I build on woman's vow,
  Unstable as the tide?
Too well the flatterer's lip allureth—
On firmer ground my faith endureth;
The Count Von Savern's wife unto
No smooth seducer comes to woo!"

"Right!"—quoth the other—"and your scorn
  The fool enow the fool chastises,
Who though a simple vassal born,
  Himself so highly prizes;
Who buoys his heart with rash desires,
And to the Dame he serves aspires."

"How!" cried the Count, and trembled—"How!
Of One who lives, then, speakest thou?"

"Surely; can that to all reveal'd
  Be all unknown to you?
Yet, from your ear if thus conceal'd,
  Let me be silent too."
Out burst the Count, with gasping breath,
"Fool—fool!—thou speak'st the words of death!
What brain has dared so bold a sin?"
"My Lord, I spoke of Fridolin!

"His face is comely to behold"—
  He adds—then paused with art.
The Count grew hot—the Count grew cold—
  The words had pierced his heart.
"My gracious master sure must see
That only in her eyes lives he;
Behind your board he stands unheeding,
Close by her chair—his passion feeding.

"And then the rhymes..." "The rhymes!" "The
    same—
  Confess'd the frantic thought."
"Confess'd!" "Ay, and a *mutual* flame
  The foolish boy besought!
No doubt the Countess, soft and tender,
Forbore the lines to you to render, ...
And I repent the babbling word
That 'scaped my lips—What ails my lord?"

Straight to a wood, in scorn and shame,
  Away Count Savern rode—
Where, in the soaring furnace-flame,
  The molten iron glow'd.
Here, late and early, still the brand
Kindled the smiths, with crafty hand;
The bellows heave and the sparkles fly,
As if they would melt down the mountains high.

Their strength the Fire, the Water gave,
    In interleagued endeavour;
The mill-wheel, whirl'd amidst the wave,
    Rolls on for aye and ever—
Here, day and night, resounds the clamour,
While measured beats the heaving hammer;
And, suppled in that ceaseless storm,
Iron to iron stamps a form.

Two smiths before Count Savern bend,
    Forth-beckon'd from their task.
" The first whom I to you may send,
    And who of you may ask—
' *Have you my lord's command obey'd ?* '
—Thrust in the hell-fire yonder made;
Shrunk to the cinders of your ore,
Let him offend mine eyes no more ! "

Then gloated they—the griesly pair—
    They felt the hangman's zest;
For senseless as the iron there,
    The heart lay in the breast.
And hied they, with the bellows' breath,
To strengthen still the furnace-death;
The murder-priests nor flag nor falter—
Wait the victim—trim the altar!

The huntsman seeks the page—God wot,
    How smooth a face hath he!
" Off, comrade, off! and tarry not;
    Thy lord hath need of thee! "
Thus spoke his lord to Fridolin,
" Haste to the forge the wood within,
And ask the serfs who ply the trade—
' *Have you my lord's command obey'd ?* ' "

" It shall be done "—and to the task
    He hies without delay.
Had *she* not hest?—'twere well to ask,
    To make less long the way.
So, wending backward at the thought,
The youth the gracious lady sought.

FRIDOLIN.

"Ere I go to the forge, I have come to thee:
Hast thou any commands, by the road for me?"

"I fain," thus spake that lady fair,
  In winsome tone and low,
"But for mine infant ailing there,
  To hear the mass would go.
Go thou, my child—and on the way,
For me and mine thy heart shall pray;
Repent each sinful thought of thine—
So shall thy soul find grace for mine!"

Forth on the welcome task he wends,
  Her wish the task endears,
Till, where the quiet hamlet ends
  A sudden sound he hears.
To and fro the church-bell, swinging,
Cheerily, clearly forth is ringing;
Knolling souls that would repent
To the Holy Sacrament.

He thought, "Seek God upon thy way,
  And he will come to thee!"
He gains the House of Prayer to pray,
  But all stood silently.
It was the Harvest's merry reign,
The scythe was busy in the grain,
One clerkly hand the rites require
To serve the mass and aid the choir.

At once the good resolve he takes,
  As sacristan to serve:
"No halt," quoth he, "the footstep makes,
  That doth but heavenward swerve!"
So, on the priest, with humble soul,
He hung the cingulum and stole,
And eke prepares each holy thing
To the high mass administ'ring.

Now, as the ministrant, before
  The priest he took his stand;
Now towards the altar moved, and bore
  The mass-book in his hand.

Rightward, leftward kneeleth he,
Watchful every sign to see;
Tinkling, as the *sanctus* fell,
Thrice at each holy name, the bell.

Now the meek priest, bending lowly,
   Turns unto the solemn shrine,
And with lifted hand and holy,
   Rears the cross divine.
While the clear bell, lightly swinging,
That boy-sacristan is ringing;—
Strike their breasts, and down inclining,
Kneel the crowd, the symbol signing.

Still in every point excelling,
   With a quick and nimble art—
Every custom in that dwelling
   Knew the boy by heart!
To the close he tarried thus,
Till *Vobiscum Dominus;*
To the crowd inclines the priest,
And the crowd have sign'd—and ceased!

Now back in its appointed place,
   His footsteps but delay
To range each symbol-sign of grace—
   Then forward on his way.
So, conscience calm, he lightly goes;
Before his steps the furnace glows;
His lips, the while, (the count completing,)
Twelve paternosters slow-repeating.

He gain'd the forge—the smiths survey'd,
   As there they grimly stand:
"How fares it, friends?—*have ye obey'd,*"
   He cried, "*my lord's command?*"
"Ho! ho!" they shout and ghastly grin,
And point the furnace-throat within:
"With zeal and heed, we did the deed—
The master's praise, the servants' meed."

On, with this answer, onward home,
   With fleeter step he flies;
Afar, the Count beheld him come—
   He scarce could trust his eyes.
" Whence com'st thou ? " " From the furnace." ' So !
Not elsewhere ? troth, thy steps are slow;
Thou hast loiter'd long ! "—" Yet only till
I might the trust consign'd fulfil.

" My noble lord, 'tis true, to-day,
   I'd chanced, on quitting thee,
To ask my duties, on the way,
   Of her who guideth me.
She bade me, (and how sweet and dear
It was!) the holy mass to hear;
Rosaries four I told, delaying,
Grace for thee and thine heart-praying."

All stunn'd, Count Savern heard the speech—
   A wondering man was he;
"And when thou didst the furnace reach,
   What answer gave they thee ? "
" An answer hard the sense to win ;
Thus spake the men with ghastly grin,
' With zeal and heed, we did the deed—
The master's praise, the servants' meed.' "

" And *Robert ?* "—gasp'd the Count, as lost
   In awe, he shuddering stood—
" Thou must, be sure, his path have cross'd ?
   I sent him to the wood."
" In wood nor field where I have been,
No single trace of him was seen."
All deathlike stood the Count : " Thy might,
O God of heaven, hath judged the right ! "

Then meekly, humbled from his pride,
   He took the servant's hand;
He led him to his lady's side,
   She nought mote understand.
This child—no angel is more pure—
Long may thy grace for him endure;

Our strength how weak, our sense how dim—
GOD AND HIS HOSTS ARE OVER HIM!"

THE YOUTH BY THE BROOK.

[Sung in "The Parasite," a comedy which Schiller translated from Picard
—much the best comedy, by the way, that Picard ever wrote.]

BESIDE the brook the Boy reclin'd
  And wove his flowery wreath,
And to the waves the wreath consign'd—
  The waves that danced beneath.
"So fleet mine hours," he sighed, "away
  Like waves that restless flow:
And, so my flowers of youth decay
  Like those that float below.

"Ask not why I, alone on earth,
  Am sad in life's young time;
To all the rest are hope and mirth
  When spring renews its prime.
Alas! the music Nature makes,
  In thousand songs of gladness—
While charming all around me, wakes
  My heavy heart to sadness.

"Ah! vain to me the joys that break
  From Spring, voluptuous are;
For only ONE 'tis mine to seek—
  The Near, yet ever Far!
I stretch my arms, that shadow-shape
  In fond embrace to hold;
Still doth the shade the clasp escape—
  The heart is unconsoled!

"Come forth, fair Friend, come forth below,
  And leave thy lofty hall,
The fairest flowers the spring can know
  In thy dear lap shall fall!
Clear glides the brook in silver roll'd,
  Sweet carols fill the air;
The meanest hut hath space to hold
  A happy loving Pair!"

TO THE IDEAL.

[To appreciate the beauty of this Poem,—the reader must remember that it preceded our own School—we will not say of Egotism, but of Self-expression; a school of which the great Byron is the everlasting master—and in which the Poet reveals the hearts of others, by confessing the emotions of his own. Of late years we have been overwhelmed with attempts at the kind of pathos which the following stanzas embody with melancholy tenderness—yet with manly resignation. But at the time Schiller wrote this elegy on departed youth, he had the merit of originality—a merit the greater, because the Poem expresses feelings which almost all of us have felt in the progress of life.—The only Poem written before it, which it resembles, is the "Ode on a Distant Prospect of Eton College," by our own illustrious Gray, whom the little critics of our day seek to depreciate.—Beautiful as the German's poem is (in his own language), the Englishman's excels it.]

Then wilt thou, with thy fancies holy—
  Wilt thou, faithless, fly from me?
With thy joy, thy melancholy,
  Wilt thou thus relentless flee?
O Golden Time, O Human May,
  Can nothing, Fleet One, thee restrain?
Must thy sweet river glide away
  Into the eternal Ocean-Main?

The suns serene are lost and vanish'd
  That wont the path of youth to gild,
And all the fair Ideals banish'd
  From that wild heart they whilome fill'd.
Gone the divine and sweet believing
  In dreams which Heaven itself unfurl'd!
What godlike shapes have years bereaving
  Swept from this real work-day world!

As once, with tearful passion fired,
  The Cyprian Sculptor clasp'd the stone,
Till the cold cheeks, delight inspired,
  Blush'd—to sweet life the marble grown:
So youth's desire for Nature!—round
  The Statue, so my arms I wreathed,
Till warmth and life in mine it found,
  And breath that poets breathe—it breathed;

With my own burning thoughts it burn'd;—
  Its silence stirr'd to speech divine;—
Its lips my glowing kiss return'd—
  Its heart in beating answer'd mine!
How fair was then the flower—the tree!—
  How silver-sweet the fountain's fall!
The soulless had a soul to me!
  My life its own life lent to all!

The Universe of things seem'd swelling
  The panting heart to burst its bound,
And wandering Fancy found a dwelling
  In every shape—thought—deed, and sound.
Germ'd in the mystic buds, reposing,
  A whole creation slumbered mute,
Alas, when from the buds unclosing,
  How scant and blighted sprung the fruit!

How happy in his dreaming error
  His own gay valour for his wing,
Of not one care as yet in terror,
  Did Youth upon his journey spring;
Till floods of balm, through air's dominion,
  Bore upward to the faintest star—
For never aught to that bright pinion
  Could dwell too high, or spread too far.

Though laden with delight, how lightly
  The wanderer heavenward still could soar,
And aye the ways of life how brightly
  The airy Pageant danced before!—
Love, showering gifts (life's sweetest) down,
  Fortune, with golden garlands gay,
And Fame, with starbeams for a crown,
  And Truth, whose dwelling is the Day.

Ah! midway soon lost evermore,
  Afar the blithe companions stray;
In vain their faithless steps explore,
  As one by one, they glide away.

TO THE IDEAL.

Fleet Fortune was the first escaper—
  The thirst for wisdom linger'd yet;
But doubts with many a gloomy vapour
  The sun-shape of the Truth beset!

The holy crown which Fame was wreathing,
  Behold! the mean man's temples wore,
And but for one short spring-day breathing,
  Bloom'd Love—the Beautiful—no more!
And ever stiller yet, and ever
  The barren path more lonely lay,
Till scarce from waning Hope could quiver
  A glance along the gloomy way.

Who, loving, lingered yet to guide me,
  When all her boon companions fled,
Who stands consoling yet beside me,
  And follows to the House of Dread?
Thine FRIENDSHIP—thine the hand so tender,
  Thine the balm dropping on the wound,
Thy task, the load more light to render,
  O! earliest sought and soonest found!—

And Thou, so pleased, with her uniting,
  To charm the soul-storm into peace,
Sweet TOIL, in toil itself delighting,
  That more it laboured, less could cease,
Tho' but by grains thou aid'st the pile
  The vast Eternity uprears,
At least thou strik'st from Time the while
  Life's debt—the minutes, days and years.*

---

* Though the Ideal images of youth forsake us, the Ideal itself still remains to the Poet. It is his task and his companion—unlike the Phantasies of Fortune, Fame, and Love, the Phantasies of the Ideal are imperishable. While, as the occupation of life, it pays off the debt of Time, as the exalter of life it contributes to the Building of Eternity.

PHILOSOPHERS.

To learn what gives to every thing
    The form and life which we survey,
The law by which the Eternal King
Moves all Creation's order'd ring,
    And keeps it from decay—
When to great Doctor Wiseman we go—
If help'd not out by Fichté's Ego—
All from his brain that we can delve,
Is this sage answer—" Ten's not Twelve." *

The snow can chill, the fire can burn,
    Men when they walk on two feet go;—
A sun in Heaven all eyes discern—
This through the senses we may learn,
    Nor go to school to know!
But the profounder student sees,
That that which burns—will seldom freeze;
And can instruct the astonish'd hearer,
How moisture moistens—light makes clearer.

Homer composed his mighty song,
    The hero danger dared to scorn,
The brave man did his duty, long
Before—(and who shall say I'm wrong)—
    Philosophers were born!

---

* " Wenn Ich nicht drauf ihm helfe
    Er heisst: zehn ist nicht zwölfe."

If the Ich in the text is correctly printed with a capital initial, the intention of Schiller must apparently be to ridicule the absolute Ego of Fichté—a philosopher whom he elsewhere treats with very little ceremony—and thus Hoffmeister seems to interpret the meaning.—Hinrichs, on the other hand, quoting the passage without the capital initial, assumes the satire to be directed against the first great law of logic, which logicians call the Principle of Contradiction, viz., that it is impossible for a thing to be and not to be at the same time; or, as Schiller expresses it, that it is impossible for ten to be both ten and twelve; a truth which is obvious to all men, and which, precisely because it is obvious to all men, Philosophers can state and explain. According to this interpretation, the sense of the translation is not correctly given, and Schiller seems rather to say, "I should call that man exceedingly clever who could explain to me the great law of the Universe, if I did not first explain it to him by saying it is this, Ten is not Twelve—i. e., No philosopher can tell a plain man anything about a profound principle, which any plain man could not just as well have told to the Philosopher."

Without Descartes and Locke—the Sun
Saw things by Heart and Genius done,
Which those great men have proved, on viewing,
The—possibility of doing!

Strength in this life prevails and sways—
    Bold Power oppresses humble Worth—
He who can nòt command obeys—
In short there's not too much to praise
    In this poor orb of earth.
But how things better might be done,
If sages had this world begun,
By moral systems of their own,
Most incontestably is shown!

"Man needs mankind, must be confest—
    In all he labours to fulfil,
Must work, or with, or for, the rest;
'Tis drops that swell the ocean's breast—
    'Tis waves that turn the mill.
The savage life for man unfit is,
So take a wife and live in cities."
Thus *ex cathedrâ* teach, we know,
Wise Messieurs Puffendorf and Co.

Yet since, what grave professors preach,
    The crowd may be excused from knowing;
Meanwhile, old Nature looks to each,
Tinkers the chain, and mends the breach,
    And keeps the clockwork going.
Some day, Philosophy, no doubt,
A better World will bring about:
Till then the Old a little longer,
Must blunder on—through Love and Hunger!

PUNCH SONG.

Four Elements, join'd in
    An emulous strife,
Fashion the world, and
    Constitute life.

From the sharp citron
  The starry juice pour;
Acid to Life is
  The innermost core.

Now, let the sugar
  The bitter one meet;
Still be life's bitter
  Tamed down with the sweet!

Let the bright water
  Flow into the bowl;
Water, the calm one,
  Embraces the Whole.

Drops from the spirit
  Pour quick'ning within;
Life but its life from
  The spirit can win.

Haste, while it gloweth,
  Your vessels to bring;
The wave has but virtue
  Drunk hot from the spring!

PUNCH SONG.

TO BE SUNG IN THE NORTH.

On the free southern hills
  Where the full summers shine,
Nature quicken'd by sunlight,
  Gives birth to the vine!

Her work the Great Mother
  Conceals from the sight,
Untrack'd is the labour,
  Unfathom'd the might.

As the child of the sunbeam,
  The wine leaps to-day,
From the tun springs the crystal,
  A fountain at play.

PUNCH SONG.

All the senses it gladdens,
  Gives Hope to the breast;
To grief a soft balsam,
  To life a new zest.

But, our zone palely gilding,
  The Sun of the North,
From the leaves it scarce tinteth
  No fruit ripens forth.

Yet life will ne'er freely
  Life's gladness resign:
Our vales know no vineyard—
  Invent we a wine!

But wan the libation,
  In truth must appear;
Living Nature alone gives
  The bright and the clear!

Yet draw from the dim fount,
  The Waters of Mirth!
For Heaven gave us Art,
  The Prometheus of Earth.

Wherever strength reacheth,
  What kingdoms await her!
From the Old, the New shaping,
  Art, ay—a Creator!—

The Elements' union
  Divides at her rod,
With the hearth-flame she mimics
  The glow of a god.

To Hesperidan Islands
  She sends the ship forth;
Lo, the southern fruits lending
  Their gold to the North!

So, this sap wrung from flame be
  A symbol-sign still,
Of the wonders man works with
  The Force and the Will!

PEGASUS IN HARNESS.

At Smithfield * once, as I've been told,
Or some such place where beasts are sold,
A bard, whose bones from flesh were all free,
Put up for sale the Muses' palfrey.
His ears how cock'd, his tail how stiff!
Loud neigh'd the prancing Hippogriff.
The crowd grew large, the crowd grew larger:
"By Jove, indeed a splendid charger!
'T would suit some coach of state!—the king's!
But, bless my soul, what frightful wings!
No doubt the breed is mighty rare—
But who would coach it through the air?
Who'd trust his neck to such a flyer?"—
In short, the bard could find no buyer.
  At last a farmer pluck'd up mettle:
"Let's see if we the thing can settle.
These useless wings my man may lop,
Or tie down tight—I likes a crop!
'T might draw my cart; it seems to frisk it;
Come, twenty pounds!—ecod, I'll risk it."
I blush to say the bard consented,
And Hodge bears off his prize, contented.
The noble beast is in the cart;
Hodge cries, "Gee hup!" and off they start.
He scarcely feels the load behind,
Skirrs, scours, and scampers like the wind.
The wings begin for heaven to itch,
The wheels go devilish near the ditch!
"So ho!" grunts Hodge, "'tis more than funny;
I've got a penn'orth for my money.
To-morrow, if I still survive,
I have some score of folks to drive;—
The load of five the beast could drag on;
I'll make him leader to the wagon.
Choler and collar wear with time;
The lively rogue is in his prime."

* Literally "Haymarket."

All's well at first; a famous start—
Wagon and team go like a dart.
The wheelers' heavy plod behind him,
But doubly speeds the task assign'd him;
Till, with tall crest, he snuffs the heaven,
Spurns the dull road so smooth and even.
True the impetuous instinct to,
Field, fen, and bog, he scampers through.
The frenzy seems to catch the team;
The driver tugs, the travellers scream.
O'er ditch, o'er hedge, splash, dash, and crash on,
Ne'er farmer flew in such a fashion.
At last, all batter'd, bruised, and broken,
(Poor Hodge's state may not be spoken,)
Wagon, and team, and travellers stop,
Perch'd on a mountain's steepest top!
Exceeding sore, and much perplext,
"I fegs," the farmer cries, "what next?
This helter-skelter sport will never do,
But break him in I'll yet endeavour to;
Let's see if work and starving diet
Can't tame the monster into quiet!"
The proof was made, and save us! if in
Three days you'd seen the hippogriffin,
You'd scarce the noble beast have known,
Starved duly down to skin and bone.
Cries Hodge, rejoiced, "I have it now,
Bring out my ox, he goes to plough."
So said, so done, and droll the tether,
Wing'd horse, slow ox, at plough together!
The unwilling griffin strains his might,
One last strong struggle yet for flight;
In vain, for well inured to labour.
Plods sober on his heavy neighbour,
And forces, inch by inch, to creep,
The hoofs that love the air to sweep;
Until, worn out, the eye grows dim,
The sinews fail the founder'd limb,
The god-steed droops, the strife is past,
He writhes amidst the mire at last!
"Accursed brute!" the farmer cries;
And, while he bawls, the cart-whip plies,

"All use it seems you think to shirk
So fierce to run—so dull to work!
My twenty pounds!—Not worth a pin!
Confound the rogue who took me in!"
He vents his wrath, he plies his thong,
When, lo! there gaily comes along,
With looks of light and locks of yellow,
And lute in hand, a buxom fellow;
Through the bright clusters of his hair
A golden circlet glistens fair.
"What's this—a wondrous yoke and pleasant?"
Cries out the stranger to the peasant.
"The bird and ox thus leash'd together—
Come, prithee, just unbrace the tether:
But let *me* mount him for a minute—
That beast!—you'll see how much is in it."
The steed released—the easy stranger
Leaps on his back, and smiles at danger;
Scarce felt that steed the master's rein,
When all his fire returns again:
He champs the bit—he rears on high,
Light, like a soul, looks from his eye;
Changed from a creature of the sod,
Behold the spirit and the god:
As sweeps the whirlwind, heavenward springs
The unfurl'd glory of his wings.
Before the eye can track the flight,
Lost in the azure fields of light.

HERO AND LEANDER,

A BALLAD.

[We have already seen, in "The Ring of Polycrates," Schiller's mode of dealing with classical subjects. In the poems that follow, derived from similar sources, the same spirit is maintained. In spite of Humboldt, we venture to think that Schiller certainly does not narrate Greek legends in the spirit of an ancient Greek. The Gothic sentiment, in its ethical depth and mournful tenderness, more or less pervades all that he translates from classic fable into modern pathos. The grief of Hero, in the ballad subjoined, touches closely on the lamentations of *Thekla*, in "Wallenstein." The Complaint of Ceres, embodies Christian Grief and Christian Hope. The Trojan Cassandra expresses the moral of the Northern Faust. Even the "Victory Feast" changes the whole spirit of Homer, on whom it is founded, by the introduction of the Ethical Sentiment at the close, borrowed, as a modern would apply what he so borrows, from the moralising Horace. Nothing can be more foreign to the Hellenic Genius (if we except the very disputable intention of the "Prometheus"), than the interior and typical design which usually exalts every conception in Schiller. But it is perfectly open to the Modern Poet to treat of ancient legends in the modern spirit. Though he selects a Greek story, he is still a modern who narrates —he can never make himself a Greek, any more than Æschylus in the "Persæ" could make himself a Persian. But this is still more the privilege of the Poet in Narrative, or lyrical composition, than in the Drama, for in the former he does not abandon his identity, as in the latter he must—yet even this *must* has its limits. Shakespeare's wonderful power of self-transfusion has no doubt enabled him, in his Plays from Roman History, to animate his characters with much of Roman life. But no one can maintain that a Roman would ever have written plays, in the least resembling "Julius Cæsar," or "Coriolanus," or "Antony and Cleopatra." The Portraits may be Roman, but they are painted in the manner of the Gothic school. The Spirit of antiquity is only in them, inasmuch as the representation of Human Nature, under certain circumstances, is accurately, though loosely outlined. When the Poet raises the dead, it is not to restore, but to remodel.]

SEE you the towers, that, gray and old,
Frown through the sunlight's liquid gold,
  Steep sternly fronting steep?
The Hellespont beneath them swells,
And roaring cleaves the Dardanelles,
  The Rock-Gates of the Deep!
Hear you the Sea, whose stormy wave,
  From Asia, Europe clove in thunder?
That sea which rent a world can nòt
  Rend Love from Love asunder!

In Hero's, in Leander's heart,
Thrills the sweet anguish of the dart
  Whose feather flies from Love.
All Hebe's bloom in Hero's cheek—
And his the hunters's steps that seek
  Delight, the hills above!
Between their sires the rival feud
  Forbids their plighted hearts to meet;
Love's fruits hang over Danger's gulf,
  By danger made more sweet.

Alone on Sestos' rocky tower,
Where upward sent in stormy shower,
  The whirling waters foam,—

Alone the maiden sits, and eyes
The cliffs of fair Abydos rise
   Afar—her lover's home.
Oh, safely thrown from strand to strand,
   No bridge can love to love convey;
No boatman shoots from yonder shore,
   Yet LOVE has found the way.—

That Love, which could the Labyrinth pierce—
Which nerves the weak, and curbs the fierce,
   And wings with wit the dull;—
That Love which o'er the furrow'd land
Bow'd—tame beneath young Jason's hand—
   The fiery-snorting Bull!
Yes, Styx itself, that nine-fold flows,
   Has Love, the fearless, ventured o'er,
And back to daylight borne the bride,
   From Pluto's dreary shore!

What marvel then that wind and wave,
Leander doth but burn to brave,
   When Love, that goads him, guides!
Still when the day, with fainter glimmer,
Wanes pale—he leaps, the daring swimmer,
   Amid the darkening tides;
With lusty arms he cleaves the waves,
   And strives for that dear strand afar;
Where high from Hero's lonely tower
   Lone streams the Beacon-star.

In vain his blood the wave may chill,
These tender arms can warm it still—
   And, weary if the way,
By many a sweet embrace, above
All earthly boons—can liberal Love
   The Lover's toil repay,
Until Aurora breaks the dream,
   And warns the Loiterer to depart—
Back to the ocean's icy bed,
   Scared from that loving heart.

So thirty suns have sped their flight—
Still in that theft of sweet delight
  Exult the happy pair;
Caress will never pall caress,
And joys that gods might envy, bless
  The single bride-night there.
Ah! never he has rapture known,
  Who has not, where the waves are driven
Upon the fearful shores of Hell,
  Pluck'd fruits that taste of Heaven!

Now changing in their Season are,
The Morning and the Hesper Star;—
  Nor see those happy eyes
The leaves that withering droop and fall,
Nor hear, when, from its northern hall,
  The neighbouring Winter sighs;
Or, if they see, the shortening days
  But seem to them to close in kindness;
For longer joys, in lengthening nights,
  They thank the heaven in blindness.

It is the time, when Night and Day,
In equal scales contend for sway *
  Lone, on her rocky steep,
Lingers the girl with wistful eyes
That watch the sun-steeds down the skies,
  Careering towards the deep.
Lull'd lay the smooth and silent sea,
  A mirror in translucent calm,
The breeze, along that crystal realm,
  Unmurmuring, died in balm.

In wanton swarms and blithe array,
The merry dolphins glide and play
  Amid the silver waves.
In gray and dusky troops are seen,
The hosts that serve the Ocean-Queen,
  Upborne from coral caves:

---

* This notes the time of year—not the time of day—viz., about the 23rd of September.—HOFFMEISTER.

They—only they—have witness'd love
  To rapture steal its secret way:
And Hecate * seals the only lips
  That could the tale betray!

She marks in joy the lullèd water,
And Sestos, thus thy tender daughter,
  Soft-flattering, woos the sea!
"Fair god—and canst thou then betray?
No! falsehood dwells with them that say
  That falsehood dwells with thee!
Ah! faithless is the race of man,
  And harsh a father's heart can prove;
But thee, the gentle and the mild,
  The grief of love can move!

"Within these hated walls of stone,
Should I, repining, mourn alone,
  And fade in ceaseless care,
But thou, though o'er thy giant tide,
Nor bridge may span, nor boat may glide,
  Dost safe my lover bear.
And darksome is thy solemn deep,
  And fearful is thy roaring wave;
But wave and deep are won by love—
  Thou smilest on the brave!

"Nor vainly, Sovereign of the Sea,
Did Eros send his shafts to thee:
  What time the Ram of Cold,
Bright Helle, with her brother bore,
How stirr'd the waves she wander'd o'er,
  How stirr'd thy deeps of old!
Swift, by the maiden's charms subdued,
  Thou cam'st from out the gloomy waves,
And, in thy mighty arms, she sank
  Into thy bridal caves.

"A goddess with a god, to keep
In endless youth, beneath the deep,
  Her solemn ocean-court!

* Hecate, as the mysterious Goddess of Nature.—HOFFMEISTER.

And still she smoothes thine angry tides,
Tames thy wild heart, and favouring guides
  The sailor to the port!
Beautiful Helle, bright one, hear
  Thy lone adoring suppliant pray!
And guide, O goddess—guide my love
  Along the wonted way!"

Now twilight dims the water's flow,
And from the tower the beacon's glow
  Waves flickering o'er the main.
Ah, where athwart the dismal stream,
Shall shine the Beacon's faithful beam
  The lover's eye shall strain!
Hark! sounds moan threat'ning from afar—
  From heaven the blessed stars are gone—
More darkly swells the rising sea—
  The tempest labours on!

Along the ocean's boundless plains
Lies Night—in torrents rush the rains
  From the dark-bosom'd cloud—
Red lightning skirs the panting air,
And, loosed from out their rocky lair,
  Sweep all the storms abroad.
Huge wave on huge wave tumbling o'er,
  The yawning gulf is rent asunder,
And shows, as through an opening pall,
  Grim earth—the ocean under!

Poor maiden! bootless wail or vow—
"Have mercy, Jove—be gracious, Thou!
  Dread prayer was mine before!
What if the gods have heard—and he,
Lone victim of the stormy sea,
  Now struggles to the shore!
There's not a sea-bird on the wave—
  Their hurrying wings the shelter seek;
The stoutest ship the storms have proved,
  Takes refuge in the creek.

"Ah, still that heart, which oft has braved
The danger where the daring saved,
  Love lureth o'er the sea;—
For many a vow at parting morn,
That nought but death should bar return,
  Breathed those dear lips to me;
And whirl'd around, the while I weep,
  Amid the storm that rides the wave,
The giant gulf is grasping down
  The rash one to the grave!

"False Pontus! and the calm I hail'd,
The awaiting murder darkly veil'd—
  The lull'd pellucid flow,
The smiles in which thou wert array'd,
Were but the snares that Love betray'd
  To thy false realm below!
Now in the midway of the main,
  Return relentlessly forbidden,
Thou loosenest on the path beyond
  The horrors thou hadst hidden."

Loud and more loud the tempest raves,
In thunder break the mountain waves,
  White foaming on the rock—
No ship that ever swept the deep
Its ribs of gnarled oak could keep
  Unshatter'd by the shock.
Dies in the blast the guiding torch
  To light the struggler to the strand;
'Tis death to battle with the wave,
  And death no less to land!

On Venus, daughter of the seas,
She calls the tempest to appease—
  To each wild-shrieking wind
Along the ocean-desert borne,
She vows a steer with golden horn—
  Vain vow—relentless wind!
On every goddess of the deep,
  On all the gods in heaven that be,
She calls—to soothe in calm, awhile,
  The tempest-laden sea!

"Hearken the anguish of my cries!
From thy green halls, arise—arise,
  Leucothoe the divine?
  Who, in the barren main afar,
Oft on the storm-beat mariner
  Dost gently-saving shine.
Oh, reach to him thy mystic veil,
  To which the drowning clasp may cling,
And safely from that roaring grave,
  To shore my lover bring!"

And now the savage winds are hushing,
And o'er the arch'd horizon, blushing,
  Day's chariot gleams on high!
Back to their wonted channels roll'd,
In crystal calm the waves behold—
  One smile on sea and sky!
All softly breaks the rippling tide,
  Low-murmuring on the rocky land,
And playful wavelets gently float
  A Corpse upon the strand!

'T is he!—who ev'n in death would still
Not fail the sweet vow to fulfil;
  She looks—sees—knows him there!
From her pale lips no sorrow speaks,
No tears glide down the hueless cheeks,
  Cold—numb'd in her despair—
She look'd along the silent deep,
  She look'd upon the bright'ning heaven,
Till to the marble face the soul
  Its light sublime had given!

"Ye solemn Powers men shrink to name,
Your might is here, your rights ye claim—
  Yet think not I repine:
Soon closed my course; yet I can bless
The life that brought me happiness—
  The fairest lot was mine!
Living have I thy temple served,
  Thy consecrated priestess been—
My last glad offering now receive
  Venus, thou mightiest queen!"

Flash'd the white robe along the air,
And from the tower that beetled there
  She sprang into the wave;
Roused from his throne beneath the waste,
Those holy forms the god embraced—
  A god himself their grave!
Pleased with his prey, he glides along—
  More blithe the murmur'd music seems,
A gush from unexhausted urns
  His Everlasting Streams!

THE PLAYING INFANT.

PLAY on thy mother's bosom, Babe, for in that holy isle
The error cannot find thee yet, the grieving, nor the guile;
Held in thy mother's arms above Life's dark and troubled wave,
Thou lookèst with thy fearless smile upon the floating grave.
Play, loveliest Innocence!—Thee, yet Arcadia circles round,
A charmèd power for thee has set the lists of fairy ground;
Each gleesome impulse Nature now can sanction and befriend,
Nor to that willing heart as yet the Duty and the End.
Play, for the haggard Labour soon will come to seize its prey,
Alas! when Duty grows thy law—Enjoyment fades away!

CASSANDRA.

[There is peace between the Greeks and Trojans—Achilles is to wed Polyxena, Priam's daughter. On entering the Temple, he is shot through his only vulnerable part by Paris.—The time of the following Poem is during the joyous preparations for the marriage.]

AND mirth was in the halls of Troy,
  Before her towers and temples fell;
High peal'd the choral hymns of joy,
  Melodious to the golden shell.

CASSANDRA.

The weary had reposed from slaughter—
   The eye forgot the tear it shed;
This day King Priam's lovely daughter
   Shall great Pelides wed!

Adorn'd with laurel boughs, they come,
   Crowd after crowd—the way divine,
Where fanes are deck'd—for gods the home—
   And to the Thymbrian's * solemn shrine.
The wild Bacchantic joy is madd'ning
   The thoughtless host, the fearless guest;
And there, the unheeded heart is sadd'ning
   One solitary breast!

Unjoyous in the joyful throng,
   Alone, and linking life with none,
Apollo's laurel groves among,
   The still Cassandra wander'd on!
Into the forest's deep recesses
   The solemn Prophet-Maiden pass'd,
And, scornful, from her loosen'd tresses,
   The sacred fillet cast!

"To all, its arms doth Mirth unfold,
   And every heart forgoes its cares—
And Hope is busy in the old—
   The bridal-robe my sister wears—
And I alone, alone am weeping;
   The sweet delusion mocks not me—
Around these walls destruction sweeping,
   More near and near I see!

"A torch before my vision glows,
   But not in Hymen's hand it shines,
A flame that to the welkin goes,
   But not from holy offering-shrines;
Glad hands the banquet are preparing,
   And near, and near the halls of state
I hear the God that comes unsparing,
   I hear the steps of Fate.

* Apollo.

"And men my prophet-wail deride!
  The solemn sorrow dies in scorn;
And lonely in the waste, I hide
  The tortured heart that would forewarn.
Amidst the happy, unregarded,
  Mock'd by their fearful joy, I trod;
Oh, dark to me the lot awarded,
  Thou evil Pythian god!

"Thine oracle, in vain to be,
  Oh, wherefore am I thus consign'd
With eyes that every truth must see,
  Lone in the City of the Blind?
Cursed with the anguish of a power
  To view the fates I may not thrall,
The hovering tempest still must lower—
  The horror must befall!

"Boots it the veil to lift, and give
  To sight the frowning fates beneath?
For error is the life we live,
  And, oh, our knowledge is but death!
Take back the clear and awful mirror,
  Shut from mine eyes the blood-red glare
Thy truth is but a gift of terror
  When mortal lips declare.

"My blindness give to me once more*
  The gay dim senses that rejoice;
The Past's delighted songs are o'er
  For lips that speak a Prophet's voice.
To me *the future* thou hast granted;
  I miss *the moment* from the chain—
The happy Present-Hour enchanted!
  Take back thy gift again!

"Never for me the nuptial wreath
  The odour-breathing hair shall twine;
My heavy heart is bow'd beneath
  The service of thy dreary shrine.

"Everywhere," says Hoffmeister truly, "Schiller exalts Ideal Belief over real wisdom;—everywhere this modern Apostle of Christianity advocates that Ideal, which exists in Faith and emotion, against the wisdom of worldly intellect, the barren experience of life," &c.

My youth was but by tears corroded,—
  My sole familiar is my pain,
Each coming ill my heart foreboded,
  And felt it first—in vain!

" How cheerly sports the careless mirth,—
  The life that loves, around I see;
Fair youth to pleasant thoughts give birth—
  The heart is only sad to me.
Not for mine eyes the young spring gloweth,
  When earth her happy feast-day keeps;
The charm of life who ever knoweth
  That looks into the deeps?

" Wrapt in thy bliss, my sister, thine
  The heart's inebriate rapture-springs;—
Longing with bridal arms to twine
  The bravest of the Grecian kings.
High swells the joyous bosom, seeming
  Too narrow for its world of love,
Nor envies, in its heaven of dreaming,
  The heaven of gods above!

" I too might know the soft controul
  Of one the longing heart could choose,
With look which love illumes with soul—
  The look that supplicates and woos.
And sweet with him, where love presiding
  Prepares our hearth, to go—but, dim,
A Stygian shadow, nightly gliding,
  Stalks between me and him!

" Forth from the grim funereal shore,
  The Hell-Queen sends her ghastly bands;
Where'er I turn—behind—before—
  Dumb in my path—a Spectre stands!
Wherever gayliest, youth assembles—
  I see the shades in horror clad,
Amidst Hell's ghastly People trembles
  One soul for ever sad!

"I see the steel of Murder gleam—
  I see the Murderer's glowing eyes—
To right—to left, one gory stream—
  One circling fate—my flight defies!
I may not turn my gaze—all seeing,
  Foreknowing all, I dumbly stand—
To close in blood my ghastly being
  In the far strangers' land!"

Hark! while the sad sounds murmur round,
  Hark, from the Temple-porch, the cries!—
A wild, confused, tumultuous sound!—
  Dead the divine Pelides lies!
Grim Discord rears her snakes devouring—
  The last departing god hath gone!
And, womb'd in cloud, the thunder, lowering,
  Hangs black on Ilion.

NOTE.—Upon this poem, Madame de Staël makes the following just and striking criticism.—*L'Allemagne*, Part II. c. 13. "One sees in this ode, the curse inflicted on a mortal by the prescience of a god. Is not the grief of the prophetess that of all who possess a superior intellect with an impassioned heart? Under a shape wholly poetic, Schiller has embodied an idea grandly moral—viz., that the true genius (that of the sentiment) is a victim to itself, even when spared by others. There are no nuptials for Cassandra: not that she is insensible—not that she is disdained, but the clear penetration of her soul passes in an instant both life and death, and can only repose in Heaven."

THE VICTORY FEAST.

[In this Lyric, Schiller had a notion of raising the popular social song from the prosaic vulgarity common to it—into a higher and more epic dignity.]

The stately walls of Troy had sunken,
  Her towers and temples strew'd the soil;
The sons of Hellas, victory-drunken,
  Richly laden with the spoil,
Are on their lofty barks reclin'd
  Along the Hellespontine strand;
A gleesome freight the favouring wind
  Shall bear to Greece's glorious land;

And gleesome chaunt the choral strain.
  As towards the household altars, now,
  Each bark inclines the painted prow—
For Home shall smile again!

And there the Trojan women, weeping,
  Sit ranged in many a length'ning row;
Their heedless locks, dishevell'd, sweeping
  Adown the wan cheeks worn with woe.
No festive sounds that peal along,
Their mournful dirge can overwhelm;
  Through hymns of joy one sorrowing song
Commingled, wails the ruin'd realm.
  "Farewell, beloved shores!" it said,
  " From home afar behold us torn,
  By foreign lords as captives borne—
Ah, happy are the dead!"

And Calchas, while the altars blaze,
  Invokes the high gods to their feast!
On Pallas, mighty or to raise
  Or shatter cities, call'd the Priest—
And Him, who wreathes around the land
  The girdle of his watery world,
And Zeus, from whose almighty hand
  The terror and the bolt are hurl'd.
Success at last awards the crown—
  The long and weary war is past;
  Time's destined circle ends at last—
And fall'n the Mighty Town!

The Son of Atreus, king of men,
  The muster of the hosts survey'd,
How dwindled from the thousands, when
  Along Scamander first array'd!
With sorrow and the cloudy thought,
  The Great King's stately look grew dim—
Of all the hosts to Ilion brought,
  How few to Greece return with him!
Still let the song to gladness call,
  For those who yet their homes shall greet!—
  For them the blooming life is sweet:
Return is not for all!

Nor all who reach their native land
　May long the joy of welcome feel—
Beside the household gods may stand
　Grim Murther with awaiting steel;
And they who 'scape the foe, may die
　Beneath the foul familiar glaive.
Thus He[*] to whose prophetic eye
　Her light the wise Minerva gave:—
　　"Ah! blest whose hearth, to memory true,
　　　The goddess keeps unstain'd and pure—
　　　For woman's guile is deep and sure,
　　And Falsehood loves the New!"

The Spartan eyes his Helen's charms,
　By the best blood of Greece recaptured;
Round that fair form his glowing arms—
　(A second bridal)—wreathe enraptured.
"Woe waits the work of evil birth—
　Revenge to deeds unblest is given!
For watchful o'er the things of earth,
　The eternal Council-Halls of Heaven.
Yes, ill shall ever ill repay—
　　Jove to the impious hands that stain
　　The Altar of Man's Hearth, again
The doomer's doom shall weigh!"

"Well they, reserved for joy to-day,"
　Cried out Oïleus' valiant son,
"May laud the favouring gods who sway
　Our earth, their easy thrones upon;
With careless hands they mete our doom,
　Our woe or welfare Hazard gives—
Patroclus slumbers in the tomb,
　And all unharm'd Thersites lives.
If Fate, then, showers without a choice
　The lots of luck and life on all,
　Let him on whom the prize may fall,—
Let him who lives—rejoice!

[*] Ulysses.

THE VICTORY FEAST.

"Yes, war will still devour the best!—
   Brother, remember'd in this hour!
His shade should be in feasts a guest,
   Whose form was in the strife a tower!
What time our ships the Trojan fired,
   Thine arm to Greece the safety gave—
The prize to which thy soul aspired,
   The crafty wrested from the brave.*
Peace to thine ever-holy rest—
   Not thine to fall before the foe!
Ajax alone laid Ajax low:
Ah—wrath destroys the best!"

To his dead sire—(the Dorian king)—
   The bright-hair'd Pyrrhus † pours the wine :—
"O'er every lot that life can bring,
   My soul, great Father, prizes thine.
Whate'er the goods of earth, of all,
   The highest and the holiest—FAME!
For when the Form in dust shall fall,
   O'er dust triumphant lives the Name!
Brave Man, thy light of glory never
   Shall fade, while song to man shall last;
The Living soon from earth are pass'd,
'THE DEAD—ENDURE FOR EVER!'"

"Since all are mute to mourn and praise
   In Victory's hour, the vanquish'd Man—
Be mine at least one voice to raise
   For HECTOR," Tydeus' son began:
"A Tower before his native town;
   He stood—and fell as fall the brave.
The conqueror wins the brighter crown,
   The conquer'd has the nobler grave!

---

* Need we say to the general reader, that allusion is here made to the strife between Ajax and Ulysses, which has furnished a subject to the Greek tragic poet, who has depicted, more strikingly than any historian, that intense emulation for glory, and that mortal agony in defeat, which constituted the main secret of the prodigious energy of the Greek character? The Tragic poet, in taking his hero from the Homeric age, endowed him with the feelings of the Athenian republicans he addressed.

† Neoptolemus, the son of Achilles.

He who brave life shall bravely close,
  For Home and Hearth, and Altar slain,
If mourn'd by Friends, shall glory gain
Out of the lips of Foes!"

Lo, Nestor now, whose stately age
  Through threefold lives of mortals lives!—
The laurel'd bowl, the kingly sage
  To Hector's tearful mother gives.
"Drink—in the draught new strength is glowing,
  The grief it bathes forgets the smart!
O Bacchus! wond'rous boons bestowing,
  Oh how thy balsam heals the heart!
Drink—in the draught new vigour gloweth,
  The grief it bathes forgets the smart—
  And balsam to the breaking heart,
The healing god bestoweth.

"As Niobe, when weeping mute,
  To angry gods the scorn and prey,
But tasted of the charmèd fruit,
  And cast despair itself away;
So, while unto thy lips, its shore,
  This stream of life enchanted flows,
Remember'd grief, that stung before,
  Sinks down to Lethè's calm repose.
  So, while unto thy lips, its shore,
    The stream of life enchanted flows—
    Drown'd deep in Lethè's calm repose,
  The grief that stung before!"

Seized by the god, behold the dark
  And dreaming prophetess arise,
She gazes from the lofty Bark
  Where Home's dim vapours wrap the skies—
"A vapour all of human birth
  Like mists ascending, seen and gone,
So fade Earth's great ones from the Earth
  And leave the changeless gods alone.
Behind the steed that skirs away;
  And on the galley's deck—sits Care,
    To-morrow comes, and we are where?
At least we'll live to-day!"

THE CRANES OF IBYCUS.

From Rhegium to the Isthmus, long
Hallow'd to steeds and glorious song,
Where, link'd awhile in holy peace,
Meet all the sons of martial Greece—
Wends Ibycus—whose lips the sweet
   And ever-young Apollo fires;
The staff supports the wanderer's feet—
   The God the Poet's soul inspires!

Soon from the mountain-ridges high,
The tower-crown'd Corinth greets his eye;
In Neptune's groves of darksome pine,
He treads with shuddering awe divine;
Nought lives around him, save a swarm
   Of Cranes, that still pursued his way—
Lured by the South, they wheel and form
   In ominous groups their wild array.

And "Hail! beloved Birds!" he cried;
"My comrades on the ocean tide,
Sure signs of good ye bode to me;
Our lots alike would seem to be;
From far, together borne, we greet
   A shelter now from toil and danger;
And may the friendly hearts we meet
   Preserve from every ill—the Stranger!"

His step more light, his heart more gay,
Along the mid-wood winds his way,
When, where the path the thickets close,
Burst sudden forth two ruffian foes;
Now strife to strife, and foot to foot!
   Ah! weary sinks the gentle hand;
The gentle hand that wakes the lute
   Has learn'd no lore that guides the brand.

He calls on men and Gods—in vain!
His cries no blest deliverer gain;
Feebler and fainter grows the sound,
And still the deaf life slumbers round—

"In the far land I fall forsaken,
　Unwept and unregarded, here;
By death from caitiff hands o'ertaken,
　Nor ev'n one late avenger near!"

Down to the earth the death-stroke bore him—
Hark, where the Cranes wheel dismal o'er him!
He hears, as darkness veils his eyes,
Near, in hoarse croak, their dirgelike cries.
"Ye whose wild wings above me hover,
　(Since never voice, save yours alone,
The deed can tell)—the hand discover—
　Avenge!"—He spoke, and life was gone.

Naked and maim'd the corpse was found—
And, still through many a mangling wound,
The sad Corinthian Host could trace
The loved—too well-remember'd face.
"And must I meet thee thus once more?
　Who hoped with wreaths of holy pine,
Bright with new fame—the victory o'er—
　The Singer's temples to entwine!"

And loud lamented every guest
Who held the Sea-God's solemn feast—
As in a single heart prevailing,
Throughout all Hellas went the wailing.
Wild to the Cóuncil Hall they ran—
　In thunder rush'd the threat'ning Flood—
"Revenge shall right the murder'd man,
　The last atonement—blood for blood!"

Yet 'mid the throng the Isthmus claims,
Lured by the Sea-God's glorious games—
The mighty many-nation'd throng—
How track the hand that wrought the wrong?—
How guess if that dread deed were done,
　By ruffian hands, or secret foes?
He who sees all on earth—the SUN—
　Alone the gloomy secret knows.

Perchance he treads in careless peace,
Amidst your Sons, assembled Greece—
Hears with a smile revenge decreed—
Gloats with fell joy upon the deed—
His steps the avenging gods may mock
 Within the very Temple's wall,
Or mingle with the crowds that flock
 To yonder solemn scenic * hall.

Wedg'd close, and serried, swarms the crowd—
Beneath the weight the walls are bow'd—
Thitherwards streaming far, and wide,
Broad Hellas flows in mingled tide—
A tide like that which heaves the deep
 When hollow-sounding, shoreward driven;
On, wave on wave, the thousands sweep
 Till arching, row on row, to heaven!

The tribes, the nations, who shall name,
That guest-like, there assembled came?
From Theseus' town, from Aulis' strand—
From Phocis, from the Spartans' land—
From Asia's wave-divided clime,
 The Isles that gem the Ægæan Sea,
To hearken on that Stage Sublime,
 The Dark Choir's mournful melody!

True to the awful rites of old,
In long and measured strides, behold
The Chorus from the hinder ground,
Pace the vast circle's solemn round.
So this World's women never strode,
 Their race from Mortals ne'er began,
Gigantic, from their grim abode,
 They tower above the Sons of Man!

Across their loins the dark robe clinging,
In fleshless hands the torches swinging,
Now to and fro, with dark red glow—
No blood that lives the dead cheeks know!

* The theatre.

Where flow the locks that woo to love
  On *human* temples—ghastly dwell
The serpents, coil'd the brow above,
  And the green asps with poison swell.

Thus circling, horrible, within
That space—doth their dark hymn begin,
And round the sinner as they go,
Cleave to the heart their words of woe.
Dismally wails, the senses chilling,
  The hymn—the FURIES' solemn song;
And froze the very marrow thrilling
  As roll'd the gloomy sounds along.

"And weal to him—from crime secure—
Who keeps his soul as childhood's pure;
Life's path he roves, a wanderer free—
We near him not—THE AVENGERS, WE!
But woe to him for whom we weave
  The doom for deeds that shun the light:
Fast to the murderer's feet we cleave,
  The fearful Daughters of the Night.

"And deems he flight from us can hide him?
Still on dark wings We sail beside him!
The murderer's feet the snare enthralls—
Or soon or late, to earth he falls!
Untiring, hounding on, we go;
  For blood can no remorse atone!
On, ever—to the Shades below,
  And there—we grasp him, still our own!"

So singing, their slow dance they wreathe,
And stillness, like a silent death,
Heavily there lay cold and drear,
As if the Godhead's self were near.
Then, true to those strange rites of old,
  Pacing the circle's solemn round,
In long and measured strides—behold,
  They vanish in the hinder ground!

Confused and doubtful—half between
The solemn truth and phantom scene,
The crowd revere the Power, presiding
O'er secret deeps, to justice guiding—
The Unfathom'd and Inscrutable
  By whom the web of doom is spun;
Whose shadows in the deep heart dwell,
  Whose form is seen not in the sun!

Just then, amidst the highest tier,
Breaks forth a voice that starts the ear;
" See there—see there, Timotheus;
Behold the Cranes of Ibycus ! "
A sudden darkness wraps the sky;
  Above the roofless building hover
Dusk, swarming wings; and heavily
  Sweep the slow Cranes—hoarse-murmuring, over!

" Of Ibycus ? "—that name so dear
Thrills through the hearts of those who hear!
Like wave on wave in eager seas,
From mouth to mouth the murmur flees—
" Of Ibycus, whom we bewail?
  The murder'd one! What mean those words?
Who is the man—knows *he* the tale?
  Why link that name with those wild birds ? "

Questions on questions louder press—
Like lightning flies the inspiring guess—
Leaps every heart—" The truth we seize;
Your might is here, EUMENIDES !
The murderer yields himself confest—
  Vengeance is near—that voice the token—
Ho !—him who yonder spoke, arrest !—
  And him to whom the words were spoken ! "

Scarce had the wretch the words let fall,
Than fain their sense he would recall.
In vain; those whitening lips, behold !
The secret have already told.

> Into their Judgment Court sublime
> The Scene is changed;—their doom is seal'd!
> Behold the dark unwitness'd Crime,
> Struck by the light'ning that reveal'd!

The principal sources whence Schiller has taken the story of Ibycus (which was well known to the ancients, and indeed gave rise to a proverb) are Suidas and Plutarch. Ibycus is said by some to have been the Inventor of the Sambuca or triangular Cithera. We must observe, however—(though erudite investigation on such a subject were misplaced here), that Athenæus and Strabo consider the Sambuca to have originated with the Syrians, and this supposition is rendered the more probable by the similarity of the Greek word with the Hebrew, which in our received translation of the Bible is rendered by the word Sackbut. The tale, in its leading incidents, is told very faithfully by Schiller: it is the moral, or interior meaning, which he has heightened and idealised. Plutarch is contented to draw from the story a moral against loquacity. "It was not," says he, "the Cranes that betrayed the murderers, but their own garrulity." With Schiller the garrulity is produced by the surprise of the Conscience, which has been awakened by the Apparition and Song of the Furies. His own conceptions as to the effect he desired to create are admirable. "It is not precisely that the Hymn of the Furies" (remarks the poet) "has roused the remorse of the murderer, whose exclamation betrays himself and his accomplice; that was not my meaning—but it has reminded him of his deed: his sense is struck with it. In this moment the appearance of the Cranes must take him by surprise; he is a rude, dull churl, over whom the impulse of the moment has all power. His loud exclamation is natural in such circumstances." "That he feels no great remorse, in this thoughtless exclamation, is evident by the quick, snappish nature of it:—'See there, see there!' &c."—"In any other state of mind," observes Hoffmeister, "perhaps the Audience might not have attended to this ejaculation—but at that moment of deep inward emotion, produced by the representation of the fearful Goddesses, and an excited belief in their might, the name of the newly-murdered man must have struck them as the very voice of Fate, in which the speaker betrayed himself."—In fact the poem is an illustration of Schiller's own lines in "The Artists," written eight years before:—

> "Here secret Murder, pale and shuddering, sees
> Sweep o'er the stage the stern Eumenides;
> Owns, where law fails, what powers to art belong,
> And, screened from justice, finds its doom in song!"

In the foregoing ballad POETRY (that is, the Dirge and dramatic representation of the Furies) acts doubly—first on the Murderer, next on the Audience; it surprises the one into self-betrayal, it prepares in the other that state of mind in which, as by a divine instinct, the quick perception seizes upon the truth. In this double effect is nobly typified the power of Poetry on the individual and on the multitude. Rightly did Schiller resolve to discard from his design whatever might seem to partake of marvellous or supernatural interposition. The appearance of the Cranes is purely accidental. . . . Whatever is of diviner agency in the punishment of crime is found not in the outer circumstances, but in the heart within—the true realm in which the gods work their miracles. As it has been finely said—"The bad conscience (in the Criminal) is its own Nemesis, the good conscience in the Many—the audience—drags at once the bad before its forum and adjudges it." The history of the composition of this

Poem affords an instance of the exquisite art of Goethe, to which it is largely indebted. In the first sketch of the ballad, it was only one Cran- that flew over Ibycus at the time he was murdered, and moreover this was only mentioned at the end of the piece. But Goethe suggested the enlargement of this leading incident—into "the long and broad phenomenon" of the swarm of Cranes, corresponding in some degree with the long and ample pageant of the Furies. Schiller at once perceived how not only the truthfulness, but the grandeur, of his picture was heightened by this simple alteration. . . . According to Goethe's suggestions, the swarm of Cranes were now introduced as the companions of Ibycus in his voyage. . . . The fine analogy between the human wanderer and his winged companions, each seeking a foreign land, was dimly outlined. . . . And the generous criticism of the one Poet finally gave its present fulness and beauty to the masterpiece of the other.—*See Goethe's Correspondence with Schiller. Hoffmeister. Heinrichs.*

THE HOSTAGE.

A BALLAD.

THE tyrant Dionys to seek,
  Stern Mœrus with his poniard crept;
  The watchful guards upon him swept;
The grim king mark'd his changeless cheek:
"What wouldst thou with thy poniard? Speak!"
"The city from the tyrant free!"—
"The death-cross shall thy guerdon be."

"I am prepared for death, nor pray,"
  Replied that haughty man, "to live;
  Enough, if thou one grace will give:
For three brief suns the death delay
To wed my sister—leagues away;
I boast one friend whose life for mine,
If I should fail the cross, is thine."

The tyrant mused,—and smil'd,—and said
  With gloomy craft, "So let it be;
  Three days I will vouchsafe to thee.
But mark—if, when the time be sped,
Thou fail'st—thy surety dies instead.
His life shall buy thine own release;
Thy guilt atoned, my wrath shall cease."

He sought his friend—" The king's decree
　　Ordains my life the cross upon
　　Shall pay the deed I would have done;
Yet grants three days' delay to me,
My sister's marriage-rites to see;
If thou, the hostage, wilt remain
Till I—set free—return again!"

His friend embraced—No word he said,
　　But silent to the tyrant strode—
　　The other went upon his road.
Ere the third sun in heaven was red,
The rite was o'er, the sister wed;
And back, with anxious heart unquailing,
He hastes to hold the pledge unfailing.

Down the great rains unending bore,
　　Down from the hills the torrents rush'd,
　　In one broad stream the brooklets gush'd.
The wanderer halts beside the shore,
The bridge was swept the tides before—
The shatter'd arches o'er and under
Went the tumultuous waves in thunder.

Dismay'd, he takes his idle stand—
　　Dismay'd, he strays and shouts around;
　　His voice awakes no answering sound.
No boat will leave the sheltering strand,
To bear him to the wish'd-for land;
No boatman will Death's pilot be;
The wild stream gathers to a sea!

Sunk by the banks, awhile he weeps,
　　Then rais'd his arms to Jove, and cried,
　　" Stay thou, oh stay the madd'ning tide!
Midway behold the swift sun sweeps,
And, ere he sinks adown the deeps,
If I should fail, his beams will see
My friend's last anguish—slain for me!"

THE HOSTAGE.

More fierce it runs, more broad it flows,
   And wave on wave succeeds and dies—
   And hour on hour remorseless flies;
Despair at last to daring grows—
Amidst the flood his form he throws;
With vig'rous arms the roaring waves
Cleaves—and a God that pities, saves.

He wins the bank—he scours the strand,
   He thanks the God in breathless prayer;
   When from the forest's gloomy lair,
With ragged club in ruthless hand,
And breathing murder—rush'd the band
That find, in woods, their savage den,
And savage prey in wandering men.

"What," cried he, pale with generous fear;
   "What think to gain ye by the strife?
   All I bear with me is my life—
I take it to the King!"—and here
He snatch'd the club from him most near:
And thrice he smote, and thrice his blows
Dealt death—before him fly the foes!

The sun is glowing as a brand;
   And faint before the parching heat,
   The strength forsakes the feeble feet:
"Thou has saved me from the robbers' hand,
Through wild floods given the blessed land;
And shall the weak limbs fail me now?
And *he*—Divine one, nerve me, thou!

Hark! like some gracious murmur by,
   Babbles low music, silver-clear—
   The wanderer holds his breath to hear;
And from the rock, before his eye,
Laughs forth the spring delightedly;
Now the swet waves he bends him o'er,
And the sweet waves his strength restore.

Through the green boughs the sun gleams dying,
  O'er fields that drink the rosy beam,
  The trees' huge shadows giant seem.
Two strangers on the road are hieing;
And as they fleet beside him flying,
These mutter'd words his ear dismay:
"Now—now the cross has claim'd its prey!"

Despair his wingèd path pursues,
  The anxious terrors hound him on—
  There, redd'ning in the evening sun,
From far, the domes of Syracuse!—
When towards him comes Philostratus,
(His leal and trusty herdsman he,)
And to the master bends his knee.

"Back—thou canst aid thy friend no more,
  The niggard time already flown—
  His life is forfeit—save thine own!
Hour after hour in hope he bore,
Nor might his soul its faith give o'er;
Nor could the tyrant's scorn deriding,
Steal from that faith one thought confiding!"

"Too late! what horror hast thou spoken!
  Vain life, since it can not requite him!
  But death with me can yet unite him;
No boast the tyrant's scorn shall make—
How friend to friend can faith forsake.
But from the double-death shall know,
That Truth and Love yet live below!"

The sun sinks down—the gate's in view,
  The cross loom is mal on the ground—
  The eager crowd gape murmuring round.
His friend is bound the cross unto . . .
Crowd—guards—all-bursts he breathless through:
"Me! Doomsman, me!" he shouts, "alone!
His life is rescued—h, mine own!"

Amazement seized the circling ring!
  Link'd in each other's arms the pair—
  Weeping for joy—yet anguish there!
Moist every eye that gazed;—they bring
The wond'rous tidings to the king—
His breast Man's heart at last hath known,
And the Friends stand before his throne.

Long silent, he, and wondering long,
  Gaz'd on the Pair—"In peace depart,
  Victors, ye have subdued my heart!
Truth is no dream!—its power is strong.
Give grace to Him who owns his wrong!
'Tis mine your suppliant now to be,
Ah, let the band of Love—be THREE!"

This story, the heroes of which are more popularly known to us under the names of Damon and Pythias (or *Phintias*), Schiller took from Hyginus, in whom the friends are called Mœrus and Selinuntius. Schiller has somewhat amplified the incidents in the original, in which the delay of Mœrus is occasioned only by the swollen stream—the other hindrances are of Schiller's invention. The subject, like "The Ring of Polycrates," does not admit of that rich poetry of description with which our author usually adorns some single passage in his narratives. The poetic spirit is rather shown in the terse brevity with which picture after picture is not only sketched, but finished—and in the great thought at the close. Still it is not one of Schiller's best ballads. His additions to the original story are not happy. The incident of the Robbers is commonplace and poor. The delay occasioned by the thirst of Mœrus is clearly open to Goethe's objection, (an objection showing very nice perception of nature)—that extreme thirst was not likely to happen to a man who had lately passed through a stream, on a rainy day, and whose clothes must have been saturated with moisture—nor in the traveller's preoccupied state of mind, is it probable that he would have so much felt the mere physical want. With less reason has it been urged by other Critics, that the sudden relenting of the Tyrant is contrary to his character. The Tyrant here has no individual character at all. He is the mere personation of Disbelief in Truth and Love—which the spectacle of sublime self-abnegation at once converts. In this idea lies the deep Philosophical Truth, which redeems all the defects of the piece—for Poetry, in its highest form, is merely this—"Truth made beautiful."

THE COMPLAINT OF CERES.

It may be scarcely necessary to treat, however briefly, of the mythological legend on which this exquisite elegy is founded; yet we venture to do so rather than that the forgetfulness of the reader should militate against his enjoyment of the poem. Proserpine, according to the Homeride (for the story is not without variations), when gathering flowers with the

Ocean Nymphs, is carried off by Aidoneus, or Pluto. Her mother, Ceres, wanders over the earth for her in vain, and refuses to return to Heaven till her daughter is restored to her. Finally, Jupiter commissions Hermes to persuade Pluto to render up his bride, who rejoins Ceres at Eleusis. Unfortunately she has swallowed a pomegranate seed in the Shades below, and is thus mysteriously doomed to spend one-third of the year with her husband in Hades, though for the remainder of the year she is permitted to dwell with Ceres and the Gods. This is one of the very few mythological fables of Greece which can be safely interpreted into an Allegory. Proserpine denotes the seed corn one-third of the year below the earth; two-thirds (that is, dating from the appearance of the ear) above it. Schiller has treated this story with admirable and artistic beauty; and, by an alteration in its symbolical character, has preserved the pathos of the external narrative, and heightened the beauty of the interior meaning—associating the productive principle of the earth with the immortality of the soul. Proserpine here is not the symbol of the buried seed, but the buried seed is the symbol of her—that is, of the Dead. The exquisite feeling of this poem consoled Schiller's friend, Sophia La Roche, in her grief for her son's death.

I.

Does pleasant Spring return once more?
  Does Earth her happy youth regain?
Sweet suns green hills are shining o'er;
  Soft brooklets burst their icy chain:
Upon the blue translucent river
  Laughs down an all-unclouded day,
The winged west winds gently quiver,
  The buds are bursting from the spray;
While birds are blithe on every tree;
  The Oread from the mountain-shore
Sighs 'Lo thy flowers come back to thee—
  Thy Child, sad Mother, comes no more!'

II.

Alas! how long an age it seems
  Since all the Earth I wander'd over,
And vainly, Titan, task'd thy beams
  The lov'd—the lost one—to discover!
Though all may seek—yet none can call
  Her tender presence back to me!
The Sun, with eyes detecting all,
  Is blind one vanish'd form to see.
Hast thou, O Zeus, hast thou away
  From these sad arms my Daughter torn?
Has Pluto, from the realms of Day,
  Enamour'd—to dark rivers borne?

III.

Who to the dismal Phantom-Strand
    The Herald of my Grief will venture?
The Boat for ever leaves the Land,
    But only Shadows there may enter.—
Veil'd from each holier eye repose
    The realms were Midnight wraps the Dead,
And, while the Stygian River flows,
    No living footstep there may tread!
A thousand pathways wind the drear
    Descent;—none upward lead to-day;—
No witness to the Mother's ear
    The Daughter's sorrows can betray.

IV.

Mothers of happy Human clay
    Can share at least their children's doom;
And when the loved ones pass away,
    Can track—can join them—in the tomb!
The race alone of Heavenly birth
    Are banish'd from the darksome portals;
The Fates—have mercy on the Earth,
    And death is only kind to mortals! *
Oh, plunge me in the Night of Nights,
    From Heaven's ambrosial halls exil'd!
Oh, let the Goddess lose the rights
    That shut the Mother from the Child!

V.

Where sits the Dark King's joyless bride,
    Where midst the Dead her home is made:
Oh that my noiseless steps might glide,
    Amidst the shades myself a shade!
I see her eyes, that search thro' tears,
    In vain the golden light to greet;
That yearn for yonder distant spheres,
    That pine the Mother's face to meet!
Till some bright moment shall renew
    The severed Hearts' familiar ties;
And softened pity still in dew,
    From Pluto's slow-relenting eyes!

* What a beautiful vindication of the shortness of human life!

VI.

Ah, vain the wish, the sorrow are!
  Calm in the changeless paths above
Rolls on the Day-God's golden Car—
  Fast are the fix'd decrees of Jove!
Far from the ever gloomy Plain,
  He turns his blissful looks away.
Alas! Night never gives again
  What once it seizes as its prey!
Till over Lethe's sullen swell,
  Aurora's rosy hues shall glow;
And arching thro' the midmost Hell
  Shine forth the lovely Iris-Bow!

VII.

And is there nought of Her;—no token—
  No pledge from that beloved hand?
To tell how Love remains unbroken,
  How far soever be the land?
Has love no link, no lightest thread,
  The Mother to the Child to bind?
Between the Living and the Dead,
  Can Hope no holy compact find?
No! every bond is not yet riven;
  We are not yet divided wholly;
To us the eternal Powers have given
  A symbol language, sweet and holy.

VIII.

When Spring's fair children pass away,
  When, in the Northwind's icy air,
The leaf and flower alike decay,
  And leave the rivell'd branches bare,
Then from Vertumnus' lavish horn
  I take Life's seeds to strew below—
And bid the gold that germs the corn
  An offering to the Styx to go!
Sad in the earth the seeds I lay—
  Laid at thy heart, my Child—to be
The mournful tokens which convey
  My sorrow and my love to Thee!

THE COMPLAINT OF CERES.

IX.

But, when the Hours, in measured dance,
   The happy smile of Spring restore,
Rife in the Sun-god's golden glance
   The buried Dead revive once more!
The germs that perish'd to thine eyes,
   Within the cold breast of the earth,
Spring up to bloom in gentler skies,
   The brighter for the second birth!
The stem its blossom rears above—
   Its roots in Night's dark womb repose—
The plant but by the equal love
   Of light and darkness fostered—grows!

X.

If half with Death the germs may sleep,
   Yet half with Life they share the beams;
My heralds from the dreary deep,
   Soft voices from the solemn streams,—
Like her, so them, awhile entombs,
   Stern Orcus, in his dismal reign,
Yet Spring sends forth their tender blooms
   With such sweet messages again,
To tell,—how far from light above,
   Where only mournful shadows meet,
Memory is still alive to love,
   And still the faithful Heart can beat!

XI.

Joy to ye children of the Field!
   Whose life each coming year renews,
To your sweet cups the Heaven shall yield
   The purest of its nectar-dews!
Steep'd in the light's resplendent streams,
   The hues that streak the Iris-Bow
Shall trim your blooms as with the beams
   The looks of young Aurora know.
The budding life of happy Spring,
   The yellow Autumn's faded leaf,
Alike to gentle Hearts shall bring
   The symbols of my joy and grief.

THE ELEUSINIAN FESTIVAL.

This, originally called the "Burger-Lay," is one of the poems which Schiller has devoted to his favourite subject—the Progress of Society.

I.

Wind in a garland the ears of gold,
    Azure Cyanes * inwoven be!
Oh how gladly shall eye behold
    The Queen who comes in her majesty.
Man with man in communion mixing,
    Taming the wild ones where she went;
Into the peace of the homestead fixing –
    Lawless bosom and shifting tent.†

II.

Darkly hid in cave and cleft
    Shy, the Troglodyte abode;
Earth, a waste, was found and left
    Where the wandering Nomad strode:
Deadly with the spear and shaft,
    Prowl'd the Hunter through the land;
Woe the Stranger, waves may waft
    On an ever-fatal strand!

III.

Thus was all to Ceres, when
    Searching for her ravish'd child,
(No green culture smiling then,)
    O'er the drear coasts bleak and wild,
Never shelter did she gain,
    Never friendly threshold trod;
All unbuilded then the Fane,
    All unheeded then the God!

---

* The corn-flowers.
† "This first strophe," observes Hoffmeister, "is opened by the chorus of the whole festive assembly. A smaller chorus, or a single narrator passes then to the *recitative*, and traces the progress of mankind through Agriculture."

THE ELEUSINIAN FESTIVAL.

IV.

Not with golden corn-ears strewed
    Were the ghastly altar-stones;
Bleaching there, and gore-embrued,
    Lay the unhallow'd Human bones!
Wide and far, where'er she roved,
    Still reigned Misery over all;
And her mighty soul was moved
    At Man's universal fall.

V.

" What! can *this* be Man—to whom
    Our own godlike form was given—
Likeness of the shapes that bloom
    In the Garden-Mount of Heaven?
Was not Earth on Man bestow'd?
    Earth itself his kingly home!
Roams he thro' his bright abode,
    Homeless wheresoe'er he roam?

VI.

" Will no God vouchsafe to aid?—
    None of the Celestial choir—
Lift the Demigod we made
    From the slough and from the mire?
No, the grief they ne'er have known,
    Calmly the Celestials scan!
I—The Mother—I, alone
    Have a heart that feels for Man!

VII.

" Let—that Men to Man may soar—
    Man and Earth with one another
Make a compact evermore—
    Man the Son, and Earth the Mother.
Let their laws the Seasons show,
    Time itself Man's teacher be;
And the sweet Moon moving slow
    To the starry Melody!"

VIII.

Gently brightening from the cloud,
  Round her image, veil-like, thrown;
On the startled savage crowd
  Lo! the Goddess-glory shone!
Soft, the Goddess-glory stole
  On their War-feast o'er the Dead;
Fierce hands offered her the bowl
  With the blood of foemen red.

IX.

Loathing, turned the gentle Queen,
  Loathing, shuddering, turned—and said,
"Ne'er a Godhead's lips have been
  With the food of tigers fed.
Offering pure that ne'er pollutes,
  Be to purer Beings given,
Summer flowers and autumn fruits
  Please the Family of Heaven."

X.

And the wrathful spear she takes
  From the Hunter's savage hand,
With the shaft of Murder,—breaks
  Into furrows the light sand;
From her spikèd wreath she singles
  Out a golden seed of corn,
With the earth the germ she mingles,
  And the mighty birth is born!

XI.

Robing now the rugged ground—
  Glints the budding lively green,
Now—a Golden Forest—round
  Waves the Mellow Harvest's Sheen!—
And the Goddess bless'd the Earth,
  Bade the earliest sheaf be bound—
Chose the landmark for a hearth,
  And serenely smiling round,

XII.

Spoke in prayer—" O Father King,
  On thine Ether-Hill divine—
Take, O Zeus, this offering,
  Let it soften Thee to thine!
From thy People's eyes—away,
  Roll the vapour coil'd below;
Let the hearts untaught to pray
  Learn the Father-God to know!"

XIII.

And his gentle Sister's prayer,
  To the High Olympian came
Thundering thro' a cloudless air
  Flashed the consecrating flame;—
On the holy sacrifice,
  Bright the wreathèd lightning leaps;
And in circles thro' the skies,
  Jove's good-omened Eagle sweeps.

XIV.

Low at the feet of the great Queen, low *
  Fall the crowd in a glad devotion;
First then, first the rude souls know
  Human channels of sweet emotion—
Cast to the Earth is the gory spear,
  Wakened a soft sense blind before;
Hush'd in delight, from her lips they hear
  Mildest accents and wisest lore!

XV.

Thither from their thrones descending,
  All the Blest ones brightly draw;
Sceptred Themis, order-blending,
  Metes the right and gives the law: †

---

* Here the Full chorus chime in again. . . The Art of Husbandry once commenced, the chorus proceed to deduce from it the improvements of all social life.—HOFFMEISTER.

† Property begins with the culture of the Earth, Law with Property.

Teaches each one to respect
 What his Neighbour's landmarks girth;
Bids attesting Styx protect
 What the mortal owns on earth.

XVI.

Hither limps the God, whom all*
 Life's inventive Arts obey,
Highly skill'd is he to call
 Shape from metal, use from clay!
Heave the bellows, rings the clamour
 Of the heavy Anvil, now;
Fashion'd from the Forge-God's hammer
 O'er the Furrow speeds the Plough!

XVII.

And Minerva, towering proudly
 Over all, with lifted spear,
Calls in accents ringing loudly
 O'er the millions far and near—†
Calls the scattered tribes around;—
 Soars the rampart—spreads the wall,
And the scattered tribes have found
 Bulwark each, and union all!

XVIII.

Forth she leads her lordly train,
 O'er the wide earth;—and where'er
Prints her conquering step the plain,
 Springs another Landmark there!
O'er the Hills her empire sweeps;
 O'er their heights her chain she throws,
Stream that thundered to the deeps
 Curb'd in green banks, gently flows.

XIX.

Nymph and Oread, all who follow
 The fleet-footed Forest-Queen,
O'er the hill, or through the hollow;
 Swinging light their spears are seen.

---

* Vulcan. Then follow the technical Arts.
† Now come the Arts of Polity.

With a merry clamour trooping,
  With bright axes—one and all
Round the doomèd forest grouping,
  Down the huge pines crackling fall!

XX.

At the hest of Jove's high daughter,
  Heavy load and groaning raft
O'er his green reed-margined Water
  Doth the River Genius waft.
In the work, glad hands have found,
  Hour on hour, light-footed, flies,
From the rude trunk, smooth and round,
  Till the polish'd mast arise!

XXI.

Up leaps now the Ocean God,
  Riving ribbèd Earth asunder;
With his wondrous Trident-rod;—
  And the granite falls in thunder.
High he swings the mighty blocks,
  As an Infant swings a ball—
Help'd by active Hermes, rocks
  Heap'd on rocks—construct the wall.*

XXII.

Then from golden strings set free
  (Young Apollo's charmed boon)
Triple flows the Harmony,
  And the Measure, and the Tune!
With their ninefold symphonies
  There the chiming Muses throng,
Stone on stone the walls arise
  To the Choral Music-song.†

---

* This refers to the building of Troy.
† A felicitous allusion to the Walls of Thebes, built according to the fable to the sound of the Muses.

XXIII.

By Cybele's cunning hand
  Set the mighty Portals are;
And the huge Lock's safety-band,
  And the force-defying Bar.
Swift from those divinest hands
  Does the Wondrous City rise—
Bright, amidst, the Temple stands
  In the pomp of sacrifice.

XXIV.

With a myrtle garland—there
  Comes the Queen,* by Gods obey'd,
And she leads the Swain most fair
  To the fairest Shepherd-maid!
Venus and her laughing Boy
  Did that earliest pair array;
All the Gods, with gifts of joy
  Bless'd the earliest Marriage Day!

XXV.

Thro' the Hospitable Gate
  Flock the City's newborn sons,
Marshall'd in harmonious state
  By that choir of Holy ones.
At the Altar-shrine of Jove
  High—the Priestess Ceres stands
Folding, the mute Crowd above,
  Blessed and all-blessing hands!

XXVI.

In the waste the Beast is free,
  And the God upon his throne!
Unto each the curb must be
  But the nature each doth own.
Yet the Man—(betwixt the two)
  Must to man allied, belong;
Only Law and Custom thro'
  Is the Mortal free and strong!"

---

* Juno, the Goddess presiding over marriage.

XXVII.

Wind in a garland the ears of gold,
   Azure Cyanes inwoven be;
Oh how gladly shall eye behold
   The Queen, who comes in her majesty!
Man to man in communion bringing,
   Hers are the sweets of Home and Hearth,
Honour and praise, and hail her, singing,
   " Hail to the Mother and Queen of Earth!"

PARABLES AND RIDDLES.

I.

FROM Pearls her lofty bridge she weaves,
   A grey sea arching proudly over;
A moment's toil the work achieves,
   And on the height behold her hover!
Beneath that arch securely go
   The tallest barks that ride the seas,
No burthen e'er the bridge may know,
   And as thou seek'st to near—it flees!
First with the floods it came, to fade
   As roll'd the waters from the land;
Say where that wondrous arch is made,
   And whose the Artist's mighty hand?*

II.

League after league it hurrieth thee,
   Yet never quits its place;
It hath no wings wherewith to flee,
   Yet wafts thee over space!
It is the fleetest boat that e'er
   The wildest wanderer bore:
As swift as thought itself to bear
   From shore to farthest shore;
'Tis here and there, and everywhere,
   Ere yet a moment's o'er! †

---

* The Rainbow.
† The Sight, or perhaps Light.

III.

O'er a mighty pasture go,
  Sheep in thousands, silver-white;
As to-day we see them, so
  In the oldest grandsire's sight.
They drink (never waxing old)
  Life from an unfailing brook;
There's a Shepherd to their fold,
  With a silver-horned crook.
From a gate of gold let out,
  Night by night he counts them over;
Wide the field they rove about,
  Never hath he lost a rover!
True the DOG, that helps to lead them,
  One gay RAM in front we see;
What the Flock and who doth heed them,
  Sheep and Shepherd—tell to me! *

IV.

There is a Mansion vast and fair,
  That doth on unseen pillars rest;
No Wanderer leaves the portals there,
  Yet each how brief a guest!
The craft by which that mansion rose
  No thought can picture to the soul;
'Tis lighted by a Lamp which throws
  Its stately shimmer through the whole.
As crystal clear, it rears aloof
The single gem which forms its roof,
And never hath the eye survey'd
The Master who that Mansion † made.

V.

Up and down two buckets ply,
  A single well within;
While the one comes full on high,
  One the deeps must win;
Full or empty, never ending,
Rising now and now descending,

  * The Moon and Stars.
  † The Earth and the Firmament.

Always—while you quaff from this,
That one lost in the abyss,
From that well the waters living
Never both together giving.*

VI.

That gentle picture dost thou know,
  Itself its hues and splendour gaining?
Some change each moment can bestow,
  Itself as perfect still remaining;
It lies within the smallest space,
  The smallest framework forms its girth,
And yet that picture can embrace
  The mightiest objects known on Earth:
Canst thou to me that crystal name
  (No gem can with its worth compare)
Which gives all light, and knows no flame;
  Absorbed is all creation there!—
That ring can in itself enclose
  The loveliest hues that light the Heaven,
Yet from it light more lovely goes
  Than all which to it can be given! †

VII.

There stands a Building vast and wide,
  Built in eldest times of yore;
Round it may the Rider ride
  For a hundred days or more;
And however fast he speed,
Shall the pile outstrip the steed.
Many a hundred years have fled,
  'Gainst it Time and Storm have striven,
Stark and strong it rears its head
  Underneath the Vault of Heaven;
Soaring here the clouds to meet,
There the ocean laves its feet.

---

* Day and Night. It has also been interpreted as Youth and Age, or Past and Present.
† The Eye.

Not some pageant-pomp to lend
  Vaunting Pride, or flaunting Power,
But to shield and to defend
  Doth that Mighty Fabric tower.
Ne'er its like hath Earth survey'd,
Tho' a mortal hand hath made!*

VIII.

Amidst the Serpent Race is one
  That Earth did never bear;
In speed and fury there be none
  That can with it compare,—
With fearful hiss—its prey to grasp
  It darts its dazzling course;
And locks in one destroying clasp
  The Horseman and the Horse.
It loves the loftiest heights to haunt—
  No bolt its prey secures,
In vain its mail may Valour vaunt,
  For steel its fury lures!
As slightest straw whirl'd by the wind,
  It snaps the starkest tree;
It can the might of metal grind,
  How hard soe'er it be!
Yet ne'er but once the Monster tries
  The prey it threats to gain,†
In its own wrath consumed it dies,
  And while it slays is slain ‡

IX.

Six Sisters, from a wondrous pair,§
  We take our common birth;
Our solemn Mother—dark as Care,
  Our Father bright as Mirth,

---

* The Wall of China.
† "Hat zwei mal nur gedroht." For *nur* should be read *nie*.
‡ Lightning.
§ Black and White. Here Schiller adopts Goethe's theory of colours, and supposes that they are formed from the mixture of Light and Darkness.

PARABLES AND RIDDLES.

Its several virtue each bequeathes;
  The soften'd shade—the merry glance;
In endless youth, around you wreathes
  Our undulating dance!
We shun the darksome hollow cave,
  And bask where daylight glows;
Our magic life to Nature gave
  The soul her beauty knows.
Blithe messengers of Spring, we lead
  Her jocund train,—we flee
The dreary chambers of the Dead,—
  Where life is—there are we!
To Happiness essential things,
  Where Man enjoys we live—
Whate'er the Pomp that blazons kings,
  'Tis ours the pomp to give! *

X.

What's that, the Poor's most precious Friend
  Nor less by kings respected—
Contrived to pierce, contrived to rend,
  And to the sword connected.
It draws no blood, and yet doth wound;—
  Makes rich, but ne'er with spoil;
It prints, as Earth it wanders round,
  A blessing on the soil.
Tho' eldest cities it hath built—
  Bade mightiest kingdoms rise, it
Ne'er fired to War, nor roused to guilt:
  Weal to the states that prize it! †

XI.

In a Dwelling of stone I conceal,
  My existence obscure and asleep;
But forth at the clash of the steel,
  From my slumber exulting I leap!

---

i. e., the Children of Night and Day. In his earlier poem of "The Artists," the noble image which concludes the Poem is taken from the different theory of Newton. According to the former theory, the Colours are six in number—according to the latter, seven.—HOFFMEISTER.
* The Colours.
† The Ploughshare.

At first, all too feeble for strife,
  As a dwarf I appear to thine eye;
A drop could extinguish my life—
  But my wings soon expand to the sky!
Let the might of my Sister * afford
  Its aid to those wings when unfurl'd,
And I grow to a terrible Lord,
  Whose anger can ravage the world.†

XII.

Revolving round a Disk I go,
  One restless journey o'er and over;
The smallest field my wanderings know,
  Thy hands the space could cover:
Yet many a thousand miles are past,
  In circling round that field so narrow;
My speed outstrips the swiftest blast—
  The strongest bowman's arrow! ‡

XIII.

It is a Bird—whose swiftness flees,
  Fast as an Eagle thro' the Air;
It is a Fish—and cleaves the seas,
  Which ne'er a mightier monster bear:
It is an Elephant, whose form
  Is crowned with a castle-keep;
And now, all like the spider-worm,
  Spinning its white webs—see it creep!
It hath an iron fang; and where
  That fang is grappled hold doth gain,
It roots its rock-like footing there,
  And braves the baffled Hurricane. §

---

* Viz.:—The Air.   ‡ The Shade on the Dial.
† Fire.   § The Ship.

THE MIGHT OF SONG.

In the two Poems—"The Might of Song"—and that to which, in the translation, we have given the paraphrastic title "Honour to Woman" (Würde der Frauen), are to be found those ideas which are the well-streams of so much of Schiller's noblest inspiration:—1st, An intense and religious conviction of the lofty character and sublime ends of the true poet. 2nd, A clear sense of what is most lovely in woman, and a chivalrous devotion to the virtues of which he regards her as the Personation and Prototype. It is these two articles in his poetical creed, which constitute Schiller so peculiarly the Poet of *Gentlemen*—not the gentlemen of convention, but the gentlemen of nature—that Aristocracy of feeling and sentiment which are the flower of the social world; chivalrously inclined to whatever is most elevated in Art—chivalrously inclined to whatever is most tender in emotion. The Nobility of the North, which Tacitus saw in its rude infancy, has found in Schiller not only the voice of its mature greatness, but the Ideal of its great essentials.

 A RAIN-FLOOD from the Mountain riven,
  It leaps in thunder forth to-day;
 Before its rush the crags are driven,
  The oaks uprooted whirl'd away!
 Awed—yet in awe all wildly gladd'ning,
  The startled wanderer halts below;
 He hears the rock-born waters madd'ning,
  Nor wits the source from whence they go,—
 So, from their high, mysterious Founts, along,
 Stream on the silenced world the Waves of Song!

 Knit with the threads of life, för ever,
  By those dread Powers that weave the woof,—
 Whose art the singer's spell can sever?
  Whose breast has mail to music proof?
 Lo, to the Bard, a wand of wonder
  The Herald * of the Gods has given:
 He sinks the soul the death-realm under,
  Or lifts it breathless up to heaven—
 Half sport, half earnest, rocking its devotion
 Upon the tremulous ladder of emotion.

    * Hermes.

As, when in hours the least unclouded
　　Portentous, strides upon the scene—
Some Fate, before from wisdom shrouded,
　　And awes the startled souls of Men—
Before that Stranger from ANOTHER,
　　Behold how THIS world's great ones bow
Mean joys their idle clamour smother,
　　The mask is vanish'd from the brow—
And from Truth's sudden, solemn flag unfurl'd,
Fly all the craven Falsehoods of the World!'

So, Song—like Fate itself—is given,
　　To scare the idler thoughts away,
To raise the Human to the Holy,
　　To wake the Spirit from the Clay!*
One with the Gods the Bard: before him
　　All things unclean and earthly fly—
Hush'd are all meaner powers, and o'er him
　　The dark fate swoops unharming by;
And while the Soother's magic measures flow,
Smooth'd every wrinkle on the brows of Woe!

Even as a child, that, after pining
　　For the sweet absent mother—hears
Her voice—and, round her neck entwining
　　Young arms, vents all his soul in tears;—
So, by harsh Custom far estranged,
　　Along the glad and guileless track,
To childhood's happy home unchanged,
　　The swift song wafts the wanderer back—
Snatch'd from the cold and formal world, and prest
By the Great Mother to her glowing breast!

---

* This somewhat obscure, but lofty comparison, by which Poetry is likened to some fate that rouses men from the vulgar littleness of sensual joy, levels all ranks for the moment, and appals conventional falsehoods with unlooked-for truth, Schiller had made, though in rugged and somewhat bombastic prose, many years before,—as far back as the first appearance of "The Robbers."

HONOUR TO WOMAN.

[Literally " Dignity of Women."]

Honour to Woman! To her it is given
To garden the earth with the roses of Heaven!
   All blessed, she linketh the Loves in their choir—
In the veil of the Graces her beauty concealing,
She tends on each altar that's hallow'd to Feeling,
   And keeps ever-living the fire!

  From the bounds of Truth careering,
    Man's strong spirit wildly sweeps,
  With each hasty impulse veering,
    Down to Passion's troubled deeps.
  And his heart, contented never,
    Greeds to grapple with the Far,
  Chasing his own dream for ever,
    On through many a distant Star!

But Woman with looks that can charm and enchain,
Lureth back at her beck the wild truant again,
   By the spell of her presence beguiled—
In the home of the Mother her modest abode,
And modest the manners by Nature bestow'd
   On Nature's most exquisite child!

  Bruised and worn, but fiercely breasting,
    Foe to foe, the angry strife;
  Man the Wild One, never resting,
    Roams along the troubled life;
  What he planneth, still pursuing;
    Vainly as the Hydra bleeds,
  Crest the sever'd crest renewing—
    Wish to wither'd wish succeeds.

But Woman at peace with all being, reposes,
And seeks from the Moment to gather the roses—
   Whose sweets to her culture belong.
Ah! richer than he, though his soul reigneth o'er
The mighty dominion of Genius and Lore,
   And the infinite Circle of Song.

Strong, and proud, and self-depending,
  Man's cold bosom beats alone;
Heart with heart divinely blending,
  In the love that Gods have known,
Souls' sweet interchange of feeling,
  Melting tears—he never knows,
Each hard sense the hard one steeling,
  Arms against a world of foes.

Alive, as the wind-harp, how lightly soever
If woo'd by the Zephyr, to music will quiver,
  Is Woman to Hope and to Fear;
Ah, tender one! still at the shadow of grieving,
How quiver the chords—how thy bosom is heaving—
  How trembles thy glance through the tear!

Man's dominion, war and labour;
  Might to right the Statute gave;
Laws are in the Scythian's sabre;
  Where the Mede reign'd—see the Slave!
Peace and Meekness grimly routing,
  Prowls the War-lust, rude and wild;
Eris rages, hoarsely shouting,
  Where the vanish'd Graces smiled.

But Woman, the Soft One, persuasively prayeth—
Of the life* that she charmeth, the sceptre she swayeth;
  She lulls, as she looks from above,
The Discord whose Hell for its victims is gaping,
And blending awhile the for-ever escaping,
  Whispers Hate to the Image of Love!

THE WORDS OF BELIEF.

THREE Words will I name thee—around and about,
  From the lip to the lip, full of meaning, they flee;
But they had not their birth in the being without,
  And the heart, not the lip, must their oracle be!
And all worth in the man shall for ever be o'er
When in those Three Words he believes no more.

* Literally, "the Manners." The French word *mœurs* corresponds best with the German.

Man is made FREE!—Man, by birthright is free,
  Though the tyrant may deem him but born for his tool.
Whatever the shout of the rabble may be—
  Whatever the ranting misuse of the fool—
Still fear not the Slave, when he breaks from his chain,
For the Man made a Freeman grows safe in his gain.

And VIRTUE is more than a shade or a sound,
  And Man may her voice, in this being, obey;
And though ever he slip on the stony ground,
  Yet ever again to the godlike way,
To the *science* of Good though the Wise may be blind,
Yet the *practice* is plain to the childlike mind.

And a GOD there is!—over Space, over Time,
  While the Human Will rocks, like a reed, to and fro,
Lives the Will of the Holy—A Purpose Sublime,
  A Thought woven over creation below;
Changing and shifting the All we inherit,
But changeless through all One Immutable Spirit!

Hold fast the Three Words of Belief—though about
  From the lip to the lip, full of meaning, they flee;
Yet they take not their birth from the being without—
  But a voice from within must their oracle be;
And never all worth in the Man can be o'er,
Till in those Three Words he believes no more.

THE WORDS OF ERROR.

THREE Errors there are, that for ever are found
  On the lips of the good, on the lips of the best;
But empty their meaning and hollow their sound—
  And slight is the comfort they bring to the breast.
The fruits of existence escape from the clasp
Of the seeker who strives but those shadows to grasp—

So long as Man dreams of some Age in *this* life
  When the Right and the Good will all evil subdue;
For the Right and the Good lead us ever to strife,
  And wherever they lead us, the Fiend will pursue.

And (till from the earth borne, and stifled at length)
The earth that he touches still gifts him with strength! *

So long as Man fancies that Fortune will live,
  Like a bride with her lover, united with Worth;
For her favours, alas! to the mean she will give—
  And Virtue possesses no title to earth!
That Foreigner wanders to regions afar,
Where the lands of her birthright immortally are!

So long as Man dreams that, to mortals a gift,
  The Truth in her fulness of splendour will shine;
The veil of the goddess no earth-born may lift,
  And all we can learn is—to guess and divine!
Dost thou seek, in a dogma, to prison her form?
The spirit flies forth on the wings of the storm!

O, Noble Soul! fly from delusions like these,
  More heavenly belief be it thine to adore;
Where the Ear never hearkens, the Eye never sees,
  Meet the rivers of Beauty and Truth evermore!
Not *without* thee the streams—there the Dull seek them;—No!
Look *within* thee—behold both the fount and the flow!

THE MERCHANT.

WHERE sails the ship?—It leads the Tyrian forth
For the rich amber of the liberal North.
Be kind ye seas—winds lend your gentlest wing,
May in each creek, sweet wells restoring spring!—
To you, ye gods, belong the Merchant!—o'er
The waves, his sails the wide world's goods explore;
And, all the while, wherever waft the gales,
The wide world's good sails with him as he sails!

---

* This simile is nobly conceived, but expressed somewhat obscurely. As Hercules contended in vain against Antæus, the Son of Earth,—so long as the Earth gave her giant offspring new strength in every fall,—so the soul contends in vain with evil—the natural earth-born enemy, while the very contact of the earth invigorates the enemy for the struggle. And as Antæus was slain at last, when Hercules lifted him from the earth, and strangled him while raised aloft, so can the soul slay the enemy (the desire, the passion, the evil, the earth's offspring), when bearing it from earth itself, and stifling it in the higher air.

THE GERMAN ART.

By no kind Augustus reared,
To no Medici endeared,
   German Art arose;
Fostering glory smil'd not on her,
Ne'er with kingly smiles to sun her,
   Did her blooms unclose.

No,—she went by Monarchs slighted—
Went unhonoured, unrequited,
   From high Frederick's throne;
Praise and Pride be all the greater,
That Man's genius did create her,
   From Man's worth alone.

Therefore, all from loftier mountains,
Purer wells and richer Fountains,
   Streams our Poet-Art;
So no rule to curb its rushing—
All the fuller flows it gushing
   From its deep—The Heart!

THE WALK.

This (excepting only "The Artists," written some years before) is the most elaborate of those Poems which, classed under the name of *Culture-Historic*, Schiller has devoted to the Progress of Civilisation. Schiller himself esteemed it amongst the greatest of the Poems he had thitherto produced—and his friends, from Goethe to Humboldt, however divided in opinion as to the relative merit of his other pieces, agreed in extolling this one. It must be observed, however, that Schiller had not then composed the narrative poems, which bear the name of Ballads, and which are confessedly of a yet higher order—inasmuch as the Narrative, in itself, demands much higher merits than the Didactic.* It is also reasonably to be objected to all Schiller's Poems of this Culture-Historic School (may we be pardoned the use of the German Barbarism), that the leading idea of the Progress of Civilisation, however varied as to form in each, is essentially repeated in all. Nor can we omit this occasion of inculcating one critical Doctrine, which seems to us highly important, and to which the theories of Schiller's intimate and over-refining friend, William Von Humboldt, were strongly opposed. The object of Poetry, differing essentially from that of abstract wisdom, is not directly to address the Reasoning faculty—but

---

* Schiller perhaps disclaimed the title of Didactic for this Poem, as for 'The Artists"—yet Didactic both Poems unquestionably are.

insensibly to rouse it through the popular medium of the emotions. Science aims at Truth, and through Truth may arrive at Beauty. Poetry or Art aims at Beauty, and through Beauty it cannot fail to arrive at Truth. The fault of "The Walk," of "The Artists,"—more than all of "The Ideal and the Actual Life," not to specify some other Poems, less elaborately scholastic—is, that they strain too much the faculty with which Poetry has least to do, viz., the mere Reason. Poetry ought, it is true, to bear aloft and to sustain the mind in a state of elevation—but through the sentiment or the passion. It fails in something when it demands a high degree of philosophy or knowledge in the reader to admire—nay to comprehend it. It ought not to ask a prepared Audience, but to raise any audience it may address. Milton takes the sublimest theme he can find—he adorns it with all his stately genius, and his multiform learning; but, except in two or three passages (which are really defects in his great whole), he contrives to keep within reach of very ordinary understandings. Because the Poet is wise, he is not for that reason to demand wisdom from his readers. In the Poem of "The Walk," it is only after repeated readings that we can arrive at what seems to us its great and distinctive purpose—apart from the mere recital of the changes of the Social State. According to our notion, the purpose is this—the intimate and necessary connexion between Man and Nature—the Social State and the Natural. The Poet commences with the actual Landscape, he describes the scenery of his walk: Rural Life, viz.—Nature in the Fields—suggests to him the picture of the Early Pelasgian or Agricultural life—Nature is then the *Companion* of Man. A sudden turn in the Landscape shows him the popular avenues which in Germany conduct to cities. He beholds the domes and towers of the distant Town—and this suggests to him the alteration from the rural life to the civic—still Nature is his guide. But in cities Man has ceased to be the companion of Nature—he has become her *Ruler* (der Herrscher). In this altered condition the Poet depicts the growth of Civilisation, till he arrives at the Invention of Printing. Light then breaks upon the Blind—Man desires not only to be Lord of Nature, but to dispense with her. "Instead of Necessity and Nature he would appoint Liberty and Reason." Reason shouts for Liberty—so do the Passions, and both burst from the wholesome control of Nature. He then reviews the corruption of Civilisation under the old French Régime; he likens Man, breaking from this denaturalised state, to the tiger escaping from its den into the wilderness; and suggests the great truth, that it is only by a return to Nature, that he can regain his true liberty and redemption. Not, indeed (as Hoffmeister truly observes), the savage Nature to which Rousseau would reduce Man—*that*, Schiller was too wise to dream of—and too virtuous to desire; but that Nature which has not more its generous liberty than its holy laws—that Nature which is but the word for Law—God's Law. He would not lead Man back to Nature in its infancy, but advance him to Nature in its perfection. The moral Liberty of a well-ordered condition of society is as different from the physical liberty lusted after by the French Revolutionists, as (to borrow Cowley's fine thought) "the solitude of a God from the solitude of a wild beast." And finally, after this general association of Nature with Mankind, the Poet awakens as from a dream, to find himself individually alone with Nature, and concludes, in some of the happiest lines he ever wrote, by insisting on that eternal youthfulness of Nature, which links itself with its companion Poetry. "The Sun of Homer smiles upon us still." In the original German, the Poem is composed in the long rhymeless metre, which no one has succeeded, or can succeed, in rendering into English melody. But happily, the true beauty of the composition, like most of Schiller's (unlike most of Goethe's), is independent of *form* :—consisting of ideas, not easily deprived of their effect, into what mould soever they may be thrown. . . . In the above remarks we have sought to remove the only drawback the general reader may find, to the pleasure to be derived from the Poem in the original—to lighten the weight upon his intellect, and define the purpose of the design. As to execution, even in translation, the sense of beauty must be dull in those who cannot perceive the exquisite merits of the preliminary description—the rapid vigour with which what Herder called "the World of Scenes," shifts and shimmers, and the grand divisions of Human History are seized and outlined—and the noble reflections which, after losing himself in the large interests of the multitude, Solitude forces upon the Poet at the close.

HAIL, mine own hill—ye bright'ning hill-tops, hail!
Hail, sun, that gild'st them with thy looks of love!
Sweet fields!—ye lindens, murmuring to the gale!
And ye gay choristers the boughs above!
And thou, the Blue Immeasurable CALM,
O'er mount and forest, motionless and bright,—
Thine airs breathe through me their reviving balm,
And the heart strengthens as it drinks thy light!
Thou gracious Heaven! man's prison-home I flee—
Loosed from the babbling world, my soul leaps up to thee!

Flowers of all hue are struggling into glow,
Along the blooming fields; yet their sweet strife
Melts into one harmonious concord. Lo,
The path allures me through the pastoral green,
And the wide world of fields!—The labouring bee
Hums round me; and on hesitating wing
O'er beds of purple clover quiveringly
Hovers the butterfly.—Save these, all life
Sleeps in the glowing sunlight's steady sheen—
Ev'n from the west, no breeze the lull'd airs bring.
Hark—in the calm aloft, I hear the skylark sing!

The thicket rustles near—the alders bow
Down their green coronals—and as I pass,
Waves, in the rising wind, the silvering grass.
Come, day's ambrosial night!—receive me now
Beneath the roof by shadowy beeches made,
Cool-breathing! Lost the gentler landscape's bloom!
And as the path mounts, snake-like, through the shade,
Deep woods close round me with mysterious gloom;
Still, through the trellice-leaves, at stolen whiles,
Glints the stray beam, or the meek azure smiles.
Again, and yet again, the veil is riven—

And the glade opening, with a sudden glare,
Lets in the blinding day! Before me, heaven
With all its Far-Unbounded!—one blue hill
Ending the gradual world—in vapour!
         Where
I stand upon the mountain-summit, lo,
As sink its sides precipitous before me,
The stream's smooth waves in flying crystal flow
Through the calm vale beneath. Wide Ether o'er me—
Beneath, alike, wide Ether endless still!
Dizzy, I gaze aloft—shuddering, I look below!—
A railèd path betwixt the eternal height—
And the eternal deep allures me on.
Still, as I pass—all laughing in delight,
The rich shores glide-along; and in glad toil,
Glories the pranksome vale with variegated soil.
Each feature that divides what labour's son
Claims for his portion from his labouring brother;—
Broidering the veil wrought by the Mighty Mother.*
Hedge-row and bound—those friendly scrolls of law,—
LAW, Man's sole guardian ever since the time
When the old Brazen Age, in sadness saw
Love fly the world!
      Now, through the harmonious meads,
One glimmering path, or lost in forests, leads,
Or up the winding hill doth labouring climb—
The highway link of lands dissever'd—glide
The quiet rafts adown the placid tide;
And through the lively fields, heard faintly, goes
The many sheep-bells' music—and the song
Of the lone herdsman, from its vex'd repose,
Rouses the gentle echo!—Calm, along
The stream, gay hamlets crown the pastoral scene,
Or peep through distant glades, or from the hill
Hang dizzy down! Man and the soil serene
Dwell neighbour-like together—and the still
Meadow sleeps peaceful round the rural door—
And, all-familiar, wreathes and clusters o'er
The lowly casement, the green bough's embrace,
As with a loving arm, clasping the gentle place!

---

   * Demeter.

O happy People of the Fields, not yet
Waken'd to freedom from the gentle will
Of the wild Nature, still content to share
With your own fields earth's elementary law!
Calm harvests to calm hopes the boundary set,
And peaceful as your daily labour, there,
Creep on your careless lives! *
      But ah! what steals
Between me and the scenes I lately saw—
A stranger spirit a strange world reveals,
A world with method, ranks, and orders rife—
And rends the simple unity of life.
The vista'd Poplars in their long array
The measured pomp of social forms betray.
That stately train proclaims the Ruler nigh;
And now the bright domes glitter to the sky,
And now from out the rocky kernel flowers
The haughty CITY, with its thousand towers!
Yet though the Fauns † back to their wilds have flown,
Devotion lends them loftier life in stone.
Man with his fellow-man more closely bound—
The world without begirts and cramps him round;
But in that world within the widening soul,
The unpausing wheels in swifter orbits roll.
See how the iron powers of thoughtful skill
Are shaped and quicken'd by the fire of strife;
Through contest great—through union greater still.
To thousand hands a single soul gives life—
In thousand breasts a single heart is beating—
Beats for the country of the common cause—
Beats for the old hereditary laws—
The earth itself made dearer by the dead—
And by the gods (whom mortal steps are meeting),
Come from their heaven, large gifts on men to shed.
Ceres, the plough—the anchor, Mercury—
Bacchus, the grape—the Sovereign of the sea,

---

* Here the Poet (after a slight and passing association of Man's more primitive state with the rural landscape before him) catches sight of the distant city; and, proceeding to idealise what he thus surveys, brings before the reader, in a series of striking and rapid images, the progressive changes of Civilisation.—See PRELIMINARY REMARKS.

† The Fauns here are meant generally to denote all the early rural gods.
—the primitive Deities of Italy.

The horse;—the olive brings the Blue-eyed Maid—
While tower'd Cybele yokes her lion-car,
Entering in peace the hospitable gate—
A Goddess-Citizen!
     All-blest ye are,
Ye Solemn Monuments! ye men and times
That did from shore to shore, and state to state,
Transplant the beauty of humanity!
Forth send far islands, from the gentler climes,
Their goodly freight—the manners and the arts.
In simple courts the Patriarchal Wise
By social Gates adjudge the unpurchased right.*
To deathless fields the ardent hero flies,
To guard the hearths that sanctify the fight;
And women from the walls, with anxious hearts
Beating beneath the infants nestled there,
Watch the devoted band, till from their eyes,
In the far space, the steel-clad pageant dies—
Then, falling by the altars, pour the prayer,
Fit for the gods to hear—that worth may earn
The fame which crowns brave souls that conquer, and—
  return!
And fame was yours and conquest!—yet alone
Fame—and not life return'd: your deeds are known
In words that kindle glory from the stone.
"Tell Sparta, we, whose record meets thine eye,
Obey'd the Spartan laws—and here we lie!" †
Sleep soft!—your blood bedews the Olive's bloom,
Peace sows its harvests in the Patriot's tomb,
And Trade's great intercourse at once is known
Where Freedom guards what Labour makes its own.
The azure River-God his watery fields
Lends to the raft;—her home the Dryad yields.
Down falls the huge oak with a thunder-groan;
Wing'd by the lever soars the quickening stone;
Up from the shaft the diving Miner brings
The metal-mass with which the anvil rings,

---

* Alluding to the ancient custom of administering Law in the open places near the town gates.

† Herodotus. The celebrated epitaph on the Spartan tumulus at Thermopylae.

THE WALK.

Anvil and hammer keeping measured time
As the steel sparkles with each heavy chime:—
The bright web round the dancing spindle gleams;
Safe guides the Pilot, through the world of streams,
The ships that interchange, where'er they roam,
The wealth of earth—the industry of home;
High from the mast the garland-banner waves,
The Sail bears life upon the wind it braves;
Life grows and multiplies where life resorts,
Life crowds the Masts—life bustles through the Ports,
And many a language the broad streets within
Blends on the wondering Ear the Babel and the din.
And all the harvests of all earth, whate'er
Hot Afric nurtures in its lurid air,
Or Araby, the blest one of the Wild,
Or the Sea's lonely and abandoned child
Uttermost Thulè,—to one mart are borne,
And the rich plenty brims starr'd Amalthæa's horn.
 The nobler Genius prospers with the rest:
Art draws its aliment from Freedom's breast;
Flush'd into life, the pictured Image breaks,
Waked by the chisel, Stone takes soul and speaks!
On slender Shafts a Heaven of Art reposes,
And all Olympus one bright Dome encloses.
Light as aloft we see the Iris spring,
Light as the arrow flying from the string,
O'er the wide river, rushing to the Deep,
The lithe bridge boundeth with its airy leap.

 But all the while, best pleased apart to dwell,
Sits musing Science in its noiseless cell;
Draws meaning circles, and with patient mind
Steals to the Spirit that the whole design'd,
Gropes through the Realm of Matter for its Laws,
Learns where the Magnet or repels or draws,
Follows the sound along the air, and flies
After the lightning through the pathless skies,
Seeks through dark Chance's wonder-teeming maze
The Guiding Law which regulates and sways,
Seeks through the shifting evanescent shows
The Central Principle's serene repose.

Now shape and voice—the immaterial Thought
Takes from th' Invented speaking page sublime;
The Ark which Mind has for its refuge wrought,
Its floating Archive down the floods of Time!
Rent from the startled gaze the veil of Night,
O'er old delusions streams the dawning light:—
Man breaks his bonds—ah, blest could he refrain,
Free from the curb, to scorn alike the rein!
"Freedom!" shouts Reason, "Freedom!" wild Desire—
And light to Wisdom is to Passion fire.
From Nature's check bursts forth one hurtling swarm—
Ah, snaps the anchor, as descends the storm!
The sea runs mountains—vanishes the shore,
The mastless wreck drifts endless ocean o'er;
Lost,—Faith—man's polar Star!—nought seems to rest,
The Heart's God, Conscience, darkens from the breast—

Yet first the foulness of the slough discern,
From which to Freedom Nature seeks return *
Gone Truth from language, and from life, belief;
The oath itself rots blighted to a lie,
On love's most solemn secrets, on the grief
Or joy that knits the Heart's familiar tie—
Intrudes the Sycophant, and glares the spy.
Suspected friendship from the soul is rent,
The hungry treason snares the Innocent—
With rabid slaver, and devouring fangs,
Fast on his prey the foul blasphemer hangs—
Shame from the reason and the heart effac'd,
The thought is abject, and the love debas'd:
Deceit—O Truth, thy holy features steals—
Watches emotion in its candid course—
Betrays what Mirth unconsciously reveals,
And desecrates Man's nature at its source;
And yet the Tribune justice can debate—
And yet the Cot of tranquil Union prate—

* The two lines in brackets are, after much hesitation, interpolated by the Translator, in order to maintain the sense, otherwise obscured, if not lost, by the abruptness of the transition. Schiller has already glanced at the French Revolution, but he now goes back to the time preceding it, and the following lines portray the corruption of the old régime.

THE WALK.

And yet a spectre which they call the Law,
Stands by the Kingly throne, the crowd to awe!
For years—for centuries, may the Mummies there,
Mock the warm life whose lying shape they wear,
Till Nature once more from her sleep awakes—
Till to the dust the hollow fabric shakes
Beneath your hands—Avenging Powers sublime,
Your heavy iron hands, NECESSITY and TIME!

Then, as some Tigress from the grated bar,
Bursts sudden, mindful of her wastes afar,
Deep in Numidian glooms—Humanity,
Fierce in the wrath of wretchedness and crime,
Forth from the City's blazing ashes breaks,
And the lost Nature it has pined for seeks.
Open ye walls and let the prisoner free!—
Safe to forsaken fields, back let the wild one flee!

But where am I—and whither would I stray?
The path is lost—the cloud-capt mountain-dome,
The rent abysses, to the dizzy sense,
Behind, before me! Far and far away,
Garden and hedgerow, the sweet Company
Of Fields, familiar speaking of man's home—
Yea, every trace of man—lie hidden from the eye.
Only the raw eternal MATTER, whence
Life buds, towers round me—the grey basalt-stone,
Virgin of human art, stands motionless and lone.
Roaringly, through the rocky cleft, and under
Gnarl'd roots of trees, the torrent sweeps in thunder—
Savage the scene, and desolate and bare—
Lo! where the eagle, his calm wings unfurl'd,
Lone-halting in the solitary air,
Knits * to the vault of heaven this ball—the world!
No plumèd wind bears o'er the Dædal soil
One breath of man's desire, and care, and toil.
Am I indeed alone, amidst thy charms,
O Nature—clasped once more within thine arms?—

* Knits—*Knüpft*. What a sublime image is conveyed in that single word!

I dreamed—and wake upon thy heart!—escaped
From the dark phantoms which my Fancy shaped;
And sinks each shape of human strife and woe
Down with the vapours to the vale below!

Purer I take my life from thy pure shrine,
Sweet Nature!—gladlier comes again to me
The heart and hope of my lost youth divine!
Both end and means, eternally our will
Varies and changes, and our acts are still
The repetitions, multiplied and stale,
Of what have been before us. But with THEE
One ancient law, that will not wane or fail,
Keeps beauty vernal in the bloom of truth!
Ever the same, thou hoardest for the man
What to thy hands the infant or the youth
Trusted familiar; and since Time began,
Thy breasts have nurtured, with impartial love,
The many-changing ages!
       Look above,
Around, below;—beneath the self-same blue,
Over the self-same green, eternally,
(Let man's slight changes wither as they will,)
All races which the wide world ever knew,
United, wander brother-like!—Ah! see,
THE SUN OF HOMER SMILES UPON US STILL!

THE LAY OF THE BELL.

"*Vivos voco—Mortuos plango—Fulgura frango.*" *

I.

FAST, in its prison-walls of earth,
 Awaits the mould of bakèd clay.
Up, comrades, up, and aid the birth—
 THE BELL that shall be born to-day!

---

* "I call the living—I mourn the Dead—I break the Lightning." These words are inscribed on the Great Bell of the Minster of Schaffhausen—also on that of the Church of Art near Lucerne. There was an old belief in Switzerland, that the undulation of air, caused by the sound of a Bell, broke the electric fluid of a thunder-cloud.

Who would honour obtain,
    With the sweat and the pain,
The praise that Man gives to the Master must buy!—
But the blessing withal must descend from on high!

And well an earnest word beseems
    The work the earnest hand prepares;
Its load more light the labour deems,
    When sweet discourse the labour shares.
So let us ponder—nor in vain—
    What strength can work when labour wills;
For who would not the fool disdain
    Who ne'er designs what he fulfils?
And well it stamps our Human Race,
    And hence the gift To UNDERSTAND,
That Man, within the heart should trace
    Whate'er he fashions with the hand.

II.

From the fir the fagot take,
    Keep it, heap it hard and dry,
That the gather'd flame may break
    Through the furnace, wroth and high.
    When the copper within
    Seethes and simmers—the tin,
Pour quick, that the fluid that feeds the Bell
May flow in the right course glib and well.

Deep hid within this nether cell,
    What force with Fire is moulding thus,
In yonder airy tower shall dwell,
    And witness wide and far of us!
It shall, in later days, unfailing,
    Rouse many an ear to rapt emotion;
Its solemn voice with Sorrow wailing,
    Or choral chiming to Devotion.
Whatever Fate to Man may bring,
    Whatever weal or woe befall,
That metal tongue shall backward ring
    The warning moral drawn from all.

III.

See the silvery bubbles spring!
  Good! the mass is melting now!
Let the salts we duly bring
  Purge the flood, and speed the flow.
    From the dross and the scum,
    Pure, the fusion must come;
For perfect and pure we the metal must keep,
That its voice may be perfect, and pure, and deep.

That voice, with merry music rife,
  The cherish'd child shall welcome in;
What time the rosy dreams of life,
  In the first slumber's arms begin.
As yet in Time's dark womb unwarning,
  Repose the days, or foul or fair;
And watchful o'er that golden morning,
  The Mother-Love's untiring care!
And swift the years like arrows fly—
No more with girls content to play,
Bounds the proud Boy upon his way,
Storms through loud life's tumultuous pleasures,
With pilgrim staff the wide world measures;
And, wearied with the wish to roam,
Again seeks, stranger-like, the Father-Home.
And, lo, as some sweet vision breaks
  Out from its native morning skies,
With rosy shame on downcast cheeks,
  The Virgin stands before his eyes.
A nameless longing seizes him!
  From all his wild companions flown;
Tears, strange till then, his eyes bedim;
  He wanders all alone.
Blushing, he glides where'er she move;
  Her greeting can transport him;
To every mead to deck his love,
  The happy wild flowers court him!
Sweet Hope—and tender Longing—ye
  The growth of Life's first Age of Gold
When the heart, swelling, seems to see
  The gates of heaven unfold!

O Love, the beautiful and brief! O prime,
Glory, and verdure, of life's summer time!

IV.

Browning o'er, the pipes are simmering,
 Dip this wand of clay * within;
If like glass the wand be glimmering,
 Then the casting may begin.
  Brisk, brisk now, and see
  If the fusion flow free;
If—(happy and welcome indeed were the sign!)
If the hard and the ductile united combine.
For still where the strong is betrothed to the weak,
And the stern in sweet marriage is blent with the meek,
 Rings the concord harmonious, both tender and strong:
So be it with thee, if for ever united,
The heart to the heart flows in one, love-delighted;
 Illusion is brief, but Repentance is long.

  Lovely, thither are they bringing,
   With her virgin wreath, the Bride!
  To the love-feast clearly ringing,
   Tolls the church-bell far and wide!
  With that sweetest holyday,
   Must the May of Life depart;
  With the cestus loosed—away
   Flies ILLUSION from the heart!
    Yet love lingers lonely,
    When Passion is mute,
   And the blossoms may only
    Give way to the fruit.
   The Husband must enter
    The hostile life,
     With struggle and strife,
     To plant or to watch,
     To snare or to snatch,
     To pray and importune,
    Must wager and venture
     And hunt down his fortune!

* A piece of clay pipe, which becomes vitrified if the metal is sufficiently heated.

Then flows in a current the gear and the gain,
And the garners are fill'd with the gold of the grain,
Now a yard to the court, now a wing to the centre!
    Within sits Another,
     The thrifty Housewife;
   The mild one, the mother—
    Her home is her life.
   In its circle she rules,
   And the daughters she schools,
    And she cautions the boys,
   With a bustling command,
   And a diligent hand
    Employ'd she employs;
   Gives order to store,
    And the much makes the more;
Locks the chest and the wardrobe, with lavender smelling,
And the hum of the spindle goes quick through the
  dwelling;
And she hoards in the presses, well polish'd and full,
The snow of the linen, the shine of the wool;
Blends the sweet with the good, and from care and en-
  deavour
Rests never!
   Blithe the Master (where the while
   From his roof he sees them smile)
    Eyes the lands, and counts the gain;
   There, the beams projecting far,
   And the laden store-house are,
   And the granaries bow'd beneath
    The blessed golden grain;
   There, in undulating motion,
   Wave the corn-fields like an ocean.
   Proud the boast the proud lips breathe:—
   " My house is built upon a rock,
   And sees unmoved the stormy shock
    Of waves that fret below!"
   What chain so strong, what girth so great,
   To bind the giant form of Fate?—
    Swift are the steps of Woe.

THE LAY OF THE BELL.

V.

Now the casting may begin;
  See the breach indented there:
Ere we run the fusion in,
    Halt—and speed the pious prayer!
      Pull the bung out—
      See around and about
What vapour, what vapour—God help us!—has risen?—
Ha! the flame like a torrent leaps forth from its prison!
    What friend is like the might of fire
    When man can watch and wield the ire?
    Whate'er we shape or work, we owe
    Still to that heaven-descended glow.
    But dread the heaven-descended glow,
    When from their chain its wild wings go,
    When, where it listeth, wide and wild
    Sweeps the free Nature's free-born Child!
    When the Frantic One fleets,
      While no force can withstand,
    Through the populous streets
      Whirling ghastly the brand;
    For the Element hates
    What Man's labour creates,
      And the work of his hand!
Impartially out from the cloud,
  Or the curse or the blessing may fall!
Benignantly out from the cloud,
  Come the dews, the revivers of all!
Avengingly out from the cloud
  Come the levin, the bolt, and the ball!
Hark—a wail from the steeple!—aloud
The bell shrills its voice to the crowd!
    Look—look—red as blood
      All on high!
It is not the daylight that fills with its flood
  The sky!
What a clamour awaking
  Roars up through the street,
What a hell-vapour breaking
  Rolls on through the street,

And higher and higher
Aloft moves the Column of Fire!
Through the vistas and rows
Like a whirlwind it goes,
And the air like the steam from a furnace glows.
Beams are crackling—posts are shrinking
Walls are sinking—windows clinking—
Children crying—
Mothers flying—
And the beast (the black ruin yet smouldering under)
Yells the howl of its pain and its ghastly wonder!
Hurry and skurry—away—away,
The face of the night is as clear as day!
As the links in a chain,
Again and again
Flies the bucket from hand to hand;
High in arches up-rushing
The engines are gushing,
And the flood, as a beast on the prey that it hounds,
With a roar on the breast of the element bounds.
To the grain and the fruits,
Through the rafters and beams,
Through the barns and the garners it crackles and
streams!
As if they would rend up the earth from its roots,
Rush the flames to the sky
Giant-high;
And at length,
Wearied out and despairing, man bows to their strength!
With an idle gaze sees their wrath consume,
And submits to his doom!
Desolate
The place, and dread
For storms the barren bed.
In the blank voids that cheerful casements were,
Comes to and fro the melancholy air,
And sits despair;
And through the ruin, blackening in its shroud
Peers, as it flits, the melancholy cloud.

One human glance of grief upon the grave
Of all that Fortune gave

The loiterer takes—Then turns him to depart,
And grasps the wanderer's staff and mans his heart:
Whatever else the element bereaves
One blessing more than all it reft—it leaves,
The *faces that he loves!*—He counts them o'er,
See—not one look is missing from *that* store!

VI.

Now clasp'd the bell within the clay—
  The mould the mingled metals fill—
Oh, may it, sparkling into day,
  Reward the labour and the skill!
    Alas! should it fail,
    For the mould may be frail—
And still with our hope must be mingled the fear—
And, ev'n now, while we speak, the mishap may be near!
  To the dark womb of sacred earth
  This labour of our hands is given,
  As seeds that wait the second birth,
  And turn to blessings watch'd by heaven!
  Ah seeds, how dearer far than they
    We bury in the dismal tomb,
  Where Hope and Sorrow bend to pray
  That suns beyond the realm of day
    May warm them into bloom!

      From the steeple
        Tolls the bell,
      Deep and heavy,
        The death-knell!
Guiding with dirge-note—solemn, sad, and slow,
To the last home earth's weary wanderers know.
    It is that worship'd wife—
    It is that faithful mother! *
Whom the dark Prince of Shadows leads benighted,
From that dear arm where oft she hung delighted.
Far from those blithe companions, born
Of her, and blooming in their morn;

---

* The translator adheres to the original, in forsaking the rhyme in these lines and some others.

On whom, when couch'd her heart above,
So often look'd the Mother-Love!

Ah! rent the sweet Home's union-band,
   And never, never more to come—
She dwells within the shadowy land,
   Who was the Mother of that Home!
How oft they miss that tender guide,
   The care—the watch—the face—the MOTHER—
And where she sate the babes beside,
   Sits with unloving looks—ANOTHER!

VII.

While the mass is cooling now,
   Let the labour yield to leisure,
As the bird upon the bough,
   Loose the travail to the pleasure.
     When the soft stars awaken,
     Each task be forsaken!
And the vesper-bell lulling the earth into peace,
If the master still toil, chimes the workman's release!

Homeward from the tasks of day,
Thro' the greenwood's welcome way
Wends the wanderer, blithe and cheerly,
To the cottage loved so dearly!
And the eye and ear are meeting,
Now, the slow sheep homeward bleating—
Now, the wonted shelter near,
Lowing the lusty-fronted steer;
Creaking now the heavy wain,
Reels with the happy harvest grain.
While, with many-coloured leaves,
Glitters the garland on the sheaves;
For the mower's work is done,
And the young folks' dance begun!
Desert street, and quiet mart;—
Silence is in the city's heart;
And the social taper lighteth
Each dear face that HOME uniteth;
While the gate the town before
Heavily swings with sullen roar!

THE LAY OF THE BELL.

Though darkness is spreading
  O'er earth—the Upright
And the Honest, undreading,
  Look safe on the night—
Which the evil man watches in awe,
For the eye of the Night is the Law!
  Bliss-dower'd! O daughter of the skies,
Hail, holy ORDER, whose employ
Blends like to like in light and joy—
Builder of cities, who of old
Call'd the wild man from waste and wold.
And, in his hut thy presence stealing,
Roused each familiar household feeling;
  And, best of all the happy ties,
The centre of the social band,—
The Instinct of the Fatherland!

United thus—each helping each,
  Brisk work the countless hands for ever;
For nought its power to Strength can teach,
  Like Emulation and Endeavour!
Thus link'd the master with the man,
  Each in his rights can each revere,
And while they march in freedom's van,
  Scorn the lewd rout that dogs the rear!
To freemen labour is renown!
  Who works—gives blessings and commands;
Kings glory in the orb and crown—
  Be ours the glory of our hands.
Long in these walls—long may we greet
Your footfalls, Peace and Concord sweet!
Distant the day. Oh! distant far,
When the rude hordes of trampling War
  Shall scare the silent vale;
    And where,
Now the sweet heaven, when day doth leave
  The air,
  Limns its soft rose-hues on the veil of Eve;
Shall the fierce war-brand tossing in the gale,
From town and hamlet shake the horrent glare!

VIII.

Now, its destin'd task fulfill'd,
    Asunder break the prison-mould ;
Let the goodly Bell we build,
    Eye and heart alike behold.
      The hammer down heave,
      Till the cover it cleave :—
For not till we shatter the wall of its cell
Can we lift from its darkness and bondage the Bell.

To break the mould, the master may,
    If skill'd the hand and ripe the hour ;
But woe, when on its fiery way
    The metal seeks itself to pour.
Frantic and blind, with thunder-knell,
    Exploding from its shattered home,
And glaring forth, as from a hell,
    Behold the red Destruction come !
When rages strength that has no reason,
There breaks the mould before the season ;
When numbers burst what bound before,
Woe to the State that thrives no more !
Yea, woe, when in the City's heart,
    The latent spark to flame is blown ;
And Millions from their silence start,
    To claim, without a guide, their own !
Discordant howls the warning Bell,
    Proclaiming discord wide and far,
And, born but things of peace to tell,
    Becomes the ghastliest voice of war :
" Freedom !   Equality !"—to blood,
    Rush the roused people at the sound !
Through street, hall, palace, roars the flood,
    And banded murder closes round !
The hyæna-shapes, (that women were !)
    Jest with the horrors they survey ;
They hound—they rend—they mangle there—
    As panthers with their prey !
Nought rests to hallow—burst the ties
    Of life's sublime and reverent awe ;
Before the Vice the Virtue flies,
    And Universal Crime is Law !

Man fears the lion's kingly tread;
　　Man fears the tiger's fangs of terror;
And still the dreadliest of the dread,
　　Is Man himself in error!
No torch, though lit from Heaven, illumes
　　The Blind!—Why place it in his hand?
It lights not him—it but consumes
　　The City and the Land!

IX.

Rejoice and laud the prospering skies!
　　The kernel bursts its husk—behold
From the dull clay the metal rise,
　　Pure-shining, as a star of gold!
　　　　Neck and lip, but as one beam,
　　　　It laughs like a sun-beam.
And even the scutcheon, clear-graven, shall tell
That the art of a master has fashion'd the Bell!

Come in—come in
My merry men—we'll form a ring
The new-born labour christening;
　　And "CONCORD" we will name her!—
To union may her heart-felt call
　　In brother-love attune us all!
May she the destined glory win
　　For which the master sought to frame her—
Aloft—(all earth's existence under,)
　　In blue-pavilion'd heaven afar
To dwell—the Neighbour of the Thunder,
　　The Borderer of the Star!
Be hers above a voice to raise
　　Like those bright hosts in yonder sphere,
Who, while they move, their Maker praise,
　　And lead around the wreathèd year!
To solemn and eternal things
　　We dedicate her lips sublime!—
As hourly, calmly, on she swings—
　　Fann'd by the fleeting wings of Time!—

a

No pulse—no heart—no feeling hers!
　　She lends the warning voice to Fate;
And still companions, while she stirs,
　　The changes of the Human State!
So may she teach us, as her tone
　　But now so mighty, melts away—
That earth no life which earth has known
　　From the last silence can delay!

　　*　　　*　　　*　　　*　　　*

Slowly now the cords upheave her!
　　From her earth-grave soars the Bell;
Mid the airs of Heaven we leave her!
　　In the Music-Realm to dwell!
　　　Up—upwards—yet raise—
　　　She has risen—she sways.
Fair Bell to our city bode joy and increase,
And oh, may thy first sound be hallow'd to—PEACE! *

IN "The Walk" we have seen the progress of Society—in "The Bell" we have the Lay of the Life of Man. This is the crowning Flower of that garland of Humanity, which, in his Culture-Historic poems, the hand of Schiller has entwined. In England, "The Lay of the Bell" has been the best known of the Poet's compositions—out of the Drama. It has been the favourite subject selected by his translators; to say nothing of others (more recent, but with which, we own we are unacquainted), the elegant version of Lord Francis Egerton has long since familiarised its beauties to the English public; and had it been possible to omit from our collection a poem of such importance, we would willingly have declined the task which suggests comparisons disadvantageous to ourselves. The idea of this poem had long been revolved by Schiller.† He went often to a bell-foundry, to make himself thoroughly master of the mechanical process, which he has applied to purposes so ideal. Even from the time in which he began the actual composition of the poem, two years elapsed before it was completed. The work profited by the delay, and as the Poet is generally clear in proportion to his entire familiarity with his own design, so of all Schiller's moral poems this is the most intelligible to the ordinary understanding; perhaps the more so, because, as one of his Commentators has remarked, the principal ideas and images he has already expressed in his previous writings, and his mind was thus free to give itself up more to the form than to the thought. Still we think that the symmetry and *oneness* of the composition have been indiscriminately panegyrised. As the Lay of Life, it begins with Birth, and when it arrives at Death, it has reached its legitimate conclusion. The reader will observe, at the seventh strophe, that there is an abrupt and final break in the individual interest which has hitherto connected the several portions. Till then, he has had before him the prominent figure of a single man—the one representative of human life—whose baptism the Bell has celebrated, whose youth, wanderings, return to his

---

* Written in the time of the French war.
† See Life of Schiller, by Madame von Wolzogen.

father's house, love, marriage, prosperity, misfortunes, to the death of the wife, have carried on the progress of the Poem; and this leading figure then recedes altogether from the scene, and the remainder of the Poem, till the ninth stanza, losing sight altogether of *individual* life, merely repeats the purpose of "The Walk," and confounds itself in illustrations of *social* life in general. The picture of the French Revolution, though admirably done, is really not only an episode in the main design, but is merely a copy of that already painted, and set in its proper place, in the Historical Poem of "The Walk."

But whatever weight may be attached, whether to this objection or to others which we have seen elsewhere urged, the "non Ego paucis offendar maculis" may, indeed, be well applied to a Poem so replete with the highest excellences,—so original in conception—so full of pathos, spirit, and variety in its plan—and so complete in its mastery over form and language. . . . Much of its beauty must escape in translation, even if an English Schiller were himself the translator. For that beauty which belongs to form—the "curiosa felicitas verborum"—is always untranslatable. Witness the Odes of Horace, the greater part of Goethe's Lyrics, and the Choruses of Sophocles. Though the life of Man is pourtrayed, it is the life of a *German* man. The wanderings, or apprenticeship, of the youth, are not a familiar feature in our own civilisation; the bustling housewife is peculiarly German; so is the incident of the fire—a misfortune very common in parts of Germany, and which the sound of the church-bell proclaims. Thus that peculiar charm which belongs to the recognition of familiar and household images, in an ideal and poetic form, must be in a great measure lost to a foreigner. The thought, too, at the end—the prayer for Peace—is of a local and temporary nature. It breathed the wish of all Germany, during the four years' war with France, and was, at the date of publication—like all temporary allusions—a strong and effective close, to become, after the interest of the allusion ceased, comparatively feeble and non-universal. These latter observations are made, not in depreciation of the Poem, but on behalf of it; to show that it has beauties peculiar to the language it was written in, and the people it addressed, of which it must be despoiled in translation.

THE POETRY OF LIFE.

"Who would himself with shadows entertain,
Or gild his life with lights that shine in vain,
Or nurse false hopes that do but cheat the true?—
Though with my dream my heaven should be resign'd—
Though the free-pinion'd soul that once could dwell
In the large empire of the Possible,
This work-day life with iron chains may bind,
Yet thus the mastery o'er ourselves we find,
And solemn duty to our acts decreed,
Meets us thus tutor'd in the hour of need,
With a more sober and submissive mind!
How front Necessity—yet bid thy youth
Shun the mild rule of life's calm sovereign, Truth."

So speak'st thou, friend, how stronger far than I;
As from Experience—that sure port serene—
Thou look'st;—and straight, a coldness wraps the sky,
The summer glory withers from the scene,
Scared by the solemn spell; behold them fly,
The godlike images that seem'd so fair!
Silent the playful Muse—the rosy Hours
Halt in their dance; and the May-breathing flowers
Fall from the sister-Graces' waving hair.
Sweet-mouth'd Apollo breaks his golden lyre,
Hermes, the wand with many a marvel rife;—
The veil, rose-woven, by the young Desire
With dreams, drops from the hueless cheeks of Life.
The world seems what it *is*—A Grave! and Love
Casts down the bondage wound his eyes above,
And *sees !*—He sees but images of clay
Where he dream'd gods; and sighs—and glides away.
The youngness of the Beautiful grows old,
And on thy lips the bride's sweet kiss seems cold;
And in the crowd of joys—upon thy throne
Thou sitt'st in state, and hardenest into stone.

THE ANTIQUE AT PARIS.

(FREE TRANSLATION.)

WHAT the Greek wrought, the vaunting Frank may gain,
And waft the pomp of Hellas to the Seine;
His proud museums may with marble groan,
And Gallia gape on Glories not her own;
But ever silent in the ungenial Halls
Shall stand the Statues on their pedestals.
By him alone the Muses are possest,
Who warms them from the marble—at his breast;
Bright, to the Greek, from stone each goddess grew—
Vandals, each goddess is but stone to you!

THE MAID OF ORLEANS.

To flaunt the fair shape of Humanity,
  Lewd Mockery dragg'd thee through the mire it trod.*
Wit wars with Beauty everlastingly—
  Yearns for no Angel—worships to no God—
Views the heart's wealth, to steal it as the thief—
Assails Delusion, but to kill Belief.

Yet the true Poetry—herself, like thee,
  Sprung from the younger race, a shepherd maid,
Gives thee her birthright of Divinity,
  Thy wrongs in life in her star-worlds repaid.
Sweet Virgin-Type of Thought, pure, brave, and high—
The Heart created thee—thou canst not die.

The mean world loves to darken what is bright,
  To see to dust each loftier image brought;
But fear not—souls there are that can delight
  In the high Memory and the stately Thought;
To ribald mirth let Momus rouse the mart,
But forms more noble glad the noble heart.

THEKLA.

(A SPIRIT VOICE.)

[It was objected to Schiller's "Wallenstein," that he had suffered Thekla to disappear from the Play without any clear intimation of her fate. These stanzas are his answer to the objection.]

  WHERE am I? whither borne? From thee
    As soars my fleeting shade above?
  Is not all being closed for me,
    And over life and love?—
  Wouldst ask, where wing their flight away
    The Nightbirds that enraptured air
  With Music's soul in happy May?
    But while they loved—they were!

* Voltaire, in "The Pucelle."

And have I found the Lost again?
　Yes, I with him at last am wed;
Where hearts are never rent in twain,
　And tears are never shed.

There, wilt thou find us welcome thee,
　When thy life to our life shall glide;
My father,* too, from sin set free,
　Nor Murther at his side—

Feels there, that no delusion won
　His bright faith to the starry spheres;
Each faith (nor least the boldest one)
　Still towards the Holy nears.

There word is kept with Hope; to wild
　Belief a lovely truth is given!
O dare to err and dream!—the child
　Has instincts of the Heaven!

WILLIAM TELL.

[Lines accompanying the copy of Schiller's Drama of William Tell, presented to the Arch-Chancellor von Dalberg.]

I.

In that fell strife, when force with force engages,
　And Wrath stirs bloodshed—Wrath with blindfold eyes—
When, midst the war which raving Faction wages,
　Lost in the roar—the voice of Justice dies,
When but for license, Sin the shameless, rages,
　Against the Holy, when the Wilful rise,
When lost the Anchor which makes Nations strong
　Amidst the storm,—*there* is no theme for song.

---

* Wallenstein:—the next stanza alludes to his belief in Astrology;—of which such beautiful uses have been made by Schiller in his solemn tragedy.

CARTHAGE.

II.

But when a Race, tending by vale and hill
   Free flocks, contented with its rude domain—
Bursts the hard bondage with its own great will,
   Lets fall the sword when once it rends the chain,
And, flush'd with Victory, can be human still—
   There blest the strife, and *then* inspired the strain.
Such is my theme—to thee not strange, 'tis true,
Thou in the Great canst never find the New! *

ARCHIMEDES.

To Archimedes once a scholar came,
"Teach me," he said, " the Art that won thy fame;—
The godlike Art which gives such boons to toil,
And showers such fruit upon thy native soil;—
The godlike Art that girt the town when all
Rome's vengeance burst in thunder on the wall!"
"Thou call'st Art godlike—it is so, in truth,
And was," replied the Master to the youth,
"Ere yet its secrets were applied to use—
Ere yet it served beleaguered Syracuse:—
Ask'st thou from Art, but what the Art is worth?
The fruit?—for fruit go cultivate the Earth.—
He who the goddess would aspire unto,
Must not the goddess as the woman woo!"

CARTHAGE.

Thou, of the nobler Mother Child degenerate;—all the
   while
That with the Roman's Might didst match the Tyrian's
   crafty guile;
The one thro' strength subdued the earth—that by its
   strength it ruled—
Thro' cunning earth the other stole, and by the cunning
   school'd—

---

* The concluding point in the original requires some paraphrase in translation.—Schiller's lines are—
    Und solch ein Bild darf ich dir freudig zeigen
    Du kennst's—denn alles Grosse ist dein eigen.

With iron as the Roman, thou (let History speak) didst gain
The empire which with gold thou as the Tyrian didst maintain.

COLUMBUS.

Steer on, bold Sailor—Wit may mock thy soul that sees the land,
And hopeless at the helm may droop the weak and weary hand,
Yet ever—ever to the West, for there the coast must lie,
And dim it dawns and glimmering dawns before thy reason's eye;
Yea, trust the guiding God—and go along the floating grave,
Though hid till now—yet now, behold the New World o'er the wave!
With Genius Nature ever stands in solemn union still,
And ever what the One foretels the Other shall fulfil.

NÆNIA.*

The Beautiful, that men and gods alike subdues, must perish;
For pity ne'er the iron breast of Stygian Jove † shall cherish!
Once only—Love, by aid of Song, the Shadow-Sovereign thrall'd,
And at the dreary threshold he again the boon recall'd.
Not Aphroditè's heavenly tears to love and life restored
Her own adored Adonis, by the grisly monster gored!
Not all the art of Thetis saved her god-like hero son,
When, falling by the Scæan gate, his race of glory run!
But forth she came, with all the nymphs of Nereus, from the deep,
Around the silence of the Dead to sorrow and to weep.

* Nænia was the goddess of funerals—and funeral songs were called Næniæ.
† Pluto.

See tears are shed by every god and goddess, to survey
How soon the Beautiful is past, the Perfect dies away!
Yet noble sounds the voice of wail—and woe the Dead can
   grace;
For never wail and woe are heard to mourn above the
   Base!

JOVE TO HERCULES.

'Twas not my nectar made thy strength divine,
But 'twas thy strength which made my nectar thine!

THE IDEAL AND THE ACTUAL LIFE.

In Schiller's Poem of "The Ideal," a translation of which has already been presented to the reader, but which was composed subsequently to "The Ideal and the Actual," the prevailing sentiment is that of simple pathos which can come home to every man who has mourned for Youth, and the illusions which belong to it—
                         for the hour
    Of glory in the grass, and splendour in the flower.

But "The Ideal and the Actual" is purely philosophical; a poem "in which," says Hoffmeister, "every object and epithet has a metaphysical back-ground." Schiller himself was aware of its obscurity to the general reader; he desires that even the refining Humboldt "should read it in a kind of holy stillness—and banish, during the meditation it required, all that was profane." Humboldt proved himself worthy of these instructions, by the enthusiastic admiration with which the poem inspired him. Previous to its composition, Schiller had been employed upon philosophical inquiries, especially his "Letters on the Æsthetic Education of Man;" and of these Letters it is truly observed, that the Poem is the crowning Flower. To those acquainted with Schiller's philosophical works and views, the poem is therefore less obscure; in its severe compression such readers behold but the poetical epitome of thoughts the depth of which they have already sounded, and the coherence of which they have already ascertained—they recognise a familiar symbol, where the general reader only perplexes himself in a riddle.

Without entering into disquisitions, out of place in this translation, and fatiguing to those who desire in a collection of poems to enjoy the poetical—not to be bewildered by the abstract—we shall merely preface the poem, with the help of Schiller's commentators, by a short analysis of the general design and meaning, so at least as to facilitate the reader's *study* of this remarkable poem—study it will require, and well repay.

The Poem begins, Stanza 1st, with the doctrine which Schiller has often inculcated, that to Man there rests but the choice between the pleasures of sense, and the peace of the soul; but both are united in the life of the Immortals, viz., the higher orders of being. Stanza 2nd.—Still it may be ours to attain, even on earth, to this loftier and holier life—provided we can raise ourselves beyond material objects. Stanza 3rd.—The Fates can only influence the body, and the things of time and matter. But, safe from the changes of matter and of life, the Platonic Archetype, *Form*, hovers in the realm of the Ideal. If we can ascend to this realm—in other words, to the domain of Beauty—we attain (Stanza 4th) to the perfection of Humanity—a perfection only found in the immaterial forms and shadows of that realm—yet in which, as in the Gods, the sensual and the intellectual powers are united. In the Actual Life we strive for a goal we cannot reach; in the Ideal, the goal is attainable, and there effort is victory. With Stanza 5th begins the antithesis, which is a key to the remainder—an antithesis constantly ballancing before us the conditions of the Actual and the privileges of the Ideal. The Ideal is not meant to relax, but to brace us for the Actual Life. From the latter we cannot escape; but when we begin to flag beneath the sense of our narrow limits, and the difficulties of the path, the eye, steadfastly fixed upon the Ideal Beauty aloft, beholds there the goal. Stanza 6th.—In Actual Life, Strength and Courage are the requisites for success, and are doomed to eternal struggle; but (Stanza 7th) in the Ideal Life, struggle exists not; the stream, gliding far from its rocky sources, is smoothed to repose. Stanza 8th.—In the Actual Life, as long as the Artist still has to contend with matter, he must strive and labour. Truth is only elicited by toil—the statue only wakens from the block by the stroke of the chisel; but when (Stanza 9th) he has once achieved the idea of Beauty—when once he has elevated the material marble into form—all trace of his human neediness and frailty is lost, and his work seems the child of the soul. Stanza 9th.—Again, in the Actual world, the man who *strives* for Virtue, finds every sentiment and every action poor compared to the rigid standard of the abstract moral law. But if (Stanza 9th), instead of *striving* for Virtue, merely from the cold sense of duty, we live that life beyond the senses, in which Virtue, becomes as it were natural to us—in which its behests are served, not through duty but inclination—then the gulf between man and the moral law is filled up; we take the Godhead, so to speak, into our will; and Heaven ceases its terrors, when man ceases to resist it. Stanza 10th.—Finally, in Actual Life, sorrows, whether our own, or those with which we sympathise, are terrible and powerful; but (Stanza 11th) in the Ideal World even Sorrow has its pleasures. We contemplate the writhings of the Laocoon in marble, with delight in the greatness of Art—not with anguish for the suffering, but with veneration for the grandeur with which the suffering is idealised by the Artist, or expressed by the subject. Over the pain of Art smiles the Heaven of the Moral world. Stanzas 11th and 12th.—Man thus aspiring to the Ideal, is compared to the Mythical Hercules. In the Actual world he must suffer and must toil; but when once he can cast aside the garb of clay, and through the Ethereal flame separate the Mortal from the Immortal, the material dross sinks downward, the spirit soars aloft, and Hebe (or Eternal Youth) pours out nectar as to the Gods. If the reader will have the patience to compare the above analysis with the subjoined version (in which the Translator has also sought to render the general sense as intelligible as possible), he will probably find little difficulty in clearing up the Author's meaning.

I.

For ever fair, for ever calm and bright,
Life flies on plumage, zephyr-light,
   For those who on the Olympian hill rejoice—

THE IDEAL AND THE ACTUAL LIFE.

Moons wane, and races wither to the tomb,
And 'mid the universal ruin, bloom
  The rosy days of Gods—
                With Man, the choice,
Timid and anxious, hesitates between
  The sense's pleasure and the soul's content;
While on celestial brows, aloft and sheen,
  The beams of both are blent.

II.

Seek'st thou on earth the life of Gods to share,
Safe in the Realm of Death ?—beware
  To pluck the fruits that glitter to thine eye;
Content thyself with gazing on their glow—
Short are the joys Possession can bestow,
  And in Possession sweet Desire will die.
'Twas not the ninefold chain of waves that bound
  Thy daughter, Ceres, to the Stygian river—
She pluck'd the fruit of the unholy ground,
  And so—was Hell's for ever!

III

The Weavers of the Web—the Fates—but sway
The matter and the things of clay;
  Safe from each change that Time to Matter gives,
Nature's blest playmate, free at will to stray
  With Gods a god, amidst the fields of Day,
  The Form, the Archetype,* serenely lives.
Would'st thou soar heavenward on its joyous wing?
  Cast from thee, Earth, the bitter and the real,
High from this cramp'd and dungeon being, spring
  Into the Realm of the Ideal!

IV.

Here, bathed, Perfection, in thy purest ray,
Free from the clogs and taints of clay,
  Hovers divine the Archetypal Man!
Dim as those phantom ghosts of life that gleam
And wander voiceless by the Stygian stream,—
  Fair as it stands in fields Elysian,

---

* "Die Gestalt"—Form, the Platonic Archetype.

Ere down to Flesh the Immortal doth descend :—
If doubtful ever in the Actual life
Each contest—*here* a victory crowns the end
Of every nobler strife.

V.

Not from the strife itself to set thee free,
But more to nerve—doth Victory
   Wave her rich garland from the Ideal clime.
Whate'er thy wish, the Earth has no repose—
Life still must drag thee onward as it flows,
   Whirling thee down the dancing surge of Time.
But when the courage sinks beneath the dull
   Sense of its narrow limits—on the soul,
Bright from the hill-tops of the Beautiful,
   Bursts the attainèd goal!

VI.

If worth thy while the glory and the strife
Which fire the lists of Actual Life—
   The ardent rush to fortune or to fame,
In the hot field where Strength and Valour are,
And rolls the whirling thunder of the car,
   And the world, breathless, eyes the glorious game—
Then dare and strive—the prize can but belong
To him whose valour o'er his tribe prevails;
In life the victory only crowns the strong—
   He who is feeble fails.

VII.

But Life, whose source, by crags around it pil'd,
Chafed while confin'd, foams fierce and wild,
   Glides soft and smooth when once its streams expand,
When its waves, glassing in their silver play,
Aurora blent with Hesper's milder ray,
   Gain the still BEAUTIFUL—that Shadow-Land!
Here, contest grows but interchange of Love,
   All curb is but the bondage of the Grace;
Gone is each foe,—Peace folds her wings above
   Her native dwelling-place.

VIII.

When, through dead stone to breathe a soul of light,
With the dull matter to unite
   The kindling genius, some great sculptor glows;
Behold him straining every nerve intent—
Behold how, o'er the subject element,
   The stately THOUGHT its march laborious goes!
For never, save to Toil untiring, spoke
   The unwilling Truth from her mysterious well—
The statue only to the chisel's stroke
    Wakes from its marble cell.

IX.

But onward to the Sphere of Beauty—go
Onward, O Child of Art! and, lo,
   Out of the matter which thy pains control
The Statue springs!—not as with labour wrung
From the hard block, but as from Nothing sprung—
   Airy and light—the offspring of the soul!
The pangs, the cares, the weary toils it cost
   Leave not a trace when once the work is done—
The Artist's human frailty merged and lost
    In Art's great victory won! *

X.

If human Sin confronts the rigid law
Of perfect Truth and Virtue,† awe
   Seizes and saddens thee to see how far
Beyond thy reach, Perfection;—if we test
By the Ideal of the Good, the best,
   How mean our efforts and our actions are!
This space between the Ideal of man's soul
   And man's achievement, who hath ever past?
An ocean spreads between us and that goal,
    Where anchor ne'er was cast!

---

* More literally translated thus by the Author of the Article on Schiller in the *Foreign and Colonial Review*, July, 1843—
     "Thence all witnesses for ever banished
     Of poor Human Nakedness."

† The Law, *i. e.*, the Kantian Ideal of Truth and Virtue. This stanza and the next embody, perhaps with some exaggeration, the Kantian doctrine of morality.

XI.

But fly the boundary of the Senses—live
The Ideal life free Thought can give;
  And, lo, the gulf shall vanish, and the chill
Of the soul's impotent despair be gone!
And with divinity thou sharest the throne,
  Let but divinity become thy will!
Scorn not the Law—permit its iron band
  The sense (it cannot chain the soul) to thrall.
Let man no more the will of Jove withstand,*
  And Jove the bolt lets fall!

XII.

If, in the woes of Actual Human Life—
If thou could'st see the serpent strife
  Which the Greek Art has made divine in stone—
Could'st see the writhing limbs, the livid cheek,
Note every pang, and hearken every shriek
  Of some despairing lost Laocoon,
The human nature would thyself subdue
  To share the human woe before thine eye—
Thy cheek would pale, and all thy soul be true
  To Man's great Sympathy.

XIII.

But in the Ideal Realm, aloof and far,
Where the calm Art's pure dwellers are,
  Lo, the Laocoon writhes, but does not groan.
Here, no sharp grief the high emotion knows—
Here, suffering's self is made divine, and shows
  The brave resolve of the firm soul alone:
Here, lovely as the rainbow on the dew
  Of the spent thunder-cloud, to Art is given,
Gleaming through Grief's dark veil, the peaceful blue
  Of the sweet Moral Heaven.

---

* "But in God's sight submission is command."
"Jonah," by the Rev. F. Hodgson. Quoted in *Foreign and Colonial Review*, July, 1843: Art. Schiller, p. 21.

XIV.

So, in the glorious parable, behold
How, bow'd to mortal bonds, of old
   Life's dreary path divine Alcides trod :
The hydra and the lion were his prey,
And to restore the friend he loved to-day,
   He went undaunted to the black-brow'd God ;
And all the torments and the labours sore
   Wroth Juno sent—the meek majestic One,
With patient spirit and unquailing, bore,
   Until the course was run—

XV.

Until the God cast down his garb of clay,
And rent in hallowing flame away
   The mortal part from the divine—to soar
To the empyreal air ! Behold him spring
Blithe in the pride of the unwonted wing,
   And the dull matter that confined before
Sinks downward, downward, downward as a dream !
   Olympian hymns receive the escaping soul,
And smiling Hebe, from the ambrosial stream,
   Fills for a God the bowl !

THE FAVOUR OF THE MOMENT.

ONCE more, then, we meet
   In the circles of yore ;
Let our song be as sweet
   In its wreaths as before.
Who claims the first place
   In the tribute of song ?
The God to whose grace
   All our pleasures belong.
Though Ceres may spread
   All her gifts on the shrine,
Though the glass may be red
   With the blush of the vine,

What boots—if the while
　Fall no spark on the hearth?
If the heart do not smile
　With the instinct of mirth?—
From the clouds, from God's breast
　Must our happiness fall,
'Mid the blessed, most blest
　Is the MOMENT of all!
Since Creation began
　All that mortals have wrought,
All that's godlike in MAN
　Comes—the flash of a Thought!
For ages the stone
　In the quarry may lurk,
An instant alone
　Can suffice to the work;
An impulse give birth
　To the child of the soul,
A glance stamp the worth
　And the fame of the whole.*
On the arch that she buildeth
　From sunbeams on high,
As Iris just gildeth,
　And fleets from the sky,
So shineth, so gloometh
　Each gift that is ours;
The lightning illumeth
　The darkness devours! †

THE FORTUNE FAVOURED.

[THE first five verses in the original of this Poem are placed as a motto on Goethe's statue in the Library at Weimar. The Poet does not here mean to extol what is vulgarly meant by the Gifts of Fortune; he but develops a favourite idea of his, that, whatever is really sublime and beautiful, comes freely down from Heaven; and vindicates the seeming

---

* The idea diffused by the translator through this and the preceding stanza, is more forcibly condensed by Schiller in four lines.

† "And ere a man hath power to say, 'behold,'
　The jaws of Darkness do devour it up,
　So quick bright things come to confusion."—SHAKESPEARE.

THE FORTUNE FAVOURED.

partiality of the Gods, by implying that the Beauty and the Genius given, without labour, to some, but serve to the delight of those to whom they are denied.]

Ah! happy He, upon whose birth each God
Looks down in love, whose earliest sleep the bright
Idalia cradles, whose young lips the rod
Of eloquent Hermes kindles—to whose eyes,
Scarce waken'd yet, Apollo steal in light,
While on imperial brows Jove sets the seal of might!
Godlike the lot ordain'd for him to share,
He wins the garland ere he runs the race;
He learns life's wisdom ere he knows life's care,
And, without labour vanquish'd, smiles the Grace.

Great is the man, I grant, whose strength of mind,
Self-shapes its objects and subdues the Fates—
Virtue subdues the Fates, but cannot bind
The fickle Happiness, whose smile awaits
Those who scarce seek it; nor can courage earn
What the Grace showers not from her own free urn!

From aught *unworthy*, the determined will
Can guard the watchful spirit—there it ends;—
The all that's *glorious* from the heaven descends;
As some sweet mistress loves us, freely still
Come the spontaneous gifts of Heaven!—Above
Favour rules Jove, as it below rules Love!
The Immortals have their bias!—Kindly they
See the bright locks of youth enamour'd play,
And where the glad one goes, shed gladness round the way.
It is not they who boast the best to see,
Whose eyes the holy Apparitions bless;
The stately light of their divinity
Hath oft but shone the brightest on the blind;—
And their choice spirit found its calm recess
In the pure childhood of a simple mind.
Unask'd they come—delighted to delude
The expectation of our baffled Pride;
No law can call their free steps to our side.
Him whom He loves, the Sire of men and gods,
(Selected from the marvelling multitude,)
Bears on his eagle to his bright abodes;
And showers, with partial hand and lavish, down,
The minstrel's laurel or the monarch's crown!

Before the fortune-favour'd son of earth,
Apollo walks—and, with his jocund mirth,
The heart-enthralling Smiler of the skies:
For him grey Neptune smooths the pliant wave—
Harmless the waters for the ship that bore
The Cæsar and his fortunes to the shore!
Charm'd at his feet the crouching lion lies,
To him his back the murmuring dolphin gave;
His soul is born a sovereign o'er the strife—
The lord of all the Beautiful of Life;
Where'er his presence in its calm has trod,
It charms—it sways as some diviner God.
  Scorn not the Fortune-favour'd, that to him
The light-won victory by the gods is given,
Or that, as Paris, from the strife severe,
The Venus draws her darling.—Whom the heaven
So prospers, love so watches, I revere!
And not the man upon whose eyes, with dim
And baleful night, sits Fate. Achaia boasts,
No less the glory of the Dorian Lord *
That Vulcan wrought for him the shield and sword—
That round the mortal hover'd all the hosts
Of all Olympus—that his wrath to grace,
The best and bravest of the Grecian race
Untimely slaughtered, with resentful ghosts
Awed the pale people of the Stygian coasts!
  Scorn not the Darlings of the Beautiful,
If without labour they Life's blossoms cull;
If, like the stately lilies, they have won
A crown for which they neither toil'd nor spun;—
If without merit, theirs be Beauty, still
Thy sense, unenvying, with the Beauty fill.
Alike for thee no merit wins the right,
To share, by simply seeing, their delight.
Heaven breathes the soul into the Minstrel's breast,
But with that soul he animates the rest;
The God inspires the Mortal—but to God,
In turn, the Mortal lifts thee from the sod.
Oh, not in vain to Heaven the Bard is dear;
Holy himself—he hallows those who hear!

* Achilles.

The busy mart let Justice still control,
Weighing the guerdon to the toil!—What then?
A God alone claims joy—all joy is his,
Flushing with unsought light the cheeks of men.
*Where is no miracle, why there no bliss!
Grow, change, and ripen all that mortal be,
Shapen'd from form to form, by toiling time;
The Blissful and the Beautiful are born
Full grown, and ripen'd from Eternity—
No gradual changes to their glorious prime,
No childhood dwarfs them, and no age has worn.—
Like Heaven's, each earthly Venus on the sight
Comes, a dark birth, from out an endless sea;
Like the first Pallas, in maturest might,
Arm'd, from the Thunderer's brow, leaps forth each Thought
    of Light.

THE SOWER.

Sure of the Spring that warms them into birth,
The golden seeds thou trustest to the Earth;
And dost thou doubt the Eternal Spring sublime,
For deeds—the seeds which Wisdom sows in Time?

SENTENCES OF CONFUCIUS.

TIME.

Threefold the stride of Time, from first to last!
  Loitering slow, the Future creepeth—
  Arrow-swift, the Present sweepeth—
And motionless for ever stands the Past.

Impatience, fret howe'er she may,
  Cannot speed the tardy goer;
Fear and Doubt—that crave delay—
  Ne'er can make the Fleet One slower:

---

* Paraphrased from—
    Aber die Freude ruft nur ein Goth auf sterbliche Wangen.
These lines furnish the key to—
    Nur ein Wunder kann dich tragen
      In das schöne Wunderland.—Schiller, *Sehnsucht*.
And the same lines, with what follow, explain also the general intention of the poem on the favour of the moment.

Nor one spell Repentance knows,
To stir the Still One from repose.
If thou would'st, wise and happy, see
Life's solemn journey close for thee,
The Loiterer's counsel thou wilt heed,
Though readier tools must shape the deed;
Not for thy friend the Fleet One know,
Nor make the Motionless thy foe!

SPACE.

A threefold measure dwells in Space—
Restless, with never-pausing pace,
LENGTH, ever stretching ever forth, is found,
And, ever widening, BREADTH extends around,
 And ever DEPTH sinks bottomless below!
In this, a type thou dost possess—
On, ever restless, must thou press,
 No halt allow, no languor know,
 If to the Perfect thou wouldst go;
Must broaden from thyself, until
Creation thy embrace can fill!
Must down the Depth for ever fleeing,
Dive to the spirit and the being.
The distant goal at last to near,
 Still lengthening labour sweeps;
The full mind is alone the clear,
 And Truth dwells in the deeps.

THE ANTIQUE TO THE NORTHERN WANDERER.

AND o'er the river hast thou past, and o'er the mighty sea,
And o'er the Alps, the dizzy bridge hath borne thy steps to me;
To look all near upon the bloom my deathless beauty knows,
And, face to face, to front the pomp whose fame through ages goes—
Gaze on, and touch my relics now! At last thou standest here,
But art thou nearer now to me—or I to thee more near?

GENIUS.

(FREE TRANSLATION.)

[The original and it seems to us the more appropriate, title of this Poem, was "Nature and the School."]

Do I believe, thou ask'st, the Master's word,
The Schoolman's shibboleth that binds the herd?
To the soul's haven is there but one chart?
Its peace a problem to be learned by art?
On system rest the happy and the good?
To base the temple must the props be wood?
Must I distrust the gentle law, imprest,
To guide and warn, by Nature on the breast,
Till, squared to rule the instinct of the soul,—
Till the School's signet stamp the eternal scroll,
Till in one mould, some dogma hath confined
The ebb and flow—the light waves—of the mind?
Say thou, familiar to these depths of gloom,
Thou, safe ascended from the dusty tomb,
Thou, who hast trod these weird Egyptian cells—
Say—if Life's comfort with yon mummies dwells!—
Say—and I grope—with saddened steps indeed—
But on, thro' darkness, if to Truth it lead!

Nay, Friend, thou know'st the golden time—the age
Whose legends live in many a poet's page?
When heavenlier shapes with Man walked side by side,
And the chaste Feeling was itself a guide;
Then the great law, alike divine amid
Suns bright in Heaven, or germs in darkness hid,—
That silent law—(call'd whether by the name
Of Nature or Necessity—the same),
To that deep sea, the heart, its movement gave—
Sway'd the full tide, and freshened the free wave.
Then sense unerring—because unreproved—
True as the finger on the dial moved,
Half-guide, half-playmate, of Earth's age of youth,
The sportive instinct of Eternal Truth.

Then, nor Initiate nor Profane were known;
Where the Heart felt—there Reason found a throne:

Not from the dust below, but life around
Warm Genius shaped what quick Emotion found.
One rule, like light, for every bosom glowed,
Yet hid from all the fountain whence it flowed.

But, gone that blessed Age!—our wilful pride
Has lost, with Nature, the old peaceful Guide.
FEELING, no more to raise us and rejoice,
Is heard and honoured as a Godhead's voice;
And, disenhallowed in its eldest cell
The Human Heart,—lies mute the Oracle; *
Save where the low and mystic whispers thrill
Some listening spirit more divinely still.
There, in the chambers of the inmost heart,
There, must the Sage explore the Magian's art;
There, seek the long-lost Nature's steps to track,
Till, found once more, she gives him Wisdom back!
Hast thou,—(O Blest, if so, whate'er betide!)—
Still kept the Guardian Angel by thy side?
Can thy Heart's guileless childhood yet rejoice
In the sweet instinct with its warning voice?
Does Truth yet limn upon untroubled eyes,
Pure and serene, her world of Iris-dies?
Rings clear the echo which her accent calls
Back from the breast, on which the music falls?
In the calm mind is doubt yet hush'd,—and will
That doubt to-morrow as to-day be still?
†Will all these fine sensations in their play,
No censor need to regulate and sway?
Fear'st thou not in the insidious Heart to find
The source of Trouble to the limpid mind?

No!—then thine Innocence thy Mentor be!
Science can teach thee nought—she learns from thee!

* Schiller seems to allude to the philosophy of Fichté and Schelling then on the ascendant, which sought to explain the enigma of the universe, and to reconcile the antithesis between man and nature, by carrying both up into the unity of an absolute consciousness, *i. e.*, a consciousness anterior to everything which is *now* known under the name of consciousness—sed de hâc re satius est silere quàm parvum dicere.

† Will this play of fine sensations (or sensibilities) require no censor to control it—*i. e.*, will it always work spontaneously for good, and run into no passionate excess?

Each law that lends lame succour to the Weak—
The cripple's crutch—the vigorous need not seek!
From thine own self thy rule of action draw;—
That which thou dost—what charms thee—is thy Law,
And founds to every race a code sublime—
What pleases Genius gives a Law to Time!
The Word—the Deed—all Ages shall command,
Pure if thy lip and holy if thy hand!
Thou, thou alone mark'st not within thy heart
The inspiring God whose Minister thou art,
Know'st not the magic of the mighty ring
Which bows the realm of Spirits to their King:
But meek, nor conscious of diviner birth,
Glide thy still footsteps thro' the conquered Earth!

ULYSSES.

To gain his home all oceans he explored—
Here Scylla frown'd—and there Charybdis roar'd;
Horror on sea—and horror on the land—
In hell's dark boat he sought the spectre land,
Till borne—a slumberer—to his native spot
He woke—and sorrowing, knew his country not!

VOTIVE TABLETS.

[Under this title Schiller arranged that more dignified and philosophical portion of the small Poems published as Epigrams in the "Musen Almanach;" which rather sought to point a general thought, than a personal satire.—Many of these, however, are either wholly without interest for the English reader, or express in almost untranslateable laconism what, in far more poetical shapes Schiller has elsewhere repeated and developed. We, therefore, content ourselves with such a selection as appears to us best suited to convey a fair notion of the object and spirit of the class.]

MOTTO TO THE VOTIVE TABLETS.

What the God taught—what has befriended all
Life's ways, I place upon the Votive Wall.

THE GOOD AND THE BEAUTIFUL.
(ZWEIERLEI WIRKUNGSARTEN.)

The Good's the Flower to Earth already given—
The Beautiful—on Earth sows flowers from Heaven!

VALUE AND WORTH.

If thou *hast* something, bring thy goods—a fair return be thine;
If thou *art* something, bring thy soul and interchange with mine.

THE DIVISION OF RANKS.

Yes, in the moral world, as ours, we see
Divided grades—a Soul's Nobility;
By deeds their titles Commoners create—
The loftier order are by birthright great.*

TO THE MYSTIC.

Spreads Life's true mystery round us evermore,
Seen by no eye, it lies all eyes before.†

THE KEY.

To know *thyself*—in others self discern;
Wouldst thou know others? read thyself—and learn!

WISDOM AND PRUDENCE.

Wouldst thou the loftiest height of Wisdom gain?
On to the rashness, Prudence would disdain;
The purblind see but the receding shore,
Not that to which the bold wave wafts thee o'er!

---

* This idea is often repeated, somewhat more clearly, in the haughty philosophy of Schiller. He himself says, elsewhere—"In a fair soul each single action is not properly moral, but the whole character is moral. The fair soul has no other service than the instincts of its own beauty." "Common Natures," observes Hoffmeister, "can only act as it were by rule and law; the Noble are of themselves morally good, and humanly beautiful."

† Query?—the Law of Creation, both physical and moral.

THE UNANIMITY.

Truth seek we both—Thou, in the life without thee and
    around ;
I in the Heart within—by both can Truth alike be found ;
The healthy eye can through the world the great Creator
    track—
The healthy heart is but the glass which gives creation
    back.

THE SCIENCE OF POLITICS.

All that thou dost be right—to that alone confine thy
    view,
And halt within the certain rule—the All that's right
    to do!
True zeal *the what already is* would sound and perfect
    see,
False zeal would sound and perfect make the something
    that's to be!

TO ASTRONOMERS.

Of the Nebulæ * and planets do not babble so to me ;
What! is Nature only mighty inasmuch as you can
    see ?
Inasmuch as you can measure her immeasurable ways ?
As she renders world on world, sun and system to your
    gaze ?
Though thro' space your object be the Sublimest to
    embrace,
Never the Sublime abideth—where you vainly search—in
    space !

---

* Nebelflecke; *i. e.*, the nebulous matter which puzzles astronomers. Is Nature, then, only great inasmuch as you can compute her almost incalculable dimensions, or inasmuch as she furnishes almost incalculable subjects for your computations ? Your object is, indeed, the sublimest in space ; but *the* Sublime does not dwell in space—*i. e.*, the Moral Law is *the* only Sublime, and its Kingdom is where Time and Space are not.

THE BEST GOVERNED STATE.

How the best state to know?—it is found out;
Like the best woman—that least talked about.

MY BELIEF.

What thy religion? those thou namest—none?
None why—because I have religion!

FRIEND AND FOE.

Dear is my friend—yet from my foe, as from my friend,
    comes good;
My friend shows what I *can* do, and my foe shows what
    I *shou'd*.

LIGHT AND COLOUR.

Dwell, Light, beside the changeless God—God spoke and
    Light began;
Come, thou, the ever-changing one—come, Colour, down
    to Man!

FORUM OF WOMEN.

Woman—to judge man rightly—do not scan
Each separate act;—pass judgment on the Man!

GENIUS.

Intellect can repeat what's been fulfill'd,
And, aping Nature, as she buildeth—build;
O'er Nature's base can haughty Reason dare
To pile its lofty castle—in the air.
But only thine, O Genius, is the charge,
In Nature's kingdom Nature to enlarge!

THE IMITATOR.

Good out of good—that art is known to all—
But Genius from the bad the good can call;
Then, Mimic, not from leading-strings escaped,
Work'st but the matter that's already shaped:
The already shaped a nobler hand awaits,
All matter asks a Spirit that *creates!*

CORRECTNESS.

(FREE TRANSLATION).

The calm correctness, where no fault we see,
Attests Art's loftiest or its least degree;
Alike the smoothness of the surface shows
The Pool's dull stagner—the great Sea's repose.

THE MASTER.

The herd of scribes, by what they tell us,
Show all in which their wits excel us;
But the True Master we behold,
In what his art leaves—just untold.

EXPECTATION AND FULFILMENT.

O'er Ocean, with a thousand masts, sails forth the stripling bold—
One boat, hard rescued from the deep, draws into port the old!

THE EPIC HEXAMETER.

(TRANSLATED BY COLERIDGE.)

Strongly it bears us along in swelling and limitless billows,
Nothing before and nothing behind but the sky and the ocean.

THE ELEGIAC METRE.

(TRANSLATED BY COLERIDGE).

In the hexameter rises the fountain's silvery column,
In the pentameter aye falling in melody back.*

OTHER EPIGRAMS, &c.

Give me that which thou know'st — I'll receive and
   attend;
But thou givest me thyself — prithee, spare me, my
   friend!

THE PROSELYTE MAKER.

"A little earth from out the Earth—and I
The Earth will move:" so spake the Sage divine.
Out of myself one little moment—try
Myself to take:—succeed, and I am thine!

THE CONNECTING MEDIUM.

What to cement the lofty and the mean
Does Nature?—what?—place vanity between!

THE MORAL POET.

[This is an Epigram on Lavater's work, called "Pontius Pilatus, oder der
   Mensch in Allen Gestalten," &c.—Hoffmeister.]

"How poor a thing is man!" alas, 'tis true
I'd half forgot it—when I chanced on you!

---

* We have ventured to borrow these two translations from Coleridge's poems, not only because what Coleridge did well, no living man could have the presumptuous hope to improve, but because they adhere to the original metre, which Germany has received from Greece, and show, we venture to think, that not even Coleridge could have made that more agreeable to the English ear and taste in poems of *any length*, nor even in small poems *if often repeated*. It is, however, in their own language the grandest which the Germans possess, and has been used by Schiller with signal success in his "Walk," and other poems.

THE SUBLIME THEME.

[Also on Lavater, and alluding to the "Jesus Messias, oder die Evangelien und Apostelgeschichte in Gesängen," &c.]

How God compassionates Mankind, thy muse, my friend,
    rehearses—
Compassion for the sins of Man!—What comfort for thy
    verses!

SCIENCE.

To some she is the Goddess great, to some the milch-cow
    of the field;
Their care is but to calculate—what butter she will
    yield.

KANT AND HIS COMMENTATORS.

How many starvelings one rich man can nourish!
When monarchs build, the rubbish-carriers flourish.

TO
THE HEREDITARY PRINCE OF SAXE WEIMAR,
ON HIS JOURNEY TO PARIS, WRITTEN FEBRUARY, 1802.

[Sung in a friendly circle.]

To the Wanderer a bowl to the brim!
    This Vale on his infancy smil'd;
Let the Vale send a blessing to him,
    Whom it cradled to sleep as a child!

He goes from his Forefathers' halls—
    From the arms that embraced him at birth—
To the City that trophies its walls
    With the spoils it has ravish'd from earth!

The thunder is silent, and now
    The War and the Discord are ended;
And Man o'er the crater may bow,
    Whence the stream of the lava descended.

O fair be the fate to secure
    Thy way through the perilous track;
The heart Nature gave thee is pure,
    Bring it pure, as it goes from us, back.

Those lands the wild hoofs of the steeds,
    War yoked for the carnage, have torn;
But Peace, laughing over the meads,
    Come, strewing the gold of the corn.

Thou the old Father Rhine wilt be greeting,
    By whom *thy* great Father * shall be
Remembered so long as is fleeting
    His stream to the beds of the Sea;—

There, honour the Heroes of old,
    And pour to our Warden, the Rhine,
Who keeps on our borders his hold,
    A cup from his own merry wine;

That thou may'st, as a guide to thy youth,
    The soul of the Fatherland find,
When thou passest the bridge where the Truth
    Of the German, thou leavest behind.

TO

A YOUNG FRIEND DEVOTING HIMSELF TO PHILOSOPHY.

SEVERE the proof the Grecian youth was doomed to undergo,
Before he might what lurks beneath the Eleusinia know—
Art *thou* prepared and ripe, the shrine—that inner shrine—to win,
Where Pallas guards from vulgar eyes the mystic prize within?
Know'st thou what bars thy way? how dear the bargain thou dost make,
When but to buy uncertain good, sure good thou dost forsake?

* Duke Bernard of Weimar, one of the great Generals of the Thirty Years' War.

Feel'st thou sufficient strength to brave the deadliest human
    fray—
When Heart from Reason—Sense from Thought, shall rend
    themselves away?
Sufficient valour, war with Doubt, the Hydra-shape, to
    wage;
And that worst Foe within thyself with manly soul
    engage?
With eyes that keep their heavenly health—the innocence
    of youth
To guard from every falsehood, fair beneath the mask of
    Truth?
Fly, if thou canst not trust thy heart to guide thee on
    the way—
Oh, fly the charmèd margin ere th' abyss engulf its prey.
Round many a step that seeks the light, the shades of
    midnight close;
But in the glimmering twilight, see—how safely Child-
    hood goes!

THE PUPPET-SHOW OF LIFE.

(DAS SPIEL DES LEBENS.)

A PARAPHRASE.

[A *literal* version of this Poem, which possibly may have been suggested by some charming passages in Wilhelm Meister, would be incompatible with the spirit which constitutes its chief merit. And perhaps, therefore, the original may be more faithfully rendered (like many of the Odes of Horace) by paraphrase than translation.—In the general idea, as in all Schiller's Poems of this kind, something more is implied than expressed. He has treated, elsewhere, the Ideal or Shadowy life in earnest. He here represents the Actual as a game; the chief images it brings to view are those of strife and contest; to see it rightly you must not approach too near; and regard the Actual Stage only by the lights of Love. True to his chivalry to the sex, even in sport, as in earnest, Schiller places the prize of life in the hand of Woman.]

    Ho—ho—my puppet-show!
    Ladies and gentlemen see my show!
    Life and the world—look here, in troth,
    Though but *in parvo*, I promise ye both!
    The world and life—they shall both appear;
    But both are best seen when you're not too near;

And every lamp from the stage to the porch,
Must be lighted by Venus, from Cupid's torch;
Never a moment, if rules can tempt ye,
Never a moment my scene is empty!
Here is the babe in his leading-strings—
　Here is the boy at play;
Here is the passionate youth with wings,
　Like a bird's on a stormy day,
To and fro, waving here and there,
Down to the earth and aloft through the air;
Now see the man, as for combat enter—
Where is the peril he fears to adventure?
　See how the puppets speed on to the race,
Each his own fortune pursues in the chase;
How many the rivals, how narrow the space!
But, hurry and scurry, O mettlesome game!
The cars roll in thunder, the wheels rush in flame.
How the brave dart onward, and pant and glow!
How the craven behind them come creeping slow—
Ha! ha! see how Pride gets a terrible fall!
See how Prudence, or Cunning, out-races them all!
See how at the goal, with her smiling eyes,
Ever waits Woman to give the prize!

THE MINSTRELS OF OLD.

WHERE now the minstrel of the large renown,
　Rapturing with living words the heark'ning throng?
Charming the Man to Heaven, and earthward down
　Charming the God!—who wing'd the soul with song?
Yet lives the minstrel, not the deeds—the lyre
　Of old demands ears that of old believed it—
Bards of bless'd time—how flew your living fire
　From lip to lip! how race from race received it!
As if a God, men hallow'd with devotion—
　What GENIUS, speaking, shaping, wrought below,
The glow of song inflamed the ear's emotion,
　The ear's emotion gave the song the glow;

Each nurturing each—back on his soul—its tone
    Whole nations echoed with a rapture-peal;
Then all around the heavenly splendour shone
    Which now the heart, and scarce the heart can feel.

THE
COMMENCEMENT OF THE NEW CENTURY.

WHERE can Peace find a refuge?—whither, say,
    Can Freedom turn?—lo, friend, before our view
The CENTURY rends itself in storm away,
    And, red with slaughter, dawns on earth the New.
The girdle of the lands is loosen'd; *—hurl'd
    To dust the forms old Custom deem'd divine,—
Safe from War's fury not the watery world;—
    Safe not the Nile-God nor the antique Rhine.
Two mighty nations make the world their field,
    Deeming the world is for their heirloom given—
Against the freedom of all lands they wield
    This—Neptune's trident; that—the Thund'rer's levin
Gold to their scales each region must afford;
    And, as fierce Brennus in Gaul's early tale,
The Frank casts in the iron of his sword,
    To poise the balance, where the right may fail—
Like some huge Polypus, with arms that roam
    Outstretch'd for prey—the Briton spreads his reign;
And, as the Ocean were his household home,
    Locks up the chambers of the liberal main.
On to the Pole where shines, unseen, the Star,
    Onward his restless course unbounded flies;
Tracks every isle and every coast afar,
    And undiscover'd leaves but—Paradise!
Alas, in vain on earth's wide chart, I ween,
    Thou seek'st that holy realm beneath the sky—
Where Freedom dwells in gardens ever green—
    And blooms the Youth of fair Humanity!
O'er shores where sail ne'er rustled to the wind,
    O'er the vast universe, may rove thy ken;
But in the universe thou canst not find
    A space sufficing for ten happy men!

* That is—the settled political question—the balance of power.

In the heart's holy stillness only beams
  The shrine of refuge from life's stormy throng;
Freedom is only in the land of Dreams;
  And only blooms the Beautiful in Song!

We have now concluded the Poems composed in the third or maturest period of Schiller's life . . . From this portion, only have been omitted in the Translation, (besides some of the moral or epigrammatic sentences to which we have before alluded) a very few pieces, which, whatever their merit in the original, would be wholly without interest for the general English reader, viz., the satirical lines on Shakespeare's Translators,—"the Philosopher," "the Rivers," "the Jeremiad," the Remonstrance, addressed to Goethe on producing Voltaire's "Mahomet" on the Stage, in which the same ideas have been already expressed by Schiller in poems of more liberal and general application; and three or four occasional pieces in albums, &c.

The "Farewell to the Reader," which properly belongs to this division of the Poems, has been transferred, as the fitting conclusion, to the last place in the entire translation.

SECOND PERIOD.

THE Poems included in the Second Period of Schiller's literary career are few, but remarkable for their beauty, and deeply interesting from the struggling and anxious state of mind which some of them depict. It was, both to his taste and to his thought, a period of visible transition. He had survived the wild and irregular power which stamps, with fierce and somewhat sensual characters, the productions of his youth; but he had not attained that serene repose of strength—that calm, bespeaking depth and fulness, which is found in the best writings of his maturer years. In point of style, the Poems in this division have more facility and sweetness than those of his youth, and perhaps more evident vigour, more popular *verve* and *gusto* than many composed in his riper manhood: in point of thought, they mark that era through which few men of inquisitive and adventurous genius—of sanguine and impassioned temperament—and of education chiefly self-formed, undisciplined, and imperfect, have failed to pass—the era of doubt and gloom, of self-conflict, and of self-torture.—In the "*Robbers*," and much of the poetry written in the same period of Schiller's life, there is a bold and wild imagination, which attacks rather than questions—innovates rather than examines—seizes upon subjects of vast social import, that float on the surface of opinion, and assails them with a blind and half-savage rudeness, according as they offend the enthusiasm of unreasoning youth. But now this eager and ardent mind had paused to contemplate; its studies were turned to philosophy and history—a more practical knowledge of life (though in this last, Schiller, like most German authors, was ever more or less deficient in variety and range) had begun to soften the stern and fiery spirit which had hitherto sported with the dangerous elements of social revolution. And while this change was working, before its feverish agitation subsided into that Kantism which is the antipodes of scepticism, it was natural that, to the energy which had asserted, denounced, and dogmatised, should succeed the reaction of despondency and distrust. Vehement indignation at "the solemn plausibilities" of the world pervades the "*Robbers*." In "*Don Carlos*," the passion is no longer vehement indignation, but mournful sorrow—not indignation that hypocrisy reigns, but sorrow that honesty cannot triumph—not indignation that formal Vice usurps the high places of the world, but sorrow that, in the world, warm and generous Virtue glows, and feels, and suffers—without reward. So, in the poems of this period, are two that made a considerable sensation at their first appearance—"*The Conflict*," published originally under the title of "*The Freethinking of Passion*," and "*Resignation*." They presented a melancholy view of the moral struggles in the heart of a noble and virtuous man. From the first of these poems, Schiller, happily and wisely, at a later period of his life, struck out the passages most calculated to offend. What hand would dare to restore them? The few stanzas that remain still suggest the outline of dark and painful thoughts, which is filled up in the more elaborate, and, in many respects, most exquisite, poem of "*Resignation*." Virtue exacting all sacrifices, and giving no reward—Belief which denies enjoyment, and has no bliss save its own faith; such is the sombre lesson of the melancholy poet—the more impressive because *so far* it is truth—deep and everlasting truth—but only, to a Christian, a part of truth. Resignation, so sad if not looking beyond the earth, becomes joy, when assured and confident of heaven. Another poem in this intermediate collection was no less subjected to severe animadversion. We mean "*The Gods of Greece*." As the Poem however now stands, though one or two expressions are not free from objection, it can only be regarded as a Poet's lament for the Mythology which was the Fount of poetry, and certainly not as a Reasoner's defence of Paganism in disparagement of Christianity. But the fact is, that Schiller's mind was so essentially religious, that we feel more angry, when he whom we would gladly hail as our light and guide, only darkens us or misleads, than we should with the absolute infidelity of a less grave and reverent genius. Yet a period—a transition state—of doubt and despondency is perhaps common to men in proportion to their natural dispositions to faith and veneration. With them, it comes from keen sympathy with undeserved sufferings—from grief at wickedness triumphant—from too intense a brooding over the mysteries involved in the government of the world. Scepticism of this nature can but little injure the frivolous, and will be charitably regarded by the wise. Schiller's mind soon outgrew the state which, to the mind of a poet, above all men, is most ungenial, but the sadness which the struggle bequeathed seems to have wrought a complete revolution in all his preconceived opinions. The wild creator of the "*Robbers*," drunk with liberty, and audacious against all restraint, becomes the champion of "Holy Order,"—the denouncer of the French Republic—the extoller of an Ideal Life, which should entirely separate Genius the Restless from Society the Settled. And as his impetuous and stormy vigour matured into the lucent and tranquil art of "*Der Spaziergang*," "*Wallenstein*," and "*Die Braut von Messina*," so his philosophy threw itself into calm respect for all that custom sanctioned, and convention hallowed.

But even during the painful transition, of which, in his minor poems, glimpses alone are visible, Scepticism, with Schiller, never insults the devoted, or mocks the earnest mind. It may have sadness—but never scorn. It is the question of a traveller who has lost his way in the great wilderness, but who mourns with his fellow-seekers, and has no bitter laughter for their wanderings from the goal. This Division begins, indeed, with a Hymn which atones for whatever pains us in the two Poems whose strain and spirit so gloomily contrast it, viz., the matchless and immortal "*Hymn to Joy*"—a poem steeped in the very essence of all-loving and all-aiding Christianity—breathing the enthusiasm of devout yet gladsome adoration, and ranking amongst the most glorious bursts of worship which grateful Genius ever rendered to the benign Creator.

And it is peculiarly noticeable, that, whatever Schiller's state of mind upon theological subjects at the time that this Hymn was composed, and though all doctrinal stamp and mark be carefully absent from it, it is yet a poem that never could have been written but in a Christian age, in a Christian land—but by a man whose whole soul and heart had been at one time (nay, *was*, at the *very moment* of composition) inspired and suffused with that firm belief in God's goodness and His justice—that full assurance of rewards beyond the grave—that exulting and seraphic cheerfulness which associates Joy with the Creator—and that animated affection for the Brotherhood of Mankind, which Christianity—and Christianity alone, in its pure, orthodox, gospel form, needing no aid from schoolman or philosopher—taught and teaches.

HYMN TO JOY.

[The origin of the following Hymn is said to be this:—Schiller, when at Leipsic, or its vicinity, saved a poor student of theology, impelled by destitution and the fear of starvation, from drowning himself in the river Pleisse. Schiller gave him what money he had; obtained his promise to relinquish the thought of suicide, at least while the money lasted; and a few days afterwards, amidst the convivialities of a marriage feast, related the circumstance so as to affect all present. A subscription was made, which enabled the student to complete his studies, and ultimately to enter into an official situation. Elated with the success of his humanity, it is to Humanity that Schiller consecrated this Ode.]

SPARK from the fire that Gods have fled—
   Joy—thou Elysian Child divine,
Fire-drunk, our airy footsteps tread,
   O Holy One! thy holy shrine.
Strong custom rends us from each other—
   Thy magic all together brings;
And man in man but hails a brother,
   Wherever rest thy gentle wings.

Chorus—Embrace ye millions—let this kiss,
      Brothers, embrace the earth below!
   Yon starry worlds that shine on this,
      One common Father know!

He who this lot from fate can grasp—
   Of one true friend the friend to be—
He who one faithful maid can clasp,
   Shall hold with us his jubilee;
Yes, each who but one single heart
   In all the earth can claim his own!—
Let him who cannot, stand apart,
   And weep beyond the pale, alone!

Chorus—Homage to holy Sympathy,
      Ye dwellers in our mighty ring;
   Up to yon star-pavilions—she
      Leads to the Unknown King!

HYMN TO JOY.

All being drinks the mother-dew
  Of joy from Nature's holy bosom;
And Vice and Worth alike pursue
  Her steps that strew the blossom.
Joy in each link—to *us* * the treasure
  Of Wine and Love;—beneath the sod,
The Worm has instincts fraught with pleasure;
  In Heaven the Cherub looks on God!

Chorus—† Why bow ye down—why down—ye millions?
  O World, thy Maker's throne to see,
Look upward—search the Star-pavilions:
  There must His mansion be!

Joy is the mainspring in the whole
  Of endless Nature's calm rotation;
Joy moves the dazzling wheels that roll
  In the great Timepiece of Creation;
Joy breathes on buds, and flowers they are;
  Joy beckons—suns come forth from heaven;
Joy rolls the spheres in realms afar,
  Ne'er to thy glass, dim Wisdom, given!

Chorus—Joyous as suns careering gay
  Along their royal paths on high,
March, Brothers, march your dauntless way,
  As Chiefs to Victory!

Joy, from Truth's pure and lambent fires,
  Smiles out upon the ardent seeker;
Joy leads to Virtue Man's desires,
  And cheers as Suffering's step grows weaker.
High from the sunny slopes of Faith,
  The gales her waving banners buoy;
And through the shatter'd vaults of Death,
  Lo, mid the choral Angels—Joy!

Chorus—Bear this life, millions, bravely bear—
  Bear this life for the Better One!
See ye the Stars?—a life is there,
  Where the reward is won.

* To *us*, emphatically. Schiller means to discriminate the measure of bliss assigned to *us*, to the *worm*, and to the *cherub*.

† The original is obscure here; and the translator is doubtful whether he has seized the meaning, which may simply be—"Have you an innate feeling of Deity—then look for Him above the starry vault!"

Men like the Gods themselves may be,
  Tho' Men may not the Gods requite;
Go soothe the pangs of Misery—
  Go share the gladness with delight.—
Revenge and hatred both forgot,
  Have nought but pardon for thy foe;
May sharp repentance grieve him not,
  No curse one tear of ours bestow!

Chorus—Let all the world be peace and love—
    Cancel thy debt-book with thy brother
    For God shall judge of *us* above,
    As we shall judge each other!

Joy sparkles to us from the bowl—
  Behold the juice whose golden colour
To meekness melts the savage soul,
  And gives Despair a Hero's valour.
Up, brothers!—Lo, we crown the cup!
  Lo, the wine flashes to the brim!
Let the bright Fount spring heavenward!—Up!
  To THE GOOD SPIRIT this glass!—To HIM!

Chorus—Praised by the ever-whirling ring
    Of Stars, and tuneful Seraphim—
    To THE GOOD SPIRIT—the Father-King
    In Heaven!—This glass to Him!

Firm mind to bear what Fate bestows;
  Comfort to tears in sinless eyes;
Faith kept alike with Friends and Foes;
  Man's Oath eternal as the skies;
Manhood—the thrones of Kings to girth,
  Tho' bought by limb or life, the prize;
Success to Merit's honest worth;
  Perdition to the Brood of Lies!

Chorus—Draw closer in the holy ring,
    Swear by the wine-cup's golden river—
    Swear by the Stars, and by their King,
    To keep our vow for ever!

THE INVINCIBLE ARMADA.

SHE comes, she comes—the Burthen of the Deeps!
Beneath her wails the Universal Sea!
With clanking chains and a new God, she sweeps,
   And with a thousand thunders, unto thee!
The ocean-castles and the floating hosts—
Ne'er on their like, look'd the wild waters!—Well
May man the monster name "Invincible."
O'er shudd'ring waves she gathers to thy coasts!
   The horror that she spreads can claim
   Just title to her haughty name.
     The trembling Neptune quails
Under the silent and majestic forms;
The Doom of Worlds in those dark sails;—
   Near and more near they sweep! and slumber all the
     Storms!

Before thee, the array,
Blest island, Empress of the Sea!
The sea-born squadrons threaten thee,
   And thy great heart, BRITANNIA!
Woe to thy people, of their freedom proud—
She rests, a thunder heavy in its cloud!
Who, to thy hand the orb and sceptre gave,
   That thou should'st be the sovereign of the nations?
To tyrant kings thou wert thyself the slave,
   Till Freedom dug from Law its deep foundations;
The mighty CHART thy citizens made kings
And kings to citizens sublimely bow'd!
And thou thyself, upon thy realm of water,
Hast thou not render'd millions up to slaughter,
   When thy ships brought upon their sailing wings
     The sceptre—and the shroud?
What should'st thou thank?—Blush, Earth, to hear and
     feel:
What should'st thou thank?—Thy genius and thy
     steel!
Behold the hidden and the giant fires!
   Behold thy glory trembling to its fall!
Thy coming doom the round earth shall appal,

And all the hearts of freemen beat for thee,
And all free souls their fate in thine foresee—
　Theirs is *thy* glory's fall!
One look below the Almighty gave,
Where stream'd the lion-flags of thy proud foe;
And near and wider yawn'd the horrent grave.
"And who," saith HE, "shall lay mine England low—
The stem that blooms with hero-deeds—
The rock when man from wrong a refuge needs—
The stronghold where the tyrant comes in vain?
Who shall bid England vanish from the main?
Ne'er be this only Eden Freedom knew,
Man's stout defence from Power, to Fate consign'd."
God the Almighty blew,
And the Armada went to every wind!

THE CONFLICT.

No! I this conflict longer will not wage,
　The conflict Duty claims—the giant task;—
Thy spells, O Virtue, never can assuage
　The heart's wild fire—this offering do not ask!

True, I have sworn—a solemn vow have sworn,
　That I myself will curb the self within;
Yet take thy wreath, no more it shall be worn—
　Take back thy wreath, and leave me free to sin.

Rent be the contract I with thee once made;—
　She loves me, loves me—forfeit be thy crown!
Blest he who, lull'd in rapture's dreamy shade,
　Glides, as I glide, the deep fall gladly down.

She sees the worm that my youth's bloom decays,
　She sees my springtime wasted as it flees;
And, marv'ling at the rigour that gainsays
　The heart's sweet impulse, my reward decrees.

Distrust this angel purity, fair soul!
　It is to guilt thy pity armeth me;
Could Being lavish its unmeasured whole,
　It ne'er could give a gift to rival *Thee!*

Thee—the dear guilt I ever seek to shun,
   O tyranny of fate, O wild desires!
My virtue's only crown can but be won
   In that last breath—when virtue's self expires!

RESIGNATION.

AND I, too, was amidst Arcadia born,
   And Nature seem'd to woo me;
And to my cradle such sweet joys were sworn:
And I, too, was amidst Arcadia born,
   Yet the short spring gave only tears unto me!
Life but one blooming holiday can keep—
   For me the bloom is fled;
The silent Genius of the Darker Sleep
Turns down my torch—and weep, my brethren, weep—
   Weep, for the light is dead!
Upon thy bridge the shadows round me press,
   O dread Eternity!
And I have known no moment that can bless;—
Take back this letter meant for Happiness—
   The seal's unbroken—see!
Before thee, Judge, whose eyes the dark-spun veil
   Conceals, my murmur came;
On this our orb a glad belief prevails,
That, thine the earthly sceptre and the scales,
   REQUITER is thy name.

Terrors, they say, thou dost for Vice prepare,
   And joys the good shall know;
Thou canst the crooked heart unmask and bare;
Thou canst the riddle of our fate declare,
   And keep account with Woe.
With thee a home smiles for the exiled one—
   There ends the thorny strife.
Unto my side a godlike vision won,
Called TRUTH, (few know her, and the many shun,)
   And check'd the reins of life.
"I will repay thee in a holier land—

Give thou to me thy youth;
All I can grant thee lies in this command."
I heard, and, trusting in a holier land,
    Gave my young joys to Truth.

"Give me thy Laura—give me her whom Love
    To thy heart's core endears;
The usurer, Bliss, pays every grief—*above!*"
I tore the fond shape from the bleeding love,
    And gave—albeit with tears!
"What bond can bind the Dead to life once more?
    Poor fool," (the scoffer cries;)
"Gull'd by the despot's hireling lie, with lore
That gives for Truth a shadow;—life is o'er
    When the delusion dies!"
"Tremblest thou," hiss'd the serpent-herd in scorn,
    "Before the vain deceit?
Made holy but by custom, stale and worn,
The phantom Gods, of craft and folly born—
    The sick world's solemn cheat?
What is this Future underneath the stone?
    But for the veil that hides, revered alone;
The giant shadow of our Terror, thrown
    On Conscience' troubled glass—
Life's lying likeness—in the dreary shroud
    Of the cold sepulchre—
Embalm'd by Hope—Time's mummy,—which the proud
Delirium, driv'ling through thy reason's cloud,
    Calls '*Immortality!*'
Giv'st thou for hope (corruption proves its lie)
    Sure joy that most delights us?
Six thousand years has Death reign'd tranquilly!—
Nor one corpse come to whisper those who die
    What *after* death requites us!"
Along Time's shores I saw the Season fly;
    Nature herself, interr'd
Among her blooms, lay dead; to those who die
There came no corpse to whisper Hope! Still I
    Clung to the Godlike Word.
Judge!—All my joys to thee did I resign,
    All that did most delight me;

And now I kneel—man's scorn I scorn'd—thy shrine
Have I adored—Thee only held divine—
  Requiter, now requite me!
" For all my sons an equal love I know
  And equal each condition,"
Answer'd an unseen Genius—"See below,
Two flowers, for all who rightly seek them, blow—
  The Hope and the Fruition.
He who has pluck'd the one, resign'd must see
  The sister's forfeit bloom:
Let Unbelief enjoy—Belief must be
All to the chooser;—the world's history
  Is the world's judgment doom.
Thou hast had Hope—in thy belief thy prize—
  Thy bliss was centred in it:
Eternity itself—(Go ask the Wise!)
Never to him who forfeits, resupplies
  The sum struck from the Minute!"

THE GODS OF GREECE.

I.

Ye in the age gone by,
Who ruled the world—a world how lovely then!—
And guided still the steps of happy men
  In the light leading-strings of careless joy!
Ah, flourish'd then your service of delight!
  How different, oh, how different, in the day
When thy sweet fanes with many a wreath were bright,
  O Venus Amathusia!

II.

Then, through a veil of dreams
  Woven by Song, Truth's youthful beauty glow'd,
And life's redundant and rejoicing streams
  Gave to the soulless, soul—where'er they flow'd
Man gifted Nature with divinity
  To lift and link her to the breast of Love;
All things betray'd to the initiate eye
  The track of gods above!

III.

Where lifeless—fix'd afar,
  A flaming ball to our dull sense is given,
Phœbus Apollo, in his golden car,
  In silent glory swept the fields of heaven!
On yonder hill the Oread was adored,
  In yonder tree the Dryad held her home;
And from her Urn the gentle Naiad pour'd
  The wavelet's silver foam.

IV.

Yon bay, chaste Daphnè wreathed,
  Yon stone was mournful Niobe's mute cell,
Low through yon sedges pastoral Syrinx breathed,
  And through those groves wail'd the sweet Philomel,
The tears of Ceres swell'd in yonder rill—
  Tears shed for Proserpine to Hades borne;
And, for her lost Adonis, yonder hill
  Heard Cytherea mourn!—

V.

Heaven's shapes were charm'd unto
  The mortal race of old Deucalion;
Pyrrha's fair daughter, humanly to woo,
  Came down, in shepherd-guise, Latona's son.
Between Men, Heroes, Gods, harmonious then
  Love wove sweet links and sympathies divine;
Blest Amathusia, Heroes, Gods, and Men,
  Equals before thy shrine!

VI.

Not to that culture gay,
  Stern self-denial, or sharp penance wan!
Well might each heart be happy in that day—
  For Gods, the Happy Ones, were kin to Man!
The Beautiful alone the Holy there!
  No pleasure shamed the Gods of that young race;
So that the chaste Camœnæ favouring were,
  And the subduing Grace!

THE GODS OF GREECE.

VII.

A palace every shrine :
  Your very sports heroic ;—Yours the crown
Of contests hallow'd to a power divine,
  As rush'd the chariots thund'ring to renown.
Fair round the altar where the incense breathed,
  Moved your melodious dance inspired ; and fair
Above victorious brows, the garland wreathed
  Sweet leaves round odorous hair !

VIII.

The lively Thyrsus-swinger,
  And the wild car the exulting Panthers bore,
Announced the Presence of the Rapture-Bringer—
  Bounded the Satyr and blithe Faun before ;
And Mænads, as the frenzy stung the soul,
  Hymn'd in the madding dance, the glorious wine—
As ever beckon'd to the lusty bowl
  The ruddy Host divine !

IX.

Before the bed of death
  No ghastly spectre stood—but from the porch
Of life, the lip—one kiss inhaled the breath,
  And the mute graceful Genius lower'd a torch.
The judgment-balance of the Realms below,
  A judge, himself of mortal lineage, held ;
The very Furies at the Thracian's woe,
  Were moved and music-spell'd.

X.

In the Elysian grove
  The shades renew'd the pleasures life held dear :
The faithful spouse rejoin'd remember'd love,
  And rush'd along the meads the charioteer ;
There Linus pour'd the old accustom'd strain ;
  Admetus there Alcestis still could greet ; his
Friend there once more Orestes could regain,
  His arrows—Philoctetes !

XI.

More glorious then the meeds
   That in their strife with labour nerved the brave,
To the great doer of renownèd deeds,
   The Hebe and the Heaven the Thunderer gave.
Before the rescued Rescuer * of the dead,
   Bow'd down the silent and Immortal Host;
And the Twin Stars † their guiding lustre shed,
   On the bark tempest-tost!

XII.

Art thou, fair world, no more?
   Return, thou virgin-bloom on Nature's face;
Ah, only on the Minstrel's magic shore,
   Can we the footstep of sweet Fable trace!
The meadows mourn for the old hallowing life;
   Vainly we search the earth of gods bereft;
Where once the warm and living shapes were rife,
   Shadows alone are left!

XIII.

Cold, from the North, has gone
   Over the Flowers the Blast that kill'd their May;
And, to enrich the worship of the ONE,
   A Universe of Gods must pass away!
Mourning, I search on yonder starry steeps,
   But thee no more, Selene, there I see!
And through the woods I call, and o'er the deeps,
   And—Echo answers me!

XIV.

Deaf to the joys she gives—
   Blind to the pomp of which she is possest—
Unconscious of the spiritual Power that lives
   Around, and rules her—by our bliss unblest—

---

* Hercules, who recovered from the Shades Alcestis, after she had given her own life to save her husband Admetus. Alcestis in the hands of Euripides (that woman-hater as he is called!) becomes the loveliest female creation in the Greek Drama.

† *i. e.* Castor and Pollux are transferred to the Stars, Hercules to Olympus, for their deeds on earth.

Dull to the Art that colours or creates,
　Like the dead timepiece, Godless NATURE creeps
Her plodding round, and, by the leaden weights,
　The slavish motion keeps.

XV.

To-morrow to receive
　New life, she digs her proper grave to-day;
And icy moons with weary sameness weave
　From their own light their fulness and decay.
Home to the Poet's Land the Gods are flown,
　Light use in *them* that later world discerns,
Which, the diviner leading-strings outgrown,
　On its own axle turns.

XVI.

Home! and with them are gone
　The hues they gaz'd on and the tones they heard;
Life's Beauty and life's Melody:—alone
　Broods o'er the desolate void the lifeless Word;
Yet rescued from Time's deluge, still they throng
　Unseen the Pindus they were wont to cherish:
Ah, that which gains immortal life in Song,
　To mortal life must perish!

THE ARTISTS.

THIS justly ranks amongst Schiller's noblest Poems. He confessed "that he had hitherto written nothing that so much pleased him—nothing to which he had given so much time."* It forms one of the many Pieces he has devoted to the progress of Man. "The Eleusinian Festival" records the social benefits of Agriculture; "The Four Ages" panegyrises the influence of Poetry in all times; "The Walk" traces, in a series of glowing pictures, the development of general civilisation; the "Lay of the Bell" commemorates the stages of Life; and "The Artists," by some years the earliest of the Series, is an elaborate exposition of the effect of Art upon the Happiness and Dignity of the Human Species—a lofty Hymn in honour of Intellectual Beauty. Herein are collected into a symmetrical and somewhat argumentative whole, many favourite ideas of Schiller, which the reader will recognise as scattered throughout his other effusions. About the time when this Poem was composed, the narrow notions of a certain School of miscalled Utilitarians were more prevalent than they deserved; and this fine composition is perhaps the most eloquent answer ever given to those

---

* Hinrichs.

thinkers, who have denied the Morality of Fiction, and considered Poets rather the Perverters than the Teachers of the World. Perhaps in his just Defence of Art, Schiller has somewhat underrated the dignity of Science: but so many small Philosophers have assailed the divine uses of Poetry that it may be pardoned to the Poet to vindicate his Art in somewhat too arrogant a tone of retaliation. And it may be fairly contended that Fiction (the several forms of which are comprehended under the name of Art) has exercised an earlier, a more comprehensive, and a more genial influence over the Civilisation and the Happiness of Man, than nine tenths of that investigation of Facts which is the pursuit of Science.

The Poem, in the original, is written in lines of irregular length, the imitation of which—considering the nature and the length of the piece—would probably displease in an English version. Occasionally too (for Schiller in all his philosophical Poems is apt to incur the fault of obscurity, from which his poems of sentiment and narrative are generally free,) it has been judged necessary somewhat to expand and paraphrase the sense—to translate the idea as well as the words. But though, verbally, the Translation may be more free than most others in this collection, yet no less pains have been taken to render the version true to the spirit and intention of the Author. For the clearer exposition of the train of thought which Schiller pursues, the Poem has been divided into sections, and the Argument of the whole prefixed. If any passages in the version should appear obscure to those readers who find the mind of Schiller worth attentive Study, even when deprived of the melodious language which clothed its thoughts, by referring to the Argument the sense will perhaps become sufficiently clear.

ARGUMENT.

SECT. 1.—Man regarded in his present palmy state of civilisation—free through Reason, strong through Law—the Lord of Nature. (2) But let him not forget his gratitude to ART, which found him the Savage, and by which his powers have been developed—his soul refined. Let him not degenerate from serving ART, the Queen—to a preference for her handmaids (the Sciences). The Bee and the Worm excel him in diligence and mechanical craft—the Seraph in knowledge—but Art is Man's alone. (3) It is through the Beautiful that Man gains the Intuition of Law and Knowledge. (4) The supposed discoveries of Philosophy were long before revealed as symbols to Feeling. Virtue charmed and Vice revolted, before the Laws of Solon. (5) That Goddess which in Heaven is Urania—the great Deity whom only pure Spirits can behold, descends to earth as the earthly Venus—viz. the Beautiful. She adapts herself to the childlike understanding. But what we now only adore as Beauty we shall, one day, recognise as Truth. (6) After the Fall of Man, this Goddess—viz. the Beautiful—(comprehending Poetry and Art) alone deigned to console him, and painted on the walls of his Dungeon the Shapes of Elysium. (7) While Men only worshipped the Beautiful, no Fanaticism hallowed Persecution and Homicide—without formal Law, without compulsion, they obeyed Virtue rather as an instinct than a Duty. (8) Those dedicated to her service (viz. the Poet and the Artist) hold the highest intellectual rank Man can obtain. (9) Before Art introduced its own symmetry and method into the world, all was chaos. (10) You, the Artists, contemplated Nature, and learned to imitate; you observed the light shaft of the cedar, the shadow on the wave. (11) Thus rose the first Column of the Sculptor—the first Design of the Painter—and the wind sighing through the reed suggested the first Music. (12) Art's first attempt was in the first choice of flowers for a posy; its second, the weaving of those flowers into a garland—*i. e.* Art first observes and selects—next blends and unites—the column is ranged with other columns—the indi-

vidual Hero becomes one of an heroic army—the rude Song becomes an Iliad. (13) The effect produced by Homeric Song, in noble emulation,—nor in this alone; Man learns to live in other woes than his own—to feel pleasures beyond animal enjoyments. (14) And as this diviner intellectual feeling is developed, are developed also Thought and Civilisation. (15) In the rudest state of Man, you, the Artists, recognise in his breast the spiritual germ, and warm it into life—true and holy Love awoke with the first Shepherd's love song. (16) It is you, the Artists, who generalising, and abstracting, gather all several excellences into one ideal.—You thus familiarise Man to the notion of the Unknown Powers, whom you invest with the attributes Man admires and adores.—He fears the Unknown, but he loves its shadow.—You suffered the Nature around him to suggest the Prototype of all Beauty. (17) You make subject to your ends—the passion, the duty, and the instinct—All that is scattered through creation you gather and concentrate, and resolve to the Song or to the Stage—Even the murderer who has escaped justice, conscience-stricken by the Eumenides on the scene, reveals himself—Long before Philosophy hazarded its dogmas an Iliad solved the riddles of Fate—And with the wain of Thespis wandered a Providence. (18) Where your symmetry, your design fail in this world, they extend into the world beyond the grave—If life be over too soon for the brave and good, Poetry imagined the Shades below, and placed the hero Castor amongst the Stars.*
(19) Not contented with bestowing immortality on Man—you furnish forth from Man, the ideal of the Immortals—Virgin Beauty grows into a Pallas—manly Strength into a Jove. (20) As the world without you is thus enlarged and the world within you agitated and enriched, your Art extends to Philosophy:—For as the essentials of Art are symmetry and design, so the Artist extends that symmetry and that design into the system of Creation, the Laws of Nature, the Government of the World;—Lends to the spheres its own harmony—to the Universe its own symmetric method. (21) The Artist thus recognising *Contrivance* everywhere, feels his life surrounded with Beauty—He has before him in Nature itself an eternal model of the Perfect and Consummate—Through joy—grief—terror—wherever goes his course—one stream of harmony murmurs by his side—The Graces are his companions—his life glides away amidst airy shapes of Beauty—His soul is merged in the divine ocean that flows around him. Fate itself which is reduced from Chance and Providence, and which furnishes him with themes of pleasurable awe, does not daunt him. (22) You, Artists, are the sweet and trusty companions of life—You gave us what life has best—Your reward is your own immortality and the gratitude of Men's hearts. (23) You are the imitators of the Divine Artist, who accompanies power with sweetness, terror with splendour, who adorns himself even in destroying—As a brook that reflects the evening landscape, so on the niggard stream of life shimmers Poetry. You lead us on, in marriage garments, to the Unknown Bourne—As your Urns deck our bones your fair semblances deck our cares.—Through the history of the world, we find that Humanity smiles in your presence and mourns in your absence. (24) Humanity came young from your hands, and when it grew old and decayed, you gave it a second youth—Time has bloomed twice from seeds sown by Art. (25) When the Barbarians chased Civilisation from Greece, you transplanted it to Italy—and, with Civilisation, freedom and gentle manners—Yet you sought not public rewards for your public benefits—In obscurity you contemplated the blessings you had diffused. (26) If the Philosopher now pursues his course without obstacles—if he now

---

* To the Poet we are indebted for the *promise* of another life (foreshadowing Divine Revelation) long before the Philosopher bewildered us by *arguing* for it.

would arrogate the crown, and hold Art but as the first Slave to Science—pardon his vain boast.—Completion and Perfection in reality rest with you.—With you dawned the Spring, in you is matured the Harvest, of the Moral World. (27) For although Art sprung first from physical materials, the clay and the stone—it soon also embraced in its scope the spiritual and intellectual—Even what Science discovers only ministers to Art.—The Philosopher obtains his first hints from the Poet or Artist—and when his wisdom flowers, as it were, into beauty—it but returns to the service, and is applied to the uses of its instructor.—When the Philosopher contemplates the Natural World, side by side with the Artist—the more the Latter accumulates images of beauty, and unites the details of the great design, the more the Former enriches the sphere of his observation—the more profound his research—the more bold his speculations—The Imagination always assists the Reason—And Art which teaches Philosophy to see Art (i. e. Symmetry and Design) everywhere, may humble the Philosopher's pride, but augments his love.—Thus scattering flowers, Poetry leads on through tones and forms, ever high and higher, pure and purer, till it shall at last attain that point when Poetry becomes but sudden inspiration and the instantaneous intuition of Truth;—when in fact the Art sought by the Poet, the Truth sought by the Philosopher, become one. (28) Then this great Goddess, whom we have hitherto served as the earthly Venus, the Beautiful—shall re-assume her blazing crown—and Man, to whose earlier and initiatory probation she has gently familiarised her splendour, shall behold her without a veil—not as the Venus of Earth, but as the Urania of Heaven—Her beauty comprehended by him in proportion to the beauty his soul took from her—So from the Mentor of his youth shone forth Minerva to Telemachus. (29) To you, O Artists, is committed the dignity of Man—It sinks with you, it revives with you. (30) In those Ages when Truth is persecuted by the Bigotry of her own time, she seeks refuge in Song.—The charm she takes from the Muse but renders her more fearful to her Foes. (31) Aspire then constantly, O Artists, to the Beautiful—covet no meaner rewards.—If Art escape you, search for her in Nature.—Remember that the excellent and the perfect ever must be found in whatsoever fair souls esteem fair.—Do not bound yourselves to your own time—Let your works reflect the shadow of the coming Age—It matters not what paths you select—You have before you the whole labyrinth of being—but all its paths for you unite at one throne—As the white breaks into seven tints, as the seven tints re-dissolve into white—so Truth is the same, whether she dazzles us with the splendour of variegated colours, or pervades the Universe in one Stream of Light.

I.

Upon the century's verge, O Man, how fair
Thou standest, stately as a silent palm
With boughs far-spreading through the solemn air,
In the full growth of mellowest years sublime;
Thro' mildness earnest, thro' achievement calm,
Each sense unfolded, all the soul matured—
The crowning work and ripest born of Time!
Free in the freedom reason has secured,
Strong in the strength that Law bestows, thou art,
Great in thy meekness—rich with countless stores,
Which slept for ages silent in thy heart;
The Lord of Nature, who thy chains adores,

Who in each strife but disciplines thy skill,
And shines from out the desert at thy will!

II.

O not, inebriate with thy victory, scorn—
Scorn not to prize and praise the fostering hand
That found thee weeping—orphan'd and forlorn,
Lone on the verge of Life's most barren strand—
That seized from lawless CHANCE its helpless prey,
And early taught thy young heart the control
Of ART—thy guide upon the upward way—
The softener and the raiser of the soul,—
Cleansing the breast it tutored to aspire,
From the rude passion and the low desire:
The good, the blessed One, who, through sweet play,
To lofty duties lured thy toilless youth;
Who by light parables revealed the ray
That gilds the mystery of each holier Truth;
And but to stranger arms consigned—once more
To clasp her darling, riper for her lore.
O fall not back from that high faith serene,
To serve the Handmaids and forsake the Queen.
In diligent toil thy master is the bee;
In craft mechanical, the worm that creeps
Through earth its dexterous way, may tutor thee;
In knowledge (couldst thou fathom all its deeps),
All to the seraph are already known.
But thine, O MAN, is ART—thine wholly and alone!

III.

But through the Morning-Gate of Beauty goes
Thy pathway to the Land of Knowledge! By
The twilight Charm,—Truth's gradual daylight grows
Familiar to the Mind's unconscious eye;
And what was first—with a sweet tremulous thrill—
Wakened within thee by melodious strings,
Grows to a Power that swells and soars until
Up to the all-pervading God it springs.*

---

* *i. e.* Poetry prepared the mind for the knowledge of God.

IV.

What first the reason of the Antique Time
Dimly discovered (many a century flown
Lay in the symbol types of the Sublime
And Beautiful—intuitively known:
True, from the seeker as a *lore* concealed,)
But as an *instinct* all to childish sense revealed.
Virtue's fair shape to Virtue love could draw,
From Vice a gentler impulse warned away,
Ere yet a Solon sowed the formal Law,
Whose fruits warmed slowly to the gradual ray;—
Ere the Idea of Space, the Infinite,
Before Philosophy, the Seeker, stole—
Who ever gazed upon the Starry Light,
Nor guess'd the large truth in the silent soul?

V.

She the URANIA, with her wreath of rays,
The glory of Orion round her brow;
On whom pure Spirits only dare to gaze,
As Heaven's bright Habitants before her bow;
And round her splendour the stars wink and fade
So awful, reigning on her sunlit throne—
When she diswreathes her of her fiery crown,
Gliding to Earth (Earth's gentle Venus) down,
Smiles on us but as BEAUTY: *—with the zone
Of the sweet Graces girded, the meek youth
Of Infancy she wears, that she may be
By Infants comprehended, and what we
Here, but as BEAUTY gazed on and obey'd,—
Will, one day, meet us in her name of TRUTH!

VI.

When the Creator from his presence cast
Man to thy dark abyss—Mortality,
Condemn'd the late return to glory past,
To seek and strive for with a weary sigh,

---

* *i. e.* She who, in Heaven, is Urania—the Daughter of Uranus:—by Light, is, on Earth, Venus—the Divinity of Love and Beauty. The Beautiful is to Mortals the revelation of Truth. Truth, in its abstract splendour too bright for the eyes of Man in his present state, familiarises itself to him in the shape of the Beautiful.

Amidst the dim paths of the sensual clay,
When every heavenlier Nature from his eye
Veil'd its bright face, and swept in scorn away;
She only—she, in the low Human cell,
Herself made human, deign'd with him to dwell—
Stoop'd round her darling, wings soft-brooding; fann'd
With freshening airs, the Sense's barren land;
And, kind in bright delusions, limn'd with all
The lost Elysium—life's sad dungeon-wall.

VII.

Ah, in that tender Nurse's cradling arms—
While yet reposed the mild Humanity—
War deck'd not Murder with Fame's holy charms,
Reek'd not the innocent blood;—but guided by
Those gentle leading-strings, the guileless soul
Shunn'd the cold duties, by compulsion taught;
Virtue was instinct—and without control,
Through ways the lovelier for their winding, sought
The Moral in the Beautiful,—and won;—
Each path a ray that guided to the Sun!
Ne'er they who tended her chaste service knew
One meaner impulse—and the frown of Fate
Paled not their courage from its healthy hue,
As in some holier realm, their happy state
Regain'd the freedom while it shunn'd the strife,
And won to Earth once more the spiritual, heavenly life.

VIII.

Oh, happy! and of many millions, they
The purest chosen, whom her service pure
Hallows and claims—whose hearts are made her throne,
Whose lips her oracle—ordain'd secure,
To lead a Priestly life, and feed the ray
Of her eternal shrine,—to them alone
Her glorious Countenance unveil'd is shown:
Ye, the high Brotherhood she links—rejoice
In the great rank allotted by her choice!—
The loftiest rank the spiritual world sublime,
Rich with its starry thrones, gives to the Sons of Time!

IX.

Ere yet unto the early world the Law
Of the harmonious Symmetry, which all
Essence and life now joyously obey,
Your Art divinely gave—wall'd round with Night
And Chaos, gloomier for one sickly ray,
Man struggled with the uncouth shapes of awe,
That through the Dark came giant on the sight,
And chained the senses in a slavish thrall:
Rude as himself press'd round the shadowy throng,
Vast without outline, without substance, strong;
So gloom'd Creation on the Savage Breast,
While brutal lusts alone allured the eye,
And unenjoy'd, unheeded, and unguest,
The lovely soul of Nature pass'd him by,—

X.

Lo, *as* it pass'd him, with a noiseless hand,
And with a gentle instinct, the fair shade
Ye seiz'd; and linked in one harmonious band
The airy images your eyes survey'd;
Ye felt, surveying, how the cedar gave
Its light shaft to the air;—how sportive, play'd
The form reflected on the crystal wave!
How could ye fail the gentle hints to read
With which free Nature met ye on the way?
By easy steps did eye observant lead
The hand to mimick the fair forms at play,
Till from the image on the water glass'd
The likeness rose—and Painting grew at last!
Yea, from the substance sever'd, Nature's fair
And phantom shadow—follow'd by the soul,
Cast itself on the silver stream, and there
Rendered its coyness to the hand that stole!

*So born the craft that imitates and takes
Shape from the shadow;—so young Art awakes
The earliest genius;—so in clay and sand
The shade is snatch'd at by the eager hand;
The sweet enjoyment in the labour grows,
And from your breast the first creation flows.

* *See Argument.*

XI.

Seized by the power of thoughtful contemplation,
Snared by the eye that steals what it surveys,
Nature, the talisman of each creation
With which her spells enamour you, betrays:
Your quicken'd sense, the wonder-working laws,
The stores in Beauty's treasure-house, conceives—
Your hand from Nature the light outline draws,
And scattered hints in gentle union weaves.
Thus rise—tall Obelisk, and vast Pyramid—
The half-formed Hermes grows—the Column springs;
Music comes lisping from the Shepherd's reed,
And Song the valour and the victory sings.

XII.

The happier choice of flowers most sweet or fair,
To weave the posy for some Shepherd Maid,
Lo the *first* Art, from nature born, is there!—
The *next*—the flowers the careless tresses braid
In garlands wreath'd:—Thus step by step ascends
The Art that notes, and gathers, shapes and blends!
 But, each once blent with each, its single grace
Each offspring of the Beautiful must lose;
The artful hand according each its place,
Confounds the separate with the common hues.
Charm'd into method by the harmonious word,
Column with column ranged—proud Fanes aspire,
The Hero melts amidst the Hero herd,
And peals the many-stringed Mæonian Lyre.

XIII.

Soon round this new Creation in great Song
Barbarian wonder gather'd and believed;
"See," cried the emulous and kindled throng,
"The deeds a Mortal like ourselves achieved!"
Grouped into social circles near and far,
Listing the wild tales of the Titan war,
Of giants piled beneath the rocks,—and caves
Grim with the lion some stout hero braves,
Still while the Minstrel sung, the listeners grew
Themselves the Heroes his high fancy drew.

Then first did Men the soul's enjoyment find,
First knew the calmer raptures of the mind
Not proved by sense—but from the distance brought;
The joy at deeds themselves had never wrought,—
The thirst for what possession cannot give,—
The power in nobler lives than life to live!

XIV.

Now from the Sensual Slumber's heavy chain,
Breaks the fair soul, which new-born pinions buoy,
And, freed by you, the ancient Slave of Pain
Springs from his travail to the breast of Joy;
Fall the dull Animal-Barriers round him wrought,
On his clear front the HUMAN halo glows,
And forth the high Majestic Stranger—THOUGHT,
Bright from the startled brain, a Pallas, goes!
Now stands sublime THE MAN, and to the star
Lifts his unclouded brow—The Kingly One;
And Contemplation, sweeping to the Far,
Speaks in the eyes commercing with the Sun.
Fair from his cheeks bloom happy smiles, and all
The rich varieties of soulful sound
Unfold in Song—divine emotions call
Sweet tears to feeling eyes;—and, sister-bound,
Kindness and Mirth upon his accents dwell,
Soul, like some happy Nymph, haunting the lips' pure
    well!

XV.

Yea, what though buried in the mire and clay
Grovels the fleshly instinct of the worm;
What though the lusts and ruder passions sway
And clasp him round—the intellectual germ
You, Sons of Art, in that dark breast behold,
Warm from its sleep and into bloom unfold:—
Love's spiritual blossom opened to the day,
First—when Man heard the first young Shepherd's lay.
Ennobled by the dignity of Thought,
Passion that blush'd the soft desire to own,
Caught chaster language from the Minstrel's tone;

And Song, the delicate Preacher, while it taught
A love outlasting what the senses sought,
Beyond Possession placed the ethereal goal,
And to the Heart proclaimed and link'd the Soul!

XVI.

The wisdom of the wise, the gentleness
The gentle know—the strength that nerves the strong—
The grace that gathers round the noble—yes
Ye blend them all to limn the Beautiful,
Each ray on Nature's brows commixed and grown
Into one pomp—a halo for your own!
Though from the Unknown Divinity, the awe
Of Man shrinks back—to what he knows no dull,
Yet with what love his young religion saw
The shadow of the Godhead downward thrown;*
Gentle the type—though fearful the Unknown.
The breasts of heroes nobly burn'd to vie
With the bright Gods that rul'd in Homer's sky;
Ye did the Ideal from the Natural call—
Ye bade Man learn how on the Earth is given
The immemorial prototype of all
Glory and Beauty, dream'd of for the Heaven!

XVII.

The wild tumultuous passions of the soul,
The playful gladness of unfetter'd joy,
The duty and the instinct—your control
Grasps at its will—can as its slaves employ
To guide the courses, and appoint the goal;
All that in restless Nature's mighty space
Wander divided—world on world afar—
Ye seize—ye gather, fix them into place,
And show them bright and living as they are,
Link'd into order stately and serene,
Limn'd in the song, or mirror'd on the scene!

---

* *i. e.* Man shrinks in awe from the notion of a Diviner Power, thoroughly unknown; but the Greek Mythology familiarised Man to the providence of the Gods, and elevated him by the contemplation of attributes in which he recognised whatever he most admired.—Art taught Man to see in the Nature round him the prototype—the ideal—of Diviner Beauty.

Here, secret Murder, pale and shuddering, sees
Sweep o'er the stage the stern Eumenides;*
Owns, where Law fails, what powers to Art belong,
And, screen'd from Justice, finds its doom in Song!
Long ere the wise their slow decrees revolved,
A fiery Iliad Fate's dark riddles solved;
And Art, the Prophetess, Heaven's mystic plan
Of doom and destiny reveal'd to Man,
When the rude goat-song spell'd the early Age,
And Providence,† spoke low from Thespis' wandering
    stage.

XVIII.

Nay, where in *this* world, Reason paus'd perplext,
Ye track'd God onward, and divined the *next*
‡ Full early wont to comprehend and meet
Harmonious systems never incomplete,
What though the vain impatient eye might fail
To pierce the dark Fate through the solemn veil—
Though the brave heart seem'd prematurely still'd,
And life's fair circle halted unfulfilled,
Yet here, ev'n here, your own unaided might
Flung its light Arch across the waves of Night;
Led the untrembling Spirit on to go
Where dark Avernus, wailing, winds below;
Bade Hope survive the Urn and Charnel, brave
In the great faith of Life beyond the grave;

---

* The Poet here seems to allude to the Story of Ibycus, which at a subsequent period furnished the theme of one of his happiest narratives.
† In the Drama the essentials are Providence and Design.

    ‡ "Doch in den grossen Weltenlauf
      Ward euer Ebenmaass zu früh getragen."

These lines are extremely obscure. Unless we may construe "zu früh," "*very* early," or "with bold prematurity." In which case, referring to the conclusion of the preceding stanza, the sense would be—That the Poet did not confine the operations of a recompensing Providence to the limited exhibitions of the Thespian wain; but, even in the infancy of society, and with a boldness which might be considered premature, ventured to transfer them to the greater stage of the actual world, and to claim compensation beyond the grave for heroic lives inevitably cut short before they had fulfilled their career. The Poet's necessary love of symmetry and system (of which justice is a part) compels him to carry on the life which fails of result and completion here, to fulfilment in a life hereafter.

Show'd there—how Love the lov'd once more could win—
How Dorian Castor gained his starry Twin—
The Shadow in the Moon's pale glimmer seen,
Ere yet she fills her horns, and rounds her orb serene!

XIX.

High, and more high, the aspiring Genius goes,
And still creation from creation flows;
What in the natural world but charms the eyes,
In Art's—to forms which awe the soul must rise;
The Maiden's majesty, at Art's commands,
Inspires the marble, and—Athenè stands!
The strength that nerves the Wrestler on the sod
Swells the vast beauty which invests a God,
And throned in Elis—wonder of his time—
With brows that sentence worlds—sits Phidian Jove sublime!

XX.

Without—the World by diligent toil transformed,
Within—by new-born passions roused the heart,
(Strengthened by each successive strife that stormed)
Wider and wider grows your realm of Art.
Still in each step that Man ascends to light
He bears the Art that first inspired the flight;
And still the teeming Nature to his gaze,
The wealth he gives her with new worlds repays.
Thus the light Victories exercise the mind,
By guess to reach what knowledge fails to find,
Practised—throughout the Universe to trace
An Artist-whole of beauty and of grace,
He sets the Columns Nature's boundary knows,
Tracks her dark course, speeds with her where she goes;
Weighs with the balance her own hands extend;
Meets with the gauge her own perfections lend,
Till all her beauty renders to his gaze
The charm that robes it and the law that sways.
In self-delighted Joy the Artist hears
His own rich harmony enchant the spheres,
And in the Universal Scheme beholds
The symmetry that reigns in all he moulds.

XXI.

Yes, in all round him can his ear divine
The voice that tells of method and design;
He sees the life mid which his lot is thrown,
Clasp'd round with beauty as a golden zone;
In all his works, before his emulous eyes,
To lead to victory, fair Perfection flies:
Where'er he hears, or gay Delight rejoice,
Or Care to stillness breathe its whispered voice,
Where starry Contemplation lingers slow,
Or stream from heavy eyes the tears of Woe,
Or Terror in her thousand shapes appal;—
Still one harmonious Sweetness glides through all,
Soft to his ear, and freshening to his look,
And winding on through earth—one haunting music brook!
In the refined and still emotion, glide
With chastened mirth the Graces to his side;
Round him the bright Companions weave their dance;
And as the curving lines of Beauty flow,
Each winding into each, as o'er his glance
The lovely apparitions gleam and go
In delicate outline—so the dreaming day
Of Life, enchanted, breathes itself away.
   His soul is mingled with the Harmonious Sea
That flows around his sense delightedly;
And Thought, where'er with those sweet waves it glide,
Bears the all-present Venus on the tide!
At peace with Fate serenely goes his race—
Here guides the Muse, and there supports the Grace;
The stern Necessity, to others dim
With Night and Terror, wears no frown for him:
Calm and serene, he fronts the threatened dart,
Invites the gentle bow, and bares the fearless heart.

XXII.

Darlings of Harmony divine,—all blest
Companions of our Beings!—whatsoe'er
Is of this life, the dearest, noblest, best,
Took life from you! If Man his fetters bear

With a glad heart that chafes not at the chain,
But clings to duty with the thoughts of love;
If now no more he wander in the reign
Of iron Chance, but with the Power above
Link his harmonious being—what can be
Your bright reward?—your Immortality,
And your own heart's high recompense! If round
The chalice-fountain, whence, to Mortals, streams
The Ideal Freedom, evermore are found
The godlike Joys and pleasure-weaving Dreams ;—
For this—for these—be yours the grateful shrine,
Deep in the Human Heart ye hallow and refine.

XXIII.

Ye are the Imitators, ye the great
Disciples of the Mighty Artist—who
Zoned with sweet grace the iron form of Fate—
Gave Heaven its starry lights and tender blue—
Whose terror more ennobles than alarms
(Its awe exalts us, and its grandeur charms)—
Who, ev'n destroying, while he scathes, illumes,
And clothes with pomp the anger that consumes.
As o'er some brook that glides its lucid way
The dancing shores in various shadow play;
As the smooth wave a faithful mirror yields
To Eve's soft blush, and flower-enamell'd fields;
So, on life's stream, that niggard steals along,
Shimmers the lively Shadow-World of Song.
Ye, to the Dread Unknown—the dismal goal
Where the stern Fates await the trembling soul—
Ye lead us on, by paths for ever gay,
And robed with joy as for a marriage-day;
And as in graceful urns your genius decks
Our very bones, and beautifies the wrecks:
So with appearances divinely fair,
Ye veil the trouble and adorn the care.
Search where I will the ages that have roll'd,
The unmeasured Past, Earth's immemorial lore,
How smil'd Humanity, where ye consoled,
How smileless mourned Humanity before!

XXIV.

All strong and mighty on the wing, and young
And fresh from your creative hands, It * sprung;
And when the Time, that conquers all, prevail'd;
When on its wrinkled cheek the roses fail'd;
When from its limbs the vigour pass'd away,
And its sad age crept on in dull decay,
And tottered on its crutch;—within your arms
It sought its shelter and regained its charms:
Out from your fresh and sparkling well, ye pour'd
The living stream that dying strength restored;
Twice into spring has Time's stern winter glow'd,
Twice Nature blossom'd from the seeds Art sow'd.

XXV.

Ye snatch'd—when chased Barbarian Hosts before—
From sacred hearths the last yet living brand;
From the dishallow'd Orient Altar bore,
And brought it glimmering to the Western Land.
As from the East the lovely Exile goes,
Fair on the West a young Aurora glows;
And all the flowers Ionian shores could yield
Blush forth, re-blooming in the Hesperian Field.
Fair Nature glass'd its image on the Soul,
From the long Night the mists began to roll;
And o'er the world of Mind, adorn'd again,
Light's holy Goddess re-assumed her reign.
Loos'd from the Millions fell the fetters then—
Slaves heard the Voice that told their rights as Men.
And the Young Race in peace to vigour grew,
In that mild brotherhood they learn'd from you!
  And you, averse the loud applause to win,
Still in the joy that overflow'd within,
Sought the mild shade, contented to survey
The World ye brighten'd, basking in the ray.

XXVI.

If on the course of Thought, now barrier-free,
Sweeps the glad search of bold Philosophy;

---

* *i. e.* Humanity.

And with self-pæans, and a vain renown,
Would claim the praise and arrogate the crown,
Holding, but as a Soldier in her band,
The nobler Art that did in truth command;
And grants, beneath her visionary throne,
To Art, her Queen—the slave's first rank alone;—
Pardon the vaunt!—For YOU Perfection all
Her star-gems weaves in one bright coronal!
With you, the first blooms of the Spring, began
Awakening Nature in the Soul of Man!
With you fulfill'd, when Nature seeks repose,
Autumn's exulting harvests ripely close.

XXVII.

If Art rose plastic from the stone and clay,
To Mind from Matter ever sweeps its sway;
Silent, but conquering in its silence, lo,
How o'er the Spiritual World its triumphs go!
What in the Land of Knowledge, wide and far,
Keen Science teaches—for *you* discovered are:
First in your arms the wise their wisdom learn—
They dig the mine you teach them to discern;
And when that wisdom ripens to the flower
And crowning time of Beauty—to the Power
From whence it rose, new stores it must impart,
The toils of Science swell the Wealth of Art.
 When to one height the Sage ascends with you,
And spreads the Vale of Matter round his view
In the mild twilight of serene repose;
The more the Artist charms, the more the Thinker
 knows.
The more the shapes—in intellectual joy,
Link'd by the Genii which your spells employ,
The more the thought with the emotion blends—
The more up-buoy'd by both the Soul ascends
To loftier Harmonies, and heavenlier things;—
And tracks the stream of Beauty to its springs.
The lovely members of the mighty whole,
Till then confused and shapeless to his soul—
Distinct and glorious grow upon his sight,
The fair enigmas brighten from the Night;

More rich the Universe his thoughts enclose—
More wide the Ocean with whose wave he flows;
The wrath of Fate grows feebler to his fears,
As from God's Scheme Chance wanes and disappears;
And as each straining impulse soars above—
How his pride lessens—how augments his love!
So scattering blooms—the still Guide—Poetry
Leads him thro' paths, tho' hid, that mount on high—
Thro' forms and tones more pure and more sublime—
Alp upon Alp of Beauty—till the time
When what we long as Poetry have nurst,
Shall as a God's swift inspiration burst,
And flash in glory, on that youngest day—
One with the Truth to which it wings the way!

XXVIII.

She, the soft Venus of the Earth, by Men
Worshipp'd but as the Beautiful till then,
Shall re-assume her blazing coronal,
Let the meek veil that shrouds her splendour fall,
And to her ripen'd Son * divinely rise
In her true shape—the Urania of the skies!
Proportion'd to the Beauty which Man's soul
Took from her culture while in her control,
Shall he, with toilless, lightly-wooing ease,
Truth in the Beautiful embrace and seize.
Thus sweet, thus heavenly, was thy glad surprise,
Son of Ulysses, when before thine eyes,
Bright from the Mentor whom thy youth had known,
Jove's radiant child—Imperial Pallas—shone!

XXIX.

O Sons of Art! into your hands consign'd
(O heed the trust, O heed it and revere!)
The liberal dignity of human kind!
With you to sink, with you to re-appear.
The hallow'd melody of Magian Song
Does to Creation as a link belong,
Blending its music with God's harmony,
As rivers melt into the mighty sea.

* Mündigen,—her Son, who has attained his majority.

THE ARTISTS.

XXX.

Truth, when the Age she would reform, expels;
Flies for safe refuge to the Muse's cells.
More fearful for the veil of charms she takes,
From Song the fulness of her splendour breaks,
And o'er the Foe that persecutes and quails
Her vengeance thunders, as the Bard prevails!

XXXI.

Rise, ye free Sons of the Free Mother, rise,
Still on the Light of Beauty, sun your eyes,
Still to the heights that shine afar, aspire,
Nor meaner meeds than those she gives, desire.
If here the Sister Art forsake awhile,
Elude the clasp, and vanish from the toil,
Go seek and find her at the Mother's heart—
Go search for Nature—and arrive at Art!
Ever the Perfect dwells in whatsoe'er
Fair souls conceive and recognise as fair!
Borne on your daring pinions soar sublime
Above the shoal and eddy of the Time.
Far-glimmering on your wizard mirror, see
The silent shadow of the Age to be.
Thro' all Life's thousand-fold entangled maze,
One godlike bourne your gifted sight surveys—
Thro' countless means one solemn end, foreshown,
The labyrinth closes at a single Throne.
   As in seven tints of variegated light
Breaks the lone shimmer of the lucid white;
As the seven tints that paint the Iris bow
Into the lucid white dissolving flow—
So Truth in many-coloured splendour plays,—
Now on the eye enchanted with the rays—
Now in one lustre gathers every beam,
And floods the World with light—a single Stream!*

---

* There is exquisite skill in concluding the Poem (after insisting so eloquently upon the maxim, that whatever Science discovers, only adds to the stores, or serves the purpose of Art) with an image borrowed from Science.

THE CELEBRATED WOMAN.

AN EPISTLE BY A MARRIED MAN—TO A FELLOW-SUFFERER.

[In spite of Mr. Carlyle's assertion of Schiller's "total deficiency in Humour,"* we think that the following Poem suffices to show that he *possessed* the gift in no ordinary degree, and that if the aims of a genius so essentially earnest had allowed him to *indulge* it, he would have justified the opinion of the experienced Iffland as to his capacities for original comedy.]

CAN I, my friend, with thee condole?—
  Can I conceive the woes that try men,
When late Repentance racks the soul
  Ensnared into the toils of Hymen?
Can *I* take part in such distress?—
Poor Martyr,—most devoutly, "Yes!"
Thou weep'st because thy Spouse has flown
To arms preferred before thine own;—
A faithless wife,—I grant the curse,—
And yet, my friend, it might be worse!
Just hear Another's tale of sorrow,
And, in comparing, comfort borrow!

What! dost thou think thyself undone,
Because thy rights are shared with *One!*
O, Happy Man—be more resign'd,
My wife belongs to all Mankind!
My wife—she's found abroad—at home;
But cross the Alps and she's at Rome;
Sail to the Baltic—there you'll find her;
Lounge on the Boulevards—kind and kinder:
In short, you've only just to drop
  Where'er they sell the last new tale,
And, bound and lettered in the shop,
  You'll find my Lady up for sale!

She must her fair proportions render
To all whose praise can glory lend her;—
Within the coach, on board the boat,
Let every pedant "take a note;"
Endure, for public approbation,
Each critic's "close investigation,"

* Carlyle's Miscellanies, vol. iii. p. 47.

And brave—nay court it as a flattery—
Each spectacled Philistine's battery.
Just as it suits some scurvy carcase
In which she hails an Aristarchus,
Ready to fly with kindred souls,
O'er blooming flowers or burning coals,
To fame or shame, to shrine or gallows,
Let him but lead—sublimely callous!
A Leipsic man—(confound the wretch!)
Has made her Topographic sketch,
A kind of Map, as of a Town,
Each point minutely dotted down;
Scarce to myself I dare to hint
What this d—d fellow wants to print!
Thy wife—howe'er she slight the vows—
Respects, at least, the *name* of spouse;
But mine to regions far too high
  For that terrestrial Name is carried;
My wife's "THE FAMOUS NINON!"—I
  "The Gentleman that Ninon married!"

It galls you that you scarce are able
To stake a florin at the table—
Confront the Pit, or join the Walk,
But straight all tongues begin to talk!
O that such luck could me befal,
Just to be talked about at all!
Behold me dwindling in my nook,
Edg'd at her left,—and not a look!
A sort of rushlight of a life,
Put out by that great Orb—my Wife!

Scarce is the Morning grey—before
Postman and Porter crowd the door;
No Premier has so dear a levée—
  She finds the Mail-bag half its trade;
My God—the parcels are so heavy!
  And not a parcel carriage-paid!
But then—the truth must be confessed—
They're all so charmingly addressed:
Whate'er they cost, they well requite her—

"To Madame Blank, The Famous Writer!"
Poor thing, she sleeps so soft! and yet
   'Twere worth my life to spare her slumber;
"Madame—from Jena—the Gazette—
   The Berlin Journal—the last number!"
Sudden she wakes; those eyes of blue
(Sweet eyes!) fall straight—on the Review!
I by her side—all undetected,
While those curs'd columns are inspected;
Loud squall the children overhead,
Still she reads on, till all is read:
At last she lays *that* darling by,
And asks—"What makes the Baby cry?"

Already now the Toilet's care
Claims from her couch the restless fair;
The Toilet's *care!*—the glass has won
Just half a glance, and all is done!
A snappish—pettish word or so
Warns the poor Maid 'tis time to go:—
Not at *her* toilet wait the Graces,
Uncombed Erynnys takes their places;
So great a mind expands its scope
Far from the mean details of—soap!

Now roll the coach-wheels to the muster—
Now round my Muse her votaries cluster;
Spruce Abbé Millefleurs—Baron Herman—
The English Lord, who don't know German,—
But all uncommonly well read
From matchless A to deathless Z!
Sneaks in the corner, shy and small,
A thing which Men the Husband call!
While every fop with flattery fires her,
Swears with what passion he admires her.—
"'Passion!' 'admire!' and still you're dumb?'"
Lord bless your soul, the worst's to come :—
I'm forced to bow, as I'm a sinner,—
And hope—the rogue will stay to dinner!
But, oh, at dinner!—there's the sting;
I see my cellar on the wing!

You know if Burgundy is dear?—
Mine once emerg'd three times a year;—
And now, to wash these learned throttles,
In dozens disappear the bottles;
They well must drink who well do eat,
(I've sunk a capital on meat).
Her immortality, I fear, a
Death-blow will prove to my Madeira;
'T has given, alas! a mortal shock
To that old friend—my Steinberg Hock! *

If Faust had really any hand
In printing, I can understand
The fate which legends more than hint;—
The devil take all hands that print!

And what my thanks for all?—a pout—
Sour looks—deep sighs; but what about?
About! O, *that* I well divine—
That such a pearl should fall to swine—
That such a literary ruby
Should grace the finger of a booby!

Spring comes;—behold, sweet mead and lea
   Nature's green splendour tapestries o'er;
Fresh blooms the flower, and buds the tree;
   Larks sing—the Woodland wakes once more.
The Woodland wakes—but not for her!
   From Nature's self the charm has flown;
No more the Spring of Earth can stir
   The fond remembrance of our own!
The sweetest bird upon the bough
Has not one note of music now;
And, oh! how dull the Grove's soft shade,
Where once—(as lovers *then*)—we stray'd!
The Nightingales have got no learning—
   Dull creatures—how can they inspire her?
The Lilies are so undiscerning,
   They never say—" how they admire her!"

---

* Literally "Nierensteiner,"—a wine not much known in England, and scarcely—according to our experience—worth the regrets of its respectable owner.

In all this Jubilee of being,
Some subject for a point she's seeing—
Some epigram—(to be impartial,
Well turn'd)—there may be worse in Martial!

But, hark! the Goddess stoops to reason:—
"The country now is quite in season,
I'll go!"—"What! to our Country Seat?"
"No!—Travelling will be such a treat;
Pyrmont's extremely full, I hear;
But Carlsbad's quite the rage this year!"
Oh yes, she loves the rural Graces;
Nature is gay—in Watering-places!
Those pleasant Spas—our reigning passion—
Where learned Dons meet folks of fashion;
Where—each with each illustrious soul
    Familiar as in Charon's boat,
All sorts of Fame sit cheek-by-jowl,
    Pearls in that string—the Table d'Hôte!
Where dames whom Man has injured—fly,
    To heal their wounds or to efface them;
While others, with the waters, try
    A course of flirting,—just to brace them!

Well, there (O Man, how light thy woes
    Compared with mine—thou need'st must see!)
My wife, undaunted, greatly goes—
    And leaves the orphans (seven!!!) to me!

O, wherefore art thou flown so soon,
Thou first fair year—Love's Honeymoon!
Ah, Dream too exquisite for life!
Home's Goddess—in the name of Wife!
Reared by each Grace—yet but to be
Man's Household Anadyomenè!
With mind from which the sunbeams fall,
Rejoicing while pervading all;
Frank in the temper pleased to please—
Soft in the feeling waked with ease.
So broke, as Native of the skies,
The Heart-enthraller on my eyes;

THE CELEBRATED WOMAN.

So saw I, like a Morn of May,
The Playmate given to glad my way;
With eyes that more than lips bespoke,
Eyes whence—sweet words—" I love thee! " broke!
So—Ah, what transports then were mine!
I led the Bride before the shrine!
And saw the future years reveal'd,
Glass'd on my Hope—one blooming field!
More wide, and widening more, were given
The Angel-gates disclosing Heaven;
Round us the lovely, mirthful troop
  Of children came—yet still to me
The loveliest—merriest of the group
  The happy Mother seemed to be!
Mine, by the bonds that bind us more
Than all the oaths the Priest before;
Mine, by the concord of content,
When Heart with Heart is music-blent;
When, as sweet sounds in unison,
  Two lives harmonious melt in one!
When—sudden (O the villain!)—came
  Upon the scene a Mind Profound!—
A Bel Esprit, who whisper'd " Fame,"
  And shook my card-house to the ground.

What have I now instead of all
The Eden lost of hearth and hall?
What comforts for the Heaven bereft?
What of the younger Angel's left?
A sort of intellectual Mule,
  Man's stubborn mind in Woman's shape,
Too hard to love, too frail to rule—
  A sage engrafted on an ape!
To what she calls the Realm of Mind,
  She leaves that throne, *her sex*, to crawl,
The cestus and the charm resign'd—
  A public gaping-show to all!
She blots from Beauty's Golden Book *
  A Name 'mid Nature's choicest Few,
To gain the glory of a nook
  In Doctor Dunderhead's Review.

---

* The Golden Book.—So was entitled in some Italian States (Venice especially) the Catalogue in which the Noble Families were enrolled.

TO A FEMALE FRIEND.

(WRITTEN IN HER ALBUM.)

[These verses were addressed to Charlotte Von Lengefeld, whom Schiller afterwards married, and were intended to dissuade her from a Court life.]

I.

As some gay child, around whose steps play all
    The laughing Graces, plays the World round thee!
Yet not as on thy soul's clear mirror fall
    The flattered shadows, deem this world to be!
The silent homages thy heart compels
By its own inborn dignity,—the spells
    That thou thyself around thyself art weaving,
The charms with which thy being is so rife,—
'Tis *these* thou countest as the charms of life,
    In Human Nature, as thine own—believing!
Alas! this Beauty but exists, in sooth,
In thine own talisman of holy youth,
    [Who can resist it?]—mightiest while deceiving? *

II.

Enjoy the lavish flowers that glad thy way,
    The happy ones whose happiness thou art;
The souls thou winnest—in these bounds survey
    Thy world!—to *this* world why shouldst thou depart?
Nay, let yon flowers admonish thee and save!
Lo, how they bloom while guarded by the fence!
    So plant Earth's pleasures—not too near the sense!

---

* The sense of the original is very shadowy and impalpable, and the difficulty of embodying it in an intelligible translation is great. It may be rendered thus:—"The silent homage which thy nobility of heart compels,—the miracles which thou thyself hast wrought,—the charms with which thy existence has invested life,—these thou lookest on as the substantial attractions of life itself, and as constituting the very staple of human nature. But in this thou art mistaken. What appears to thee to be the grace and beauty of life, is but the reflection of the witchery of thine own undesecrated youth, and the talisman of thine own innocence and virtue, though these certainly are powers which no man can resist. Enjoy the flowers of life, then; but do not take them for more than they are worth. Theirs is but a surface-beauty; let the glance, therefore, which thou bestowest on them be superficial too. Gaze on them from a distance, and never expect that the core of life will wear the same attractive hues as those which ornament its "exterior." Schiller has repeated this thought in the Poem of the "Actual and Ideal."

Nature to see, but not to pluck them, gave:
  Afar they charm thee—leave them on the stem;
  Approached by thee, the glory fades from them—
And, in thy touch, their sweetness has a grave!

Here conclude the Poems classed under the Second Period of Schiller's career; we have excepted only his translations from Virgil.

FIRST PERIOD;
OR,
EARLY POEMS.

We now trace back the stream to its source. We commenced with Schiller's maturest Poems—we close with his earliest. The contrast between the compositions in the first and third period is sufficiently striking. In the former there is more fire and action—more of that lavish and exuberant energy which characterised the earlier tales of Lord Byron, and redeemed, in that wonderful master of animated and nervous style, a certain poverty of conception by a vigour and *gusto* of execution, which no English poet, perhaps, has ever surpassed. In his poems lies the life, and beats the heart, of Schiller. They conduct us through the various stages of his spiritual education, and indicate each step in the progress. In this division, *effort* is no less discernible than power—both in language and thought there is a struggle at something not yet achieved, and not, perhaps, even yet definite and distinct to the poet himself. Here may be traced, though softened by the charm of genius (which softens all things), the splendid errors that belong to a passionate youth, and that give such distorted grandeur to the giant melodrame of "The Robbers." But here are to be traced also, and in far clearer characters, the man's strong heart, essentially human in its sympathies—the thoughtful and earnest intellect giving ample promise of all it was destined to receive. In these earlier poems, extravagance is sufficiently noticeable—yet never the sickly eccentricities of diseased weakness, but the exuberant overflowings of a young Titan's strength. There is a distinction, which our critics do not always notice, between the *extravagance* of a great genius, and the *affectation* of a pretty poet.

HECTOR AND ANDROMACHE.

[This and the following poem are, with some alterations, introduced in the Play of "The Robbers."]

ANDROMACHE.

Will Hector leave me for the fatal plain,
Where, fierce with vengeance for Patroclus slain,
  Stalks Peleus' ruthless son?
Who, when thou glid'st amid the dark abodes,
To hurl the spear and to revere the Gods,
  Shall teach thine Orphan One?

HECTOR.

Woman and wife belovèd—cease thy tears;
My soul is nerved—the war-clang in my ears!
  Be mine in life to stand
Troy's bulwark!—fighting for our hearths, to go
In death, exulting to the streams below,
  Slain for my father-land!

ANDROMACHE.

No more I hear thy martial footsteps fall—
Thine arms shall hang, dull trophies, on the wall—
  Fallen the stem of Troy!
Thou go'st where slow Cocytus wanders—where
Love sinks in Lethe, and the sunless air
  Is dark to light and joy!

HECTOR.

Longing and thought—yea, all I feel and think
May in the silent sloth of Lethe sink,
  But my love not!
Hark, the wild swarm is at the walls!—I hear!
Gird on my sword—Belov'd one, dry the tear—
  Lethe for love is not!

AMALIA.

FAIR as an angel from his blessed hall*—
 Of every fairest youth the fairest he!
Heaven-mild his look, as maybeams when they fall,
 Or shine reflected from a clear blue sea!
His kisses—feelings rife with paradise!
 Ev'n as two flames, one on the other driven—
Ev'n as two harp-tones their melodious sighs
 Blend in some music that seems born of heaven—

So rush'd, mix'd, melted life with life united!
 Lips, cheeks burn'd, trembled—soul to soul was won!
And earth and heaven seem'd chaos, as, delighted,
 Earth—heaven were blent round the belovèd one!
Now, he is gone! vainly and wearily
 Groans the full heart, the yearning sorrow flows—
Gone! and all zest of life, in one long sigh,
 Goes with him where he goes.

   * Literally, Walhalla.

A FUNERAL FANTASIE.

I.

Pale, at its ghastly noon,
Pauses above the death-still wood—the moon;
The night-sprite, sighing, through the dim air stirs;
   The clouds descend in rain;
   Mourning, the wan stars wane,
Flickering like dying lamps in sepulchres!
Haggard as spectres—vision-like and dumb,
   Dark with the pomp of Death, and moving slow,
Towards that sad lair the pale Procession come
   Where the Grave closes on the Night below.

II.

With dim, deep-sunken eye,
Crutch'd on his staff, who trembles tottering by?
As wrung from out the shatter'd heart, one groan
   Breaks the deep hush alone!
Crush'd by the iron Fate, he seems to gather
   All life's last strength to stagger to the bier,
And hearken—Do those cold lips murmur "Father?"
   The sharp rain, drizzling through that place of fear,
Pierces the bones gnaw'd fleshless by despair,
And the heart's horror stirs the silver hair.

III.

Fresh bleed the fiery wounds
   Through all that agonizing heart undone—
Still on the voiceless lips "my Father" sounds,
   And still the childless Father murmurs "Son!"
Ice-cold—ice-cold, in that white shroud he lies—
   Thy sweet and golden dreams all vanish'd there—
The sweet and golden name of "Father" dies
   Into thy curse,—ice-cold—ice-cold—he lies!
   Dead, what thy life's delight and Eden were!

IV.

Mild, as when, fresh from the arms of Aurora,
  While the air like Elysium is smiling above,
Steep'd in rose-breathing odours, the darling of Flora
  Wantons over the blooms on his winglets of love.—
So gay, o'er the meads, went his footsteps in bliss,
  The silver wave mirror'd the smile of his face;
Delight, like a flame, kindled up at his kiss,
  And the heart of the maid was the prey of his chase.

V.

Boldly he sprang to the strife of the world,
  As a deer to the mountain-top carelessly springs;
As an eagle whose plumes to the sun are unfurl'd,
  Sweet his Hope round the Heaven on its limitless wings.
Proud as a war-horse that chafes at the rein,
  That, kingly, exults in the storm of the brave;
That throws to the wind the wild stream of its mane,
  Strode he forth by the prince and the slave!

VI.

Life, like a spring-day, serene and divine,
  In the star of the morning went by as a trance;
His murmurs he drown'd in the gold of the wine,
  And his sorrows were borne on the wave of the dance.
Vorlds lay conceal'd in the hopes of his youth!—
  When once he shall ripen to Manhood and Fame!
Fond Father exult!—In the germs of his youth
  What harvests are destined for Manhood and Fame!

VII.

Not to be was that Manhood!—The death-bell is knelling,
  The hinge of the death-vault creaks harsh on the ears—
How dismal, O Death, is the place of thy dwelling!
  Not to be was that Manhood!—Flow on bitter tears!
Go, belovèd, thy path to the sun,
  Rise, world upon world, with the perfect to rest;
Go—quaff the delight which thy spirit has won,
  And escape from   grief in the Halls of the Blest.

VIII.

Again (in that thought what a healing is found!)
  To meet in the Eden to which thou art fled!—
Hark, the coffin sinks down with a dull, sullen sound,
  And the ropes rattle over the sleep of the dead.
And we cling to each other!—O Grave, he is thine!
  The eye tells the woe that is mute to the ears—
And we dare to resent what we grudge to resign,
  Till the heart's sinful murmur is choked in its tears.
  Pale at its ghastly noon,
Pauses above the death-still wood—the moon!
The night-sprite, sighing, through the dim air stirs:
  The clouds descend in rain;
  Mourning. the wan stars wane,
Flickering like dying lamps in sepulchres.
The dull clods swell into the sullen mound!
  Earth, one look yet upon the prey we gave!
The Grave locks up the treasure it has found;
Higher and higher swells the sullen mound—
  Never gives back the Grave!

FANTASIE TO LAURA.

What, Laura, say, the vortex that can draw
  Body to body in its strong control;
Beloved Laura, what the charmèd law
  That to the soul attracting plucks the soul?
It is the charm that rolls the stars on high,
  For ever round the sun's majestic blaze—
When, gay as children round their parent, fly
  Their circling dances in delighted maze.
Still, every star that glides its gladsome course,
  Thirstily drinks the luminous golden rain;
Drinks the fresh vigour from the fiery source,
  As limbs imbibe life's motion from the brain;
With sunny motes, the sunny motes united
  Harmonious lustre both receive and give,
Love spheres with spheres still interchange delighted,
  Only through love the starry systems live.

Take love from Nature's universe of wonder,
   Each jarring each, rushes the mighty All.
See, back to Chaos shock'd, Creation thunder;
   Weep, starry Newton—weep the giant fall!
Take from the spiritual scheme that Power away,
   And the still'd body shrinks to Death's abode.
Never—love *not*—would blooms revive for May,
   And, love extinct, all life were dead to God.
And what the charm that at my Laura's kiss,
   Pours the diviner brightness to the cheek;
Makes the heart bound more swiftly to its bliss,
   And bids the rushing blood the magnet seek?—
Out from their bounds swell nerve, and pulse, and sense,
   The veins in tumult would their shores o'erflow;
Body to body rapt—and, charmèd thence,
   Soul drawn to soul with intermingled glow.

Mighty alike to sway the flow and ebb
   Of the inanimate Matter, or to move
The nerves that weave the Arachnèan web
   Of Sentient Life—rules all-pervading Love!
Ev'n in the Moral World, embrace and meet
   Emotions—Gladness clasps the extreme of Care;
And Sorrow, at the worst, upon the sweet
   Breast of young Hope, is thaw'd from its despair.
Of sister-kin to melancholy Woe,
   Voluptuous Pleasure comes, and happy eyes
Delivered of the tears, their children, glow
   Lustrous as sunbeams—and the Darkness flies! *

        * Und entbunden von den gold'nen Kindern
          Strahlt das Auge Sonnenpracht.

Schiller, in his earlier poems, strives after poetry in expression, as our young imitators of Shelley and Keates do, sanctioned generally by our critics, who quote such expressions in italics with three notes of admiration! He here, for instance, calls tears "the Golden Children of the Eye." In his later poems Schiller had a much better notion of true beauty of diction. The general meaning of this poem is very obscure, but it seems to imply that Love rules all things in the inanimate or animate creation; that, even in the moral world, opposite emotions or principles meet and embrace each other. The idea is pushed into an extravagance natural to the youth, and redeemed by the passion, of the Author. But the connecting links are so slender, nay, so frequently omitted, in the original, that a certain degree of paraphrase in many of the stanzas is absolutely necessary to supply them, and render the general sense and spirit of the poem intelligible to the English reader.

The same great Law of Sympathy is given
　　To Evil as to Good, and if we swell
The dark account that life incurs with Heaven,
　　'Tis that our Vices are thy Wooers, Hell!
In turn those Vices are embraced by Shame
　　And fell Remorse, the twin Eumenides.
Danger still clings in fond embrace to Fame,
　　Mounts on her wing, and flies where'er she flees.
Destruction marries its dark self to Pride,
　　Envy to Fortune: when Desire most charms,
'Tis that her brother Death is by her side,
　　For him she opens those voluptuous arms.
The very Future to the Past but flies
　　Upon the wings of Love—as I to thee;
O, long swift Saturn, with unceasing sighs,
　　Hath sought his distant bride, Eternity!
When—so I heard the oracle declare—
　　When Saturn once shall clasp that bride sublime,
Wide-blazing worlds shall light his nuptials there—
　　'Tis thus Eternity shall wed with Time.
In *those* shall be *our* nuptials! ours to share
　　That bridenight, waken'd by no jealous sun;
Since Time, Creation, Nature, but declare
　　Love,—in our love rejoice, Beloved One!

TO LAURA PLAYING.

WHEN o'er the chords thy fingers steal,
A soulless statue now I feel,
　　And now a soul set free!
Sweet Sovereign! ruling over death and life—
Seizes the heart, in a voluptuous strife
　　As with a thousand strings—the SORCERY!*

Then the vassal airs that woo thee,
Hush their low breath hearkening to thee.

---

* "The Sorcery."—In the original, Schiller, with very questionable taste, compares Laura to a conjuror of the name of Philadelphia, who exhibited before Frederick the Great.

TO LAURA PLAYING.

In delight and in devotion,
Pausing from her whirling motion,
Nature, in enchanted calm,
Silently drinks the floating balm.
Sorceress, *her* heart with thy tone
Chaining—as thine eyes my own!

O'er the transport-tumult driven,
   Doth the music gliding swim;
From the strings, as from their heaven,
   Burst the new-born Seraphim.
As when from Chaos' giant arms set free,
'Mid the Creation-storm, exultingly
Sprang sparkling thro' the dark the Orbs of Light—
So streams the rich tone in melodious might.

Soft gliding now, as when o'er pebbles glancing,
   The silver wave goes dancing;
Now with majestic swell, and strong,
As thunder peals in organ-tones along;
   And now with stormy gush,
As down the rock, in foam, the whirling torrents rush;
      To a whisper now
        Melts it amorously,
     Like the breeze through the bough
       Of the aspen tree;
Heavily now, and with a mournful breath,
Like midnight's wind along those wastes of death,
Where Awe the wail of ghosts lamenting hears,
And slow Cocytus trails the stream whose waves are tears.

Speak, maiden, speak!—Oh, art thou one of those
Spirits more lofty than our region knows?
Should we in *thine* the mother-language seek
   Souls in Elysium speak?

TO LAURA.

(RAPTURE.)

Laura—above this world methinks I fly,
And feel the glow of some May-lighted sky,
    When thy looks beam on mine!
And my soul drinks a more ethereal air,
When mine own shape I see reflected, there,
    In those blue eyes of thine!
A lyre-sound from the Paradise afar,
A harp-note trembling from some gracious star,
    Seems the wild ear to fill;
And my muse feels the Golden Shepherd-hours,
When from thy lips the silver music pours
    Slow, as against its will
I see the young Loves flutter on the wing—
Move the charm'd trees, as when the Thracian's string
    Wild life to forests gave;
Swifter the globe's swift circle seems to fly,
When in the whirling dance thou glidest by,
    Light as a happy wave.
Thy looks, when there Love's smiles their gladness wreathe,
Could life itself to lips of marble breathe,
    Lend rocks a pulse divine;
Reading thine eyes—my veriest life but seems
Made up and fashioned from my wildest dreams,—
    Laura, sweet Laura, mine!

TO LAURA.

(THE MYSTERY OF REMINISCENCE.)*

Who, and what gave to me the wish to woo thee—
Still, lip to lip, to cling for aye unto thee?
Who made thy glances to my soul the link—
Who bade me burn thy very breath to drink—
    My life in thine to sink?

---

* This most exquisite love-poem is founded on the Platonic notion, that souls were united in a pre-existent state, that love is the yearning of the spirit to reunite with the spirit with which it formerly made one—and which it discovers on earth. The idea has often been made subservient to poetry, but never with so earnest and elaborate a beauty.

TO LAURA.

As from the conqueror's unresisted glaive,
Flies, without strife subdued, the ready slave—
So, when to life's unguarded fort, I see
Thy gaze draw near and near triumphantly—
    Yields not my soul to thee?
Why from its lord doth thus my soul depart?—
Is it because its native home thou art?
Or were they brothers in the days of yore,
Twin-bound, both souls, and in the links they bore
    Sigh to be bound once more?
Were once our beings blent and intertwining,
And therefore still my heart for thine is pining?
Knew we the light of some extinguished sun—
The joys remote of some bright realm undone,
    Where once our souls were ONE?
Yes, it *is* so!—And thou wert bound to me
In the long-vanish'd Eld eternally!
In the dark troubled tablets which enroll
The Past—my Muse beheld this blessed scroll—
    "One with thy love my soul!"
Oh yes, I learn'd in awe, when gazing there,
How once one bright inseparate life we were,
How once, one glorious essence as a God,
Unmeasured space our chainless footsteps trod—
    All Nature our abode!
Round us, in waters of delight, for ever
Voluptuous flow'd the heavenly Nectar river;
We were the master of the seal of things,
And where the sunshine bathed Truth's mountain-springs
    Quiver'd our glancing wings.
Weep for the godlike life we lost afar—
Weep!—thou and I its scatter'd fragments are;
And still the unconquer'd yearning we retain—
Sigh to restore the rapture and the reign,
    And grow divine again.
And therefore came to me the wish to woo thee—
Still, lip to lip, to cling for aye unto thee;
This made thy glances to my soul the link—
This made me burn thy very breath to drink—
    My life in thine to sink:
And therefore, as before the conqueror's glaive,
Flies, without strife subdued, the ready slave,

So, when to life's unguarded fort, I see
Thy gaze draw near and near triumphantly—
    Yieldeth my soul to thee!
Therefore my soul doth from its lord depart,
Because, beloved, its native home thou art;
Because the twins recall the links they bore,
And soul with soul, in the sweet kiss of yore,
    Meets and unites once more!
Thou too—Ah, there thy gaze upon me dwells,
And thy young blush the tender answer tells;
Yes! with the dear relation still we thrill,
Both lives—tho' exiles from the homeward hill—
    One life—all glowing still!

MELANCHOLY; TO LAURA.

I.

Laura! a sunrise seems to break
  Where'er thy happy looks may glow,
Joy sheds its roses o'er thy cheek,
Thy tears themselves do but bespeak
  The rapture whence they flow:
Blest youth to whom those tears are given—
The tears that change his earth to heaven;
His best reward those melting eyes—
For him new suns are in the skies!

II.

Thy soul—a crystal river passing,
Silver-clear, and sunbeam-glassing,
Mays into bloom sad Autumn by thee;
Night and desert, if they spy thee,
To gardens laugh—with daylight shine,
Lit by those happy smiles of thine!
Dark with cloud the Future far
Goldens itself beneath thy star.

MELANCHOLY; TO LAURA.

Smil'st thou to see the Harmony
   Of charm the laws of Nature keep?
Alas! to me the Harmony
   Brings only cause to weep!

III.

Holds not Hades its domain
   Underneath this earth of ours?
Under Palace, under Fane,
   Underneath the cloud-capt Towers?
Stately cities soar and spread
O'er your mouldering bones, ye Dead!
From corruption, from decay,
   Springs yon clove pink's fragrant bloom;
Yon gay waters wind their way
   From the hollows of a tomb.

IV.

From the Planets thou may'st know
All the change that shifts below,
Fled—beneath that zone of rays,
Fled to Night a thousand Mays;
Thrones a thousand—rising—sinking,
Earth from thousand slaughters drinking
Blood profusely pour'd as water;—
Of the sceptre—of the slaughter—
Wouldst thou know what trace remaineth?
Seek them where the dark king reigneth!

V.

Scarce thine eye can ope and close
Ere Life's dying sunset glows;
Sinking sudden from its pride
Into Death—the Lethe tide.
Ask'st thou whence thy beauties rise?
Boastest thou those radiant eyes?—
Or that cheek in roses dy'd?
All their beauty (thought of sorrow!)
From the brittle mould they borrow.
Heavy interest in the tomb
For the brief loan of the bloom,

For the beauty of the Day,
Death, the Usurer, thou must pay,
  In the long to-morrow!

VI.

Maiden!—Death's too strong for scorn;
  In the cheek the fairest, He
  But the fairest throne doth see;
Though the roses of the morn
Weave the veil by Beauty worn—
Aye, beneath that broidered curtain,
Stands the Archer stern and certain!
Maid—thy Visionary hear—
Trust the wild one as the seer,
When he tells thee that thine eye,
  While it beckons to the wooer,
Only lureth yet more nigh
  Death, the dark undoer!

VII.

Every ray shed from thy beauty
  Wastes the life-lamp while it beams,
And the pulse's playful duty,
  And the blue veins' merry streams,
Sport and run unto the pall—
Creatures of the Tyrant, all!
As the wind the rainbow shatters,
Death thy bright smiles rends and scatters,
Smile and rainbow leave no traces;—
From the spring-time's laughing graces,
From all life, as from its germ,
Grows the revel of the worm!

VIII.

Woe, I see the wild wind wreak
  Its wrath upon thy rosy bloom,
Winter plough thy rounded cheek,
  Cloud and darkness close in gloom;
Blackening over, and for ever,
Youth's serene and silver river!
Love alike and Beauty o'er,
Lovely and belov'd no more!

MELANCHOLY; TO LAURA.

IX.

Maiden, an oak that soars on high,
  And scorns the whirlwind's breath,
Behold thy Poet's youth defy
  The blunted dart of Death!
His gaze as ardent as the light
  That shoots athwart the Heaven,
His soul yet fiercer than the light
  In the Eternal Heaven
Of Him, in whom as in an ocean-surge
Creation ebbs and flows—and worlds arise and merge!
Thro' Nature steers the Poet's thought to find
No fear but this—one barrier to the Min l ?

X.

And dost thou glory so to think ?'
  And heaves thy bosom?—Woe!
This Cup, which lures him to the brink,
As if Divinity to drink—
  Has poison in its flow!
Wretched, oh, wretched, they who trust
To strike the God-spark from the dust!
The mightiest tone the Music knows,
  But breaks the harp-string with the sound;
And Genius, still the more it glows,
But wastes the lamp whose life bestows
  The light it sheds around.
Soon from existence dragg'd away,
The watchful gaoler grasps his prey;
Vowed on the altar of the abusèd fire,
The spirits I raised against myself conspire!
Let—yes, I feel it—two short springs away
  Pass on their rapid flight;
And life's faint spark shall, fleeting from the clay,
  Merge in the Fount of Light!

XI.

And weep'st thou, Laura?—be thy tears forbid;
Wouldst thou my lot, life's dreariest years amid,
  Protract and doom?—No; sinner, dry thy tears!

Wouldst thou, whose eyes beheld the eagle wing
Of my bold youth through air's dominion spring,
Mark my sad age (life's tale of glory done)—
Crawl on the sod and tremble in the sun?
Hear the dull frozen heart condemn the flame
That as from Heaven to youth's blithe bosom came;
And see the blind eyes loathing turn from all
The lovely sins Age curses to recall?
 Let me die young!—sweet sinner, dry thy tears!
Yes, let the flower be gathered in its bloom!
And thou, young Genius, with the brows of gloom,
 Quench thou Life's torch, while yet the flame is strong!
Ev'n as the curtain falls; while still the scene
Most thrills the hearts which have its audience been;
As fleet the shadows from the stage—and long
When all is o'er, lingers the breathless throng!

THE INFANTICIDE.

I.

Hark where the bells toll, chiming, dull and steady,
 The clock's slow hand hath reach'd the appointed time.
Well, be it so—prepare, my soul is ready,
 Companions of the Grave—the rest for crime!
Now take, O world! my last farewell—receiving
 My parting kisses—in these tears they dwell!
Sweet are thy poisons while we taste believing,
 Now we are quits—heart-poisoner, fare-thee-well!

II.

Farewell, ye suns that once to joy invited,
 Changed for the mould beneath the funeral shade;
Farewell, farewell, thou rosy Time delighted,
 Luring to soft desire the careless maid.
Pale gossamers of gold, farewell, sweet-dreaming
 Fancies—the children that an Eden bore!
Blossoms that died while Dawn itself was gleaming,
 Opening in happy sunlight never more.

THE INFANTICIDE.

III.

Swanlike the robe which Innocence bestowing,
  Deck'd with the virgin favours, rosy fair,
In the gay time when many a young rose glowing,
  Blush'd through the loose train of the amber hair.
Woe, woe! as white the robe that decks me now—
  The shroud-like robe Hell's destin'd victim wears;
Still shall the fillet bind this burning brow—
  That sable braid the Doomsman's hand prepares!

IV.

Weep ye, *who never fell*—for whom, unerring,
  The soul's white lilies keep their virgin hue,
Ye who when thoughts so danger-sweet are stirring,
  Take the stern strength that Nature gives the few!
Woe, for too human was this fond heart's feeling—
  Feeling!—my sin's avenger * doom'd to be;
Woe—for the false man's arm around me stealing,
  Stole the lull'd Virtue, charm'd to sleep, from me.

V.

Ah, he perhaps shall, round another sighing,
  (Forgot the serpents stinging at my breast,)
Gaily, when I in the dumb grave am lying,
  Pour the warm wish or speed the wanton jest,
Or play, perchance with his new maiden's tresses,
  Answer the kiss her lip enamour'd brings,
When the dread block the head he cradled presses,
  And high the blood his kiss once fever'd springs.

VI.

Thee, Francis, Francis,† league on league, shall follow
  The death-dirge of the Lucy once so dear;
From yonder steeple, dismal, dull, and hollow,
  Shall knell the warning horror on thy ear.

---

* "Und Empfindung soll mein Richtschwert soyn."
A line of great vigour in the original, but which, if literally translated, would seem extravagant in English.
† Joseph, in the original.

On thy fresh leman's lips when Love is dawning,
   And the lisp'd music glides from that sweet well—
Lo, in that breast a red wound shall be yawning,
   And, in the midst of rapture, warn of hell!

VII.

Betrayer, what! thy soul relentless closing
   To grief—the woman-shame no art can heal—
To that small life beneath my heart reposing!
   Man, man, the wild beast for its young can feel!
Proud flew the sails—receding from the land,
   I watch'd them wanning from the wistful eye,
Round the gay maids on Seine's voluptuous strand,
   Breathes the false incense of his fatal sigh.

VIII.

And there the Babe! there, on the mother's bosom,
   Lull'd in its sweet and golden rest it lay,
Fresh in life's morning as a rosy blossom,
   It smiled, poor harmless one, my tears away.
Deathlike yet lovely, every feature speaking
   In such dear calm and beauty to my sadness,
And cradled still the mother's heart, in breaking,
   The soft'ning love and the despairing madness.

IX.

"Woman, where is my father?"—freezing through me,
   Lisp'd the mute Innocence with thunder-sound;
"Woman, where is thy husband?"—call'd unto me,
   In every look, word, whisper, busying round!
Alas, for thee, there is no father's kiss;—
   He fondleth *other* children on his knee.
How thou wilt curse our momentary bliss,
   When Bastard on thy name shall branded be!

X.

Thy mother—oh, a hell her heart concealeth,
   Lone-sitting, lone in social Nature's All!
Thirsting for that glad fount thy love revealeth,
   While still thy look the glad fount turns to gall.

In every infant cry my soul is heark'ning,
    The haunting happiness for ever o'er,
And all the bitterness of death is dark'ning
    The heavenly looks that smiled mine eyes before.

XI.

Hell, if my sight those looks a moment misses—
    Hell, when my sight upon those looks is turn'd—
The avenging furies madden in *thy* kisses,
    That slept in *his* what time my lips they burn'd.
Out from their graves his oaths spoke back in thunder!
    The perjury stalk'd like murder in the sun—
For ever—God!—sense, reason, soul, sunk under—
    The deed was done!

XII.

Francis, O Francis! league on league, shall chase thee
    The shadows hurrying grimly on thy flight—
Still with their icy arms they shall embrace thee,
    And mutter thunder in thy dream's delight!
Down from the soft stars, in their tranquil glory,
    Shall look thy dead child with a ghastly stare;
That shape shall haunt thee in its cerements gory,
    And scourge thee back from heaven — its home is there!

XIII.

Lifeless—how lifeless!—see, oh see, before me
    It lies cold—stiff!—O God!—and with that blood
I feel, as swoops the dizzy darkness o'er me,
    Mine own life mingled—ebbing in the flood—
Hark, at the door they knock—more loud within me—
    More awful still—its sound the dread heart gave!
Gladly I welcome the cold arms that win me—
    Fire, quench thy tortures in the icy grave!

XIV.

Francis—a God that pardons dwells in heaven—
    Francis, the sinner—yes—she pardons thee—
So let my wrongs unto the earth be given:
    Flame seize the wood!—it burns—it kindles—see!

There—there his letters cast—behold are ashes—
His vows—the conquering fire consumes them here:
His kisses—see—see all—all are only ashes—
All, all—the all that once on earth were dear!

XV.

Trust not the roses which your youth enjoyeth,
  Sisters, to man's faith, changeful as the moon!
Beauty to me brought guilt—its bloom destroyeth:
  Lo, in the judgment court I curse the boon:
Tears in the headsman's gaze—what tears?—'tis spoken!
  Quick, bind mine eyes—all soon shall be forgot—
Doomsman—the lily hast thou never broken?
  Pale Doomsman—tremble not!

The poem we have just concluded was greatly admired at the time of its first publication, and it so far excels in art most of the earlier efforts by the author, that it attains one of the highest secrets in true pathos;—it produces interest for the *criminal* while creating terror for the *crime*. This, indeed, is a triumph in art never achieved but by the highest genius. The inferior writer, when venturing upon the grandest stage of passion (which unquestionably exists in the delineation of great guilt as of heroic virtue), falls into the error either of gilding the crime, in order to produce sympathy for the criminal, or, in the spirit of a spurious morality, of involving both crime and criminal in a common odium. It is to discrimination between the doer and the deed, that we owe the sublimest revelations of the human heart: in this discrimination lies the key to the emotions produced by the Œdipus and Macbeth. In the brief poem before us a whole drama is comprehended. Marvellous is the completeness of the pictures it presents—its mastery over emotions the most opposite—its fidelity to nature in its exposition of the disordered and despairing mind in which tenderness becomes cruelty, and remorse for error tortures itself into scarce conscious crime.

But the art employed, though admirable of its kind, still falls short of the perfection which, in his later works, Schiller aspired to achieve, viz. the point at which *Pain* ceases. The tears which Tragic Pathos, when purest and most elevated, calls forth, ought not to be tears of pain. In the ideal world, as Schiller has inculcated, even sorrow should have its charm—all that harrows, all that revolts, belongs but to that inferior school in which Schiller's fiery youth formed itself for nobler grades—the school of "Storm and Pressure" (Sturm und Drang, as the Germans have expressively described it). If the reader will compare Schiller's poem of the "Infanticide," with the passages which represent a similar crime in the Medea (and the author of "Wallenstein" deserves comparison even with the Euripides), he will see the distinction between the art that seeks an *elevated* emotion, and the art which is satisfied with creating an *intense* one. In Euripides, the detail—the reality—all that can degrade terror into pain—are loftily dismissed. The Titan grandeur of the Sorceress removes us from too close an approach to the crime of the unnatural Mother—the emotion of pity changes into awe—just at the pitch before the coarse sympathy of actual pain can be effected. And it is the avoidance of reality—it is the all-purifying Presence of the Ideal, which make the vast distinction in our emotions between following, with shocked and displeasing pity, the crushed, broken-hearted, mortal criminal to the scaffold, and gazing with an awe which has pleasure of its own upon the mighty Murderess—soaring out of the reach of humanity, upon her Dragon-Car!

THE GREATNESS OF CREATION.

Upon the winged winds, among the rolling worlds I flew,
Which, by the breathing spirit, erst from ancient Chaos grew;
    Seeking to land
    On the farthest strand,
Where life lives no longer to anchor alone,
And gaze on Creation's last boundary-stone.

Star after star around me now its shining youth uprears,
To wander through the Firmament its day of thousand years—
    Sportive they roll
    Round the charmèd goal:
Till, as I look'd on the deeps afar,
The space waned—void of a single star.

On to the Realm of Nothingness—on still in dauntless flight,
Along the splendours swiftly steer my sailing wings of light;
    Heaven at the rear,
    Paleth, mist-like and drear;
Yet still as I wander, the worlds in their glee
Sparkle up like the bubbles that glance on a Sea!

And towards me now, the selfsame path I see a Pilgrim steer!
"Halt, Wanderer, halt—and answer me—What, Pilgrim, seek'st thou here?"
    "To the World's last shore
    I am sailing o'er,
Where life lives no longer to anchor alone,
And gaze on Creation's last boundary-stone."

"Thou sail'st in vain—Return! Before thy path, IN-
    FINITY!"
"And thou in vain!—Behind me spreads INFINITY to
    thee!
        Fold thy wings drooping,
        O Thought, eagle-swooping!—
O Fantasie, anchor!—The Voyage is o'er:
Creation, wild sailor, flows on to no shore!"

ELEGY ON THE DEATH OF A YOUTH.*

[Said to be the Poet Rudolf Weckherlin.]

HEAVY moans, as when Nature the storm is foretelling,
    From the Dark House of Mourning come sad on the ear;
The Death-note on high from the steeple is knelling,
    And slowly comes hither a youth on the Bier;—
A youth not yet ripe for that garner—the tomb,
    A blossom pluck'd off from the sweet stem of May,
Each leaf in its verdure, each bud in its bloom:
A youth—with the eyes yet enchanted by day:
A Son—to the Mother, O word of delight!
A Son—to the Mother, O thought of despair!
My Brother, my friend!—To the grave and the night
    Follow, ye that are human, the treasure we bear.

Ye Pines, do ye boast that unshattered your boughs
    Brave the storm when it rushes, the bolt when it falls?
Ye Hills, that the Heavens rest their pomp on your brows?
    Ye Heavens, that the Suns have their home in your
        halls?
Does the Aged exult in the works he has done—
    The Ladders by which he has climb'd to Renown?
Or the Hero, in deeds by which valour has won
    To the heights where the Temple of Glory looks down?

---

* Of this Poem, as of Gray's divine and unequalled Elegy, it may be truly
said that it abounds in thoughts so natural, that the reader at first believes
they have been often expressed before, but his memory will not enable him
to trace a previous owner. The whole Poem has the rare beauty of being
at once familiar and original.

ELEGY ON THE DEATH OF A YOUTH.

When the canker the bud doth already decay,
  Who can deem that *his* ripeness is free from the worm;
Who can hope to endure, when the young fade away,
  Who can count on life's harvest—the blight at the germ?

How lovely with youth,—and with youth how delighted,
  His days, in the hues of the Rose glided by!
How sweet was the world and how fondly invited
  The Future, that Fairy enchanting his eye!
All life like a Paradise smil'd on his way,
  And, lo! see the Mother weep over his bed,
See the gulf of the Hades yawn wide for its prey,
  See the shears of the Parcæ gleam over the thread!
Earth and Heaven which such joy to the living one gave,
  From his gaze darkened dimly!—and sadly and sighing
The dying one shrunk from the Thought of the grave,—
  The World, oh! the World is so sweet to the Dying!

Dumb and deaf is all sense in the Narrow House!—deep
  Is the slumber the Grave's heavy curtains unfold!
How silent a Sabbath eternally keep,
  O Brother—the Hopes ever Busy of old!
Oft the Sun shall shine down on thy green native hill,
  But the glow of his smile thou shalt feel never more!
Oft the west wind shall rock the young blossoms, but still
  Is the breeze for the heart that can hear never more!
Love gilds not for thee all the world with its glow,
  Never Bride in the clasp of thine arms shall repose;
Thou canst see not our tears, though in torrents they flow,
  Those eyes in the calm of eternity close!
Yet happy—oh, happy, at least in thy slumber—
  Serene is the rest, where all trouble must cease;
For the sorrows must die with the joys they outnumber,
  And the pains of the flesh with its dust—are at peace!
The tooth of sharp slander thou never canst feel,
  The poison of Vice cannot pierce to thy cell;
Over thee may the Pharisee thunder his zeal,
  And the rage of the Bigot devote thee to Hell!
Though the mask of the saint may the swindler disguise;
  Though Earth's Justice, that Bastard of Right, we may see
At play with mankind as the cheat with his dies,
  As now so for ever—what matters to thee?

Over thee too may Fortune (her changes unknown)
  Blindly give to her minions the goods they desire;
Now raising her darling aloft to the throne,
  Now hurling the wretch whom she raised—to the mire!
Happy thou, happy thou—in the still narrow cell!
  To this strange tragi-comedy acted on earth,
To these waters where Bliss is defil'd at the well,
  To this lottery of chances in sorrow and mirth,
To this rot and this ferment—this sloth and this strife,
  To the day and the night of this toilsome repose,
To this Heaven full of Devils—O, Brother!—TO LIFE—
  Thine eyes in the calm of Eternity close!

Fare-thee-well, fare-thee-well, O Belov'd of the soul!
  Our yearnings shall hallow the loss we deplore;
Slumber soft in the Grave till we win to thy goal—
  Slumber soft, slumber soft, till we see thee once more!
Till the Trumpet that heralds God's coming in thunder,
  From the hill-tops of light shall ring over thy bed—
Till the portals of Death shall be riven asunder,
  And the storm-wind of God whirl the dust of the Dead;
Till the breath of Jehovah shall pass o'er the Tombs,
  Till their seeds spring to bloom at the life of the Breath,
Till the pomp of the Stars into vapour consumes,
  And the spoils he hath captured are ravished from Death.
If not in the worlds dream'd by sages, nor given
  In the Eden the Multitude hope to attain,
If not where the Poet hath painted his Heaven,
  Still, Brother, we know we shall meet thee again!
Is there truth in the hopes which the Pilgrim beguile?
  Does the thought still exist when Life's journey is o'er?
Does Virtue conduct o'er the dreary defile?
  Is the faith we have cherish'd a dream and no more?
Already the riddle is bared to thy sight,
  Already thy soul quaffs the Truth it has won,
The Truth that streams forth in its waters of light
  From the chalice the Father vouchsafes to the Son!
Draw near, then, O silent and dark gliding Train,
  Let the feast for the Mighty Destroyer be spread;
Cease the groans which so loudly, so idly complain,
  Heap the mould o'er the mould—heap the dust o'er the
    Dead!

Who can solve the decrees of God's Senate?—the heart
  Of the groundless abyss, what the eye that explores?
Holy!—holy!—all holy in darkness thou art,
  O God of the Grave, whom our shudder adores!
Earth to Earth may return, the material to matter,
  But high from the cell soars the spirit above;
His ashes the winds of the tempest may scatter—
  The life of Eternity lives in his love!

THE BATTLE.

HEAVY and solemn,
A cloudy column,
  Thro' the green plain they marching came!
Measureless spread, like a table dread,
For the wild grim dice of the iron game.
The looks are bent on the shaking ground,
And the heart beats loud with a knelling sound;
Swift by the breasts that must bear the brunt,
Gallops the Major along the front—
    "Halt!"
And fetter'd they stand at the stark command,
And the warriors, silent, halt!

  Proud in the blush of morning glowing,
What on the hill-top shines in flowing!
" See you the Foeman's banners waving?"
" We see the Foeman's banners waving!"
" God be with ye—children and wife!"
Hark to the Music—the trump and the fife,
How they ring thro' the ranks which they rouse to the
    strife!
Thrilling they sound with their glorious tone,
Thrilling they go through the marrow and bone!
Brothers, God grant when this life is o'er,
In the life to come that we meet once more!
  See the smoke how the lightning is cleaving asunder!
Hark the guns, peal on peal, how they boom in their
    thunder!
From host to host, with kindling sound,
. The shouting signal circles round,

Ay, shout it forth to life or death—
Freer already breathes the breath!
The war is waging, slaughter raging,
And heavy through the reeking pall,
   The iron Death-dice fall!
Nearer they close—foes upon foes
"Ready!"—From square to square it goes,
   Down on the knee they sank,
And the fire comes sharp from the foremost rank.
Many a man to the earth it sent,
Many a gap by the balls is rent—
O'er the corpse before springs the hinder-man,
That the line may not fail to the fearless van.
To the right, to the left, and around and around,
Death whirls in its dance on the bloody ground.
God's sunlight is quench'd in the fiery fight,
Over the host falls a brooding Night!
*Brothers, God grant when this life is o'er,
In the life to come that we meet once more!*

   The dead men lie bathed in the weltering blood,
And the living are blent in the slippery flood,
And the feet, as they reeling and sliding go,
Stumble still on the corpses that sleep below.
"What, Francis!" "Give Charlotte my last farewell."
As the dying man murmurs, the thunders swell—
"I'll give—Oh God! are their guns so near?
Ho! comrades!—yon volley!—look sharp to the rear!—
I'll give thy Charlotte thy last farewell,
Sleep soft! where Death thickest descendeth in rain,
The friend thou forsakest thy side shall regain!"
Hitherward—thitherward reels the fight,
Dark and more darkly Day glooms into night—
*Brothers, God grant when this life is o'er,
In the life to come that we meet once more!*
Hark to the hoofs that galloping go!
   The Adjutants flying,—
The horsemen press hard on the panting foe,
   Their thunder booms in dying—
        Victory!
The terror has seized on the dastards all,
   And their colours fall!
        Victory!

Closed is the brunt of the glorious fight:
And the day, like a conqueror, bursts on the night.
Trumpet and fife swelling choral along,
The triumph already sweeps marching in song.
*Farewell, fallen brothers, tho' this life be o'er,
There's another, in which we shall meet you once more!*

ROUSSEAU.

(FREE TRANSLATION.)

O MONUMENT of Shame to this our time!
Dishonouring record to thy mother clime;
Hail Grave of Rousseau!—here thy troubles cease!
Thy life one search for Freedom and for Peace:
Thee, Peace and Freedom life did ne'er allow,
Thy search is ended, and thou find'st them now!
When will the old wounds scar!—In the dark age
Perish'd the wise;—Light comes—How fares the sage?
The same in darkness or in light his fate,
Time brings no mercy to the Bigot's hate!
Socrates charmed Philosophy to dwell
On Earth—by false philosophers he fell;
In Rousseau, Christians mark'd their victim—when
Rousseau enlisted Christians into Men!

FRIENDSHIP.

[From "Letters of Julius to Raphael," an unpublished Novel.]

FRIEND!—the Great Ruler, easily content,
  Needs not the laws it has laborious been
The task of small Professors to invent;
  A single wheel impels the whole machine
Matter and spirit;—yea that simple law,
Pervading Nature, which our Newton saw.

This taught the spheres, slaves to one golden rein,
   Their radiant labyrinths to weave around
Creation's mighty heart; this made the chain,
   Which into interwoven systems bound
All spirits streaming to the spiritual Sun,
As brooks that ever into ocean run!

Did not the same strong mainspring urge and guide
   Our Hearts to meet in Love's eternal bond?
Link'd to thine arm, O Raphael, by thy side
   Might I aspire to reach to souls beyond
Our earth, and bid the bright Ambition go
To that Perfection which the Angels know!

Happy, O happy—I have found thee—I
   Have out of millions found thee, and embraced;
Thou, out of millions, mine!—Let earth and sky
   Return to darkness, and the antique waste—
To chaos shock'd, let warring atoms be,
Still shall each heart unto the other flee!

Do I not find within thy radiant eyes
   Fairer reflections of all joys most fair?
In thee I marvel at myself—the dyes
   Of lovely earth seem lovelier painted there,
And in the bright looks of the Friend is given
A heavenlier mirror even of the Heaven!

Sadness casts off its load, and gaily goes
   From the intolerant storm to rest awhile,
In Love's true heart, sure haven of repose;
   Does not Pain's veriest transports learn to smile
From that bright eloquence Affection gave
To friendly looks?—there, finds not Pain a grave?

In all Creation did I stand alone,
   Still to the rocks my dreams a soul should find,
Mine arms should wreathe themselves around the stone,
   My grief should feel a listener in the wind;
My joy—its echo in the caves should be!
Fool, if ye will—Fool, for sweet Sympathy!

We are dead groups of matter when we hate;
  But when we love we are as Gods!—Unto
The gentle fetters yearning, through each state
  And shade of being multiform, and thro'
All countless spirits (save of all the sire)—
Moves, breathes, and blends the one divine Desire.

Lo! arm in arm, thro' every upward grade,
  From the rude Mongol to the starry Greek,
Who the fine link between the Mortal made,
  And Heaven's last Seraph—everywhere we seek
Union and bond—till in one sea sublime
Of Love be merg'd all measure and all time!

Friendless ruled God His solitary sky;
  He felt the want, and therefore Souls were made,
The blessed mirrors of His bliss!—His Eye
  No equal in His loftiest works surveyed;
And from the source whence souls are quickened—He
Called His Companion forth—ETERNITY!

A GROUP IN TARTARUS.

HARK, as hoarse murmurs of a gathering sea—
  As brooks that howling through black gorges go,
Groans sullen, hollow, and eternally,
  One wailing Woe!
Sharp Anguish shrinks the shadows there;
And blasphemous Despair
Yells its wild curse from jaws that never close;
  And ghastly eyes for ever
  Stare on the bridge of the relentless River,
Or watch the mournful wave as year on year it flows,
  And ask each other, with parch'd lips that writhe
Into a whisper, "When the end shall be?"
  The *end?*—Lo, broken in Time's hand the scythe,
And round and round revolves Eternity!

ELYSIUM.

Past the despairing wail—
And the bright banquets of the Elysian Vale
   Melt every care away!
Delight, that breathes and moves for ever,
Glides through sweet fields like some sweet river!
   Elysian life survey!
There, fresh with youth, o'er jocund meads,
His merry west-winds blithely leads
   The ever-blooming May!
Through gold-woven dreams goes the dance of the Hours,
In space without bounds swell the soul and its powers,
   And Truth, with no veil, gives her face to the day.
And joy to-day and joy to-morrow,
   But wafts the airy soul aloft;
The very name is lost to Sorrow,
   And Pain is Rapture tuned more exquisitely soft.
Here the Pilgrim reposes the world-weary limb,
And forgets in the shadow, cool-breathing and dim,
   The load he shall bear never more;
Here the Mower, his sickle at rest, by the streams,
Lull'd with harp-strings, reviews, in the calm of his dreams,
   The fields, when the harvest is o'er.
Here, He, whose ears drank in the battle roar,
Whose banners stream'd upon the startled wind
   A thunder-storm,—before whose thunder tread
The mountains trembled,—in soft sleep reclined,
   By the sweet brook that o'er its pebbly bed
In silver plays, and murmurs to the shore,
Hears the stern clangour of wild spears no more!
Here the true Spouse the lost-beloved regains,
And on the enamell'd couch of summer-plains
   Mingles sweet kisses with the zephyr's breath.
Here, crown'd at last, Love never knows decay,
Living through ages its one BRIDAL DAY,
   Safe from the stroke of Death!

THE REFUGEE.

FRESH breathes the living air of dawning Day,
 The young Light reddens thro' the dusky pines,
Ogling the tremulous leaves with wanton ray:
  The cloud-capt hill-tops shine,
  With golden-flame divine;
And all melodious thrills the lusty song
 Of sky-larks, greeting the delighted Sun;
As to Aurora's arms he steals along—
 And now in bright embrace she clasps the glowing one!
  O Light, hail to thee!
  How the mead and the lea
The warmth and the wave of thy splendour suffuse!
  How silver-clear, shimmer
  The fields, and how glimmer
The thousand suns glass'd in the pearl of the dews!
  How frolic and gay
  Is young Nature at play,
Where the cool-breathing shade with low whispers is sweet;
  Sighing soft round the rose,
  The Zephyr, its lover, caressingly goes,
 And over the Meadow the light vapours fleet!
How, high o'er the city the smoke-cloud is reeking,
What snorting, and rattling, and trampling, and creaking;
  Neighs the horse—the bull lows,
  And the heavy wain goes
 To the valley that groans with the tumult of Day;
The life of the Woodlands leaps up to the eye—
The Eagle, the Falcon, the Hawk, wheel on high,
 On the wings that exult in the ray!
  Where shall I roam,
  O Peace, for thy home?
With the staff of the Pilgrim, where wander to Thee?
  The face of the Earth
  With the smile of its mirth
Has only a grave for me!
Rise up, O rosy Morn, whose lips of love
 Kiss into blushing splendour grove and field;
Sink down, O rosy Eve, that float'st above
 The weary world, in happy slumbers seal'd.

Morn, in the joyous world thou reddenest over
But one dark Burial-place the Pilgrim knows!
O Eve, the sleep thy rosy veil shall cover
Is—but my long repose!

THE FLOWERS.

CHILDREN of Suns restored to youth,
　In purfled Fields ye dwell,
Reared to delight and joy—in sooth,
　Kind Nature loves ye well;
Broidered with light the robes ye wear,
And liberal Flora decks ye fair,
　In gorgeous-coloured pride:
Yet woe—Spring's harmless Infants—Woe,
Mourn, for ye wither while ye glow—
　Mourn for the soul denied!

The Skylark and the Nightbird sing
　To you their Hymns of Love,
And Sylphs that wanton on the wing
　Embrace your blooms above;
Woven for Love's soft pillow, were
The Chalice crowns ye blushing bear,
　By the Idalian Queen:
Yet weep, soft Children of the Spring,
The feelings Love alone can bring
　To you denied have been!

But me in vain my Laura's * eyes,
　Her Mother hath forbidden;
For in the buds I gather, lies
　Love's symbol-language hidden—
Mute Heralds of voluptuous pain
I touch ye—life, speech, heart, ye gain,
　And soul, denied before:
And silently your leaves enclose
The mightiest God in arch repose,
　Soft cradled in the core!

* *Nanny*, in the Editions of Schiller's collected Works; but Laura, when the Poem was first printed in the Anthology. In the earlier form of the poem, it was not, however, the Poet who sent the flowers to Laura, but Laura who sent the flowers to him.

TO MINNA.

I.

Do I dream? can I trust to my eye?
   My sight sure some vapour must cover?
Or, there, did my Minna pass by—
   My Minna—and knew not her lover?
On the arm of the coxcomb she crost,
   Well the fan might its zephyr bestow;
Herself in her vanity lost,
   That wanton my Minna?—Ah, no!

II.

In the gifts of my love she was drest,
   My plumes o'er her summer-hat quiver;
The ribbons that flaunt in her breast
   Might bid her—remember the giver!
And still do they bloom on thy bosom,
   The flowerets I gathered for thee!
Still as fresh is the leaf of each blossom,
   'Tis the Heart that has faded from me!

III.

Go and take, then, the incense they tender;
   Go, the one that adored thee forget!
Go, thy charms to the Feigner surrender,
   In my scorn is my comforter yet!
Go, for thee with what trust and belief
   There beat not ignobly a heart,
That has strength yet to strive with the grief
   To have worshipp'd the trifler thou art!

IV.

Thy beauty *thy* heart hath betray'd—
   Thy beauty—shame, Minna, to thee!
To-morrow its glory will fade,
   And its roses all withered will be!
The swallows that swarm in the sun
   Will fly when the north winds awaken,
The false ones thine Autumn will shun,
   For whom thou the true hast forsaken!

V.

'Mid the wrecks of thy charms in December,
　　I see thee alone in decay,
And each Spring shall but bid thee remember
　　How brief for thyself was the May!
Then they who so wantonly flock
　　To the rapture thy kiss can impart,
Shall scoff at thy winter, and mock
　　Thy beauty as wreck'd as thy heart;

VI.

Thy beauty thy heart hath betray'd—
　　Thy beauty—shame, Minna, to thee!
To-morrow its glory will fade—
　　And its roses all withered will be!
O, what scorn for thy desolate years
　　Shall I feel!—God forbid it in me!
How bitter will then be the tears
　　Shed, Minna, O, Minna, for thee!

TO THE SPRING.

Welcome, gentle Stripling
　　Nature's darling, thou!
With thy basket full of blossoms,
　　A happy welcome now!
Aha!—and thou returnest,
　　Heartily we greet thee—
The loving and the fair one,
　　Merrily we meet thee!
Think'st thou of my Maiden
　　In thy heart of glee?

I love her yet, the Maiden—
　　And the Maiden yet loves me!
For the Maiden, many a blossom
　　I begg'd—and not in vain!
I came again, a-begging,
　　And thou—thou giv'st again:

Welcome, gentle Stripling,
  Nature's darling thou—
With thy basket full of blossoms,
  A happy welcome, now!

THE TRIUMPH OF LOVE.

A HYMN.

BLESSED through love are the Gods above—
  Through love like the Gods may man be;
Heavenlier through love is the heaven above,
  Through love like a heaven earth can be!
Once, as the poet sung,
  In Pyrrha's time 'tis known,
From rocks Creation sprung,
  And Men leapt up from stone;
Rock and stone, in night
  The souls of men were seal'd,
Heaven's diviner light
  Not as yet reveal'd;
As yet the Loves around them
Had never shone—nor bound them
  With their rosy rings;
As yet their bosoms knew not
Soft song—and music grew not
  Out of the silver strings:
No gladsome garlands cheerily
  Were love-y-woven then;
And o'er Elysium drearily
  The May-time flew for men,*
The morning rose ungreeted
  From ocean's joyless breast;
Unhail'd the evening fleeted
  To ocean's joyless breast—
Wild through the tangled shade,
By clouded moons they stray'd,

---

* "The World was sad, the garden was a wild,
  And Man, the Hermit, sigh'd—till Woman smiled."—
                            CAMPBELL.

The iron race of Men!
Sources of mystic tears,
Yearnings for starry spheres,
　No God awaken'd then!

* * * * *

Lo, mildly from the dark-blue water,
Comes forth the Heaven's divinest Daughter,
　Borne by the Nymphs fair-floating o'er
　　To the intoxicated shore!
Like the light-scattering wings of morning
Soars universal May, adorning
As from the glory of that birth
Air and the ocean, heaven and earth!
Day's eye looks laughing, where the grim
Midnight lay coil'd in forests dim;
And gay narcissuses are sweet
Wherever glide those holy feet—
　Now, pours the bird that haunts the eve
The earliest song of love,
　Now in the heart—their fountain—heave
The waves that murmur love!
O blest Pygmalion—blest art thou—
It melts, it glows, thy marble now!
　O Love, the God, thy world is won!
　Embrace thy children, Mighty One.

* * * * *

Blessed through love are the Gods above—
　Through love like the Gods may man be;
Heavenlier through love is the heaven above,
　Through love like a heaven earth can be.

* * * * *

Where the nectar bright-streams,
Like the dawn's happy dreams,
Eternally one holiday,
The life of the Gods glides away.
Throned on his seat sublime,
Looks He whose years know not time;
At his nod, if his anger awaken,
At the wave of his hair all Olympus is shaken.
Yet He from the throne of his birth,
Bow'd down to the sons of the earth,

Through dim Arcadian glades to wander sighing,
    Lull'd into dreams of bliss—
    Lull'd by his Leda's kiss—
Lo, at his feet the harmless thunders lying!

The Sun's majestic coursers go
    Along the Light's transparent plain,
    Curb'd by the Day-god's golden rein;
The nations perish at his bended bow;
    Steeds that majestic go,
    Shafts from the bended bow,
    Gladly he leaves above—
    For Melody and Love!
Low bend the dwellers of the sky,
When sweeps the stately Juno by;
Proud in her car, the Uncontroll'd
    Curbs the bright birds that breast the air,
    As flames the sovereign crown of gold
    Amidst the ambrosial waves of hair—
Ev'n thou, fair Queen of Heaven's high throne,
Hast Love's subduing sweetness known;
From all her state, the Great One bends
    To charm the Olympian's bright embraces,
The Heart-Enthraller only lends
    The rapture-cestus of the Graces!
    o   o   o   o   •
Blessed through love are the Gods above—
    Through love like a God may man be;
Heavenlier through love is the heaven above,
    Through love like a heaven earth can be!
    o   o   o   o   •
Love can sun the Realms of Night—
Orcus owns the magic might—
Peaceful where She sits beside,
Smiles the swart King on his Bride;
Hell feels the smile in sudden light—
Love can sun the Realms of Night!
Heavenly o'er the startled Hell,
Holy, where the Accursed dwell,
    O Thracian, went thy silver song!
Grim Minos, with unconscious tears,
Melts into Mercy as he hears—

The serpents in Megara's hair,
Kiss, as they wreathe enamour'd there;
　All harmless rests the madding thong;—
From the torn breast the Vulture mute
Flies, scared before the charmèd lute—
Lull'd into sighing from their roar
The dark waves woo the listening shore—
Listening the Thracian's silver song!—
Love was the Thracian's silver song!
　○　　○　　○　　●　　○

Blessed through love are the Gods above—
　Through love like a God may man be;
Heavenlier through love is the heaven above,
　Through love like a heaven earth can be!
　○　　○　　○　　●　　○

Through Nature, blossom-strewing,
One footstep we are viewing,
　One flash from golden pinions!—
If from Heaven's starry sea,
　If from the moonlit sky;
If from the Sun's dominions,
　Look'd not Love's laughing eye;
Then Sun and Moon and Stars would be
Alike, without one smile for me!
　　But, oh, wherever Nature lives
　　　Below, around, above—
　　Her happy eye the mirror gives
　　　To thy glad beauty, Love!
Love sighs through brooklets silver-clear,
　Love bids their murmur woo the vale;
Listen, O list! Love's soul ye hear
　In his own earnest nightingale.
No sound from Nature ever stirs,
But Love's sweet voice is heard with hers!
Bold Wisdom, with her sunlit eye,
Retreats when Love comes whispering by—
　For Wisdom's weak to Love!
To victor stern or monarch proud,
Imperial Wisdom never bow'd
　The knee she bows to Love!
Who through the steep and starry sky,
Goes onward to the Gods on high,

TO A MORALIST.

Before thee, hero-brave?
Who halves for thee the land of Heaven;
Who shows thy heart, Elysium, given
    Through the flame-rended Grave?
Below, if we were blind to Love,
Say, should we soar o'er Death, above?
Would the weak soul, did Love forsake her,
E'er gain the wing to seek the Maker?
Love, only Love, can guide the creature
Up to the Father-fount of Nature;
What were the soul did Love forsake her?
Love guides the Mortal to the Maker!

  o   o   o   o   o

Blessed through love are the Gods above—
    Through love like a God may man be;
Heavenlier through love is the heaven above,
    Through love like a heaven earth can be!

TO A MORALIST.

Are the sports of our youth so displeasing?
    Is love but the folly you say?
Benumb'd with the Winter, and freezing,
    You scold at the revels of May.

For you once a nymph had her charms,
    And oh! when the waltz you were wreathing,
All Olympus embraced in your arms—
    All its nectar in Julia's breathing.

If Jove at that moment had hurl'd
    The earth in some other rotation,
Along with your Julia whirl'd,
    You had felt not the shock of creation.

Learn this—that Philosophy beats
    Sure time with the pulse,—quick or slow
As the blood from the heyday retreats,—
    But it cannot make gods of us—No!

It is well, icy Reason should thaw
  In the warm blood of Mirth now and then,
The Gods for themselves have a law
  Which they never intended for men.

The Spirit is bound by the ties
  Of its Gaoler the Flesh;—if I can
Not reach as an Angel the skies,
  Let me feel on the earth as a Man!

FORTUNE AND WISDOM.

In a quarrel with her lover
  To Wisdom Fortune flew;
"I'll all my hoards discover—
  Be but my friend—to you.
Like a mother I presented
  To one each fairest gift,
Who still is discontented,
  And murmurs at my thrift.
Come, let's be friends. What say you?
  Give up that weary plough,
My treasures shall repay you,
  For both I have enow!"
"Nay, see thy Friend betake him
  To death from grief for thee—
He dies if thou forsake him—
  Thy gifts are nought to *me!*"

COUNT EBERHARD, THE QUARRELLER (DER GREINER) OF WURTEMBERG.

[Count Eberhard reigned from 1344–92. His son Ulrick was defeated before Reutling in 1377, and fell the next year in battle, at Doffingen, near Stuttgard, in a battle in which Eberhard was victorious. There is something of national feeling in this fine war-song, composed in honour of the old Suabian hero, by a poet himself a Suabian.]

COUNT EBERHARD, THE QUARRELLER

Ha, ha!—take heed,—ha, ha! take heed—*
   Ye knaves both South and North!
For many a man both bold in deed,
And wise in peace the land to lead,
   Old Suabia has brought forth.

Proud boasts your Edward and your Charles,
   Your Ludwig, Frederick—are!
Yet Eberhard's worth, ye bragging carles!
Your Ludwig, Frederick, Edward, Charles—
   A thunder-storm in war!

And Ulrick, too, his noble son,
   Ha, ha! his might ye know;
Old Eberhard's boast, his noble son,
Not he the boy, ye rogues, to run,
   How stout soe'er the foe!

The Reutling lads with envy saw
   Our glories, day by day;
The Reutling lads shall give the law—
The Reutling lads the sword shall draw—
   O Lord—how hot were they!

Out Ulrick went, and beat them not—
   To Eberhard back he came—
A lowering look young Ulrick got—
Poor lad, his eyes with tears were hot—
   He hung his head for shame.

"Ho—ho"—thought he—"ye rogues beware;
   Nor you nor I forget—
For by my father's beard † I swear
Your blood shall wash the blot I bear,
   And Ulrick pay you yet!"

---

* "Don't bear the head too high."
   Ihr, ihr dort aussen in der Welt,
   Die Nasen eingespannt!—

† Count Eberhard had the nickname of Rush-Beard, from the rustling of that appendage, with which he was favoured to no ordinary extent.

Soon came the hour! with steeds and men
   The battle-field was gay;
Steel closed on steel at Doffingen—
And joyous was our stripling then,
   And joyous the hurra!

"The battle lost" our battle-cry;
   The foe once more advances:
As some fierce whirlwind cleaves the sky,
We skirr, through blood and slaughter, by,
   Amidst a night of lances!

On, lion-like, grim Ulrick sweeps—
   Bright shines his hero-glaive—
Her chase before him Fury keeps,
Far-heard behind him, Anguish weeps,
   And round him—is the Grave!

Woe—woe! it gleams—the sabre-blow—
   Swift-sheering down it sped—
Around, brave hearts the buckler throw—
Alas! our boast in dust is low!
   Count Eberhard's boy is dead!

Grief checks the rushing Victor-van—
   Fierce eyes strange moisture know—
On rides old Eberhard, stern and wan,
"My son is like another man—
   March, children, on the Foe!"

And fiery lances whirr'd around,
   Revenge, at least, undying—
Above the blood-red clay we bound—
Hurra! the burghers break their ground,
   Through vale and woodland flying!

Back to the camp, behold us throng,
   Flags stream, and bugles play—
Woman and child with choral song,
And men, with dance and wine, prolong
   The warrior's holyday.

And our old Count—and what doth he?
  Before him lies his son,
Within his lone tent, lonelily,
The old man sits with eyes that see
  Through one dim tear—his son!

So heart and soul, a loyal band,
  Count Eberhard's band, we are!
His front the tower that guards the land,
A thunderbolt his red right hand—
  His eye a guiding star!

Then take ye heed —Aha! take heed,
  Ye knaves both South and North!
For many a man, both bold in deed
And wise in peace, the land to lead,
  Old Suabia has brought forth!

With this ballad conclude all in the First Period, or early Poems which Schiller himself thought worth preserving, and which are retained in the editions of his collected works;—except the sketch of "Semele," which ought to be classed amongst his dramatic compositions.

FAREWELL TO THE READER.

(TRANSFERRED FROM THE THIRD PERIOD.)

THE Muse is silent; with a virgin cheek,
  Bow'd with the blush of shame, she ventures near—
She waits the judgment that thy lips may speak,
  And feels the deference, but disowns the fear.
Such praise as Virtue gives, 'tis hers to seek—
  Bright Truth, not tinsel Folly to revere;
He only for her wreath the flowers should cull
Whose heart, with hers, beats for the Beautiful.

Nor longer yet these lays of mine would live,
  Than to one genial heart, not idly stealing,
There some sweet dreams and fancies fair to give,
  Some hallowing whispers of a loftier feeling.

Not for the far posterity they strive,
  Doom'd with the time, its impulse but revealing,
Born to record the Moment's smile or sigh,
And with the light dance of the Hours to fly.

Spring wakes—and life, in all its youngest hues,
  Shoots through the mellowing meads delightedly;
Air the fresh herbage scents with nectar-dews;
  Livelier the choral music fills the sky;
Youth grows more young, and age its youth renews,
  In that field-banquet of the ear and eye;
Spring flies—and with it all the train it leads,
And flowers in fading leave us but their seeds.

THE END.

BRADBURY, AGNEW, & CO., PRINTERS, WHITEFRIARS.

CPSIA information can be obtained at www.ICGtesting.com
Printed in the USA
LVOW06*1753160813

348285LV00011B/594/P